TRUE CRIME CASE HISTORIES

VOLUMES 1, 2, & 3

JASON NEAL

IDIGITAL GROUP

More books by Jason Neal

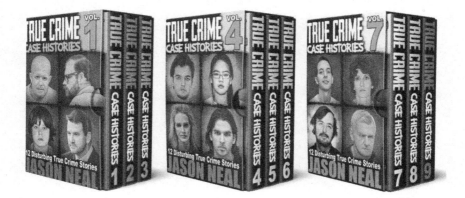

Looking for more?? I am constantly adding new volumes of True Crime Case Histories. The series **can be read in any order,** and all books are available in paperback, hardcover, and audiobook.

Check out the complete series at:

https://amazon.com/author/jason-neal

All Jason Neal books are also available in **AudioBook format at Audible.com.** Enjoy a **Free Audiobook** when you signup for a 30-Day trial using this link:

https://geni.us/AudibleTrueCrime

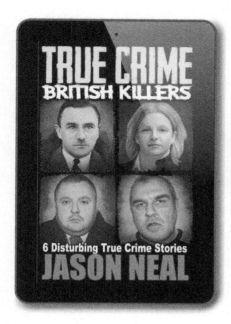

FREE BONUS EBOOK FOR MY READERS

As my way of saying "Thank you" for downloading, I'm giving away a FREE True Crime e-book I think you'll enjoy.

https://TrueCrimeCaseHistories.com

Just visit the link above to let me know where to send your free book!

CONTENTS

TRUE CRIME CASE HISTORIES
VOLUME 1

TRUE CRIME CASE HISTORIES
VOLUME 2

TRUE CRIME CASE HISTORIES
VOLUME 3

TRUE CRIME CASE HISTORIES

VOLUME 1

TRUE CRIME

CASE HISTORIES

VOL. 1

12 Disturbing True Crime Stories

JASON NEAL

INTRODUCTION

A quick word of warning: the short stories within this book are unimaginably gruesome. Most news stories and television crime shows tend to leave out the most horrible details about murder cases simply because they are too extreme for the general public.

I have done my best to include the full details of these stories, no matter how sickening they may be. In these true crime stories, you'll find that truth really is stranger – and vastly more disturbing – than fiction.

In my first book, I've started with a few stories that have haunted me for some time. Some of these stories are unbelievable in their brutality, while others are astounding in the stupidity of the perpetrator.

You'll find the story of a religious evangelical who would rather strangle his wife and two young boys than lose his prominent job with the church.

Then, there's the story of a man who filled his wife's orifices with grease so she would burn from the inside.

There's also the story of the small-town doctor who went to unbelievable lengths to perform surgery on himself to avoid jail for raping his patients.

Plus, I've included more stories of serial killers who terrorized southern California and investigations that brought seasoned crime scene officers to tears.

These stories are from around the globe and have no common thread other than they are both thought-provoking and disturbing.

The stories included in this book are dark, creepy, and will leave you with a new understanding of just how fragile the human mind can be.

Lastly, please join my mailing list for discounts, updates, and a free book. You can sign up for that at

TrueCrimeCaseHistories.com

Additional photos, videos, and documents pertaining to the cases in this volume can be found on the accompanying web page:

https://TrueCrimeCaseHistories.com/vol1/

Thank you for reading. I sincerely hope you gain some insight from this first volume of True Crime Case Histories.

- Jason

CHAPTER 1
JAMES PATTERSON SMITH

On an April afternoon in 1996, a man calmly walked into a Manchester, England, police station to report that his girlfriend had accidentally drowned in his bathtub. The man was forty-eight-year-old James Patterson Smith, and his girlfriend was just a seventeen-year-old child. The police later learned that Smith was a sadistic, controlling psychopath. Not only had the girl drowned, but she had been subjected to three weeks of some of the most brutal torture England had ever seen. The horrific crime scene brought seasoned police officers to tears.

Kelly Anne Bates was mature for her age. At age fourteen, when Kelly told her parents, Margaret and Tommy Bates, that she had a boyfriend, they thought nothing of it. As any parent would, they assumed she had a teenage crush on a young boy from school.

Wanting to raise their children with a sense of independence, they gave Kelly a long leash and let her see her boyfriend as she pleased. However, it wasn't long before Kelly started staying out overnight, and her worried parents called the police. When Kelly finally came home, she told them she had been staying at her friend Rachel's house – but her parents had a sinking feeling that her story wasn't true.

They weren't the only ones concerned about Kelly's whereabouts. Even though they had never met him, Kelly's boyfriend "Dave" occasionally called to ask where she was. Her parents didn't realize at the time that Dave was already tightening his control over their daughter.

Kelly managed to keep her parents from meeting Dave for a full two years, until she was sixteen. That's when she broke the news: she was dropping out of school and moving in with him. Her parents were livid and called both social services and the police for help. Unfortunately Kelly was sixteen, and according to UK laws, the authorities couldn't do anything. Kelly's parents demanded to meet her boyfriend, Dave.

When Margaret and Tommy finally met Dave, they were shocked to find that he was not a boy but a full-grown man. Kelly and Dave told her parents that he was thirty-two years old, but even that wasn't true. They later discovered he was actually forty-eight – older than Kelly's father at the time.

Dave's age wasn't the only thing they hid from her parents. Dave wasn't "Dave" at all: his name was actually James Patterson Smith.

Though mature for her age, Kelly was still young and naïve. She was flattered to have an older man so interested in her, but she didn't realize that their relationship was more about power and control than love. Smith controlled everything the young girl did from that point on.

Kelly's demeanor slowly changed. She was no longer the bright, bubbly girl her mother knew, and they gradually saw less and less of her. When she finally showed up at her parent's home again, she seemed troubled and depressed but refused to admit anything was wrong.

Kelly had bruises on her arms and face. Her parents' concerns reached a new level when she came home one day with the whole side of her face black from bruising.

Kelly lied and told her mother she'd been jumped by a group of girls who had beaten her up. Each time she showed up with new injuries, her story changed. Her parents had no idea that Smith had a long history of violence towards young women.

Margaret could clearly see that her daughter had been abused and went to the police, who told her to have a doctor examine Kelly so they could document the abuse. But again, Kelly was sixteen and considered an adult. Her mother was helpless. Unless Kelly went in of her own accord, neither her parents nor the police could do anything.

Kelly's mother could see that the violence was escalating when Kelly showed up with a horrible bite mark on her arm. But again, Kelly shrugged it off and claimed that she had fallen and caught her arm on a chain-link fence.

In November 1995, Margaret pleaded with Kelly to leave Smith, but it only seemed to anger her. She told her mother she would be seeing much less of her. Unfortunately, that was the last time Margaret saw Kelly alive.

Over the following months, Kelly phoned her mother and told her that she was working long hours and weekends at a factory – that was why she hadn't stopped by to visit. Eventually, however, the phone calls stopped altogether.

In March 1996, Margaret received a Mother's Day card and a birthday card for Kelly's father, Tommy. Both were obviously not written in Kelly's handwriting; Smith was now in complete control and toying with them.

On April 17, 1996, James Patterson Smith walked into the Gorton Police Department and reported that his girlfriend had drowned in his bathtub. Police arrived at a horrific bloodbath that was much more than a drowning.

Seventeen-year-old Kelly Anne Bates had indeed drowned in the bathtub, but she had also been held prisoner for at least three weeks and suffered torture beyond imagination.

The pathologist's report revealed 150 separate injuries, including having her eyes gouged out, stab wounds inside her eye sockets, and mutilation of her mouth, ears, nose, and genitalia. In addition, she had been scalded with boiling water, burned with a hot iron, stabbed and cut with knives, forks, pruning shears, and scissors, her head was partially scalped, and her knees had been kicked in.

Literally every room in the house had traces of Kelly's blood. Evidence revealed that Kelly's hair had been tied to a radiator, and her eyes were gouged out at least a week before her death. She hadn't received water for several days and had been starved, having lost about forty-five pounds.

Investigations revealed that there was a progressive pattern with Smith. They found that he had been married years before and divorced due to his violence against his wife. After the divorce, he dated a twenty-year-old who testified that he had used her as a "punching bag" even while she was pregnant. Their relationship ended when he tried to drown her. After that, he had a relationship with a fifteen-year-old girl who testified that he held her head underwater.

At the trial, Smith denied the murder charges and believed he was justified in his torture. Smith claimed that Kelly taunted him about the death of his mother and that she only had herself to blame. He also claimed she had "a habit of hurting herself to make it look worse on me." When asked why he gouged out her eyes, he said, "She dared me to do it."

The jury didn't even need a full hour to come back with a guilty verdict. The evidence and photos seen at the trial were so horrific that, after the trial, the jury members were offered psychological counseling. Every jury member accepted.

James Patterson Smith was sentenced to life imprisonment with a minimum term of twenty years. Kelly was buried the day before her eighteenth birthday.

CHAPTER 2
FRED GRABBE

The Grabbe family was wealthy by small-town standards. They were easily one of the richest families in Marshall, Illinois, a tiny farming town just ten miles west of the Indiana border. Most of their wealth came from Charlotte Grabbe's inheritance from her parents.

Both Charlotte and her husband, Fred, were extremely hard workers who spent long hours farming their soybean and corn fields, but their life together was far from perfect.

The couple had two children, Jeff and Jennie, who usually took Charlotte's side when there were problems between their parents. Fred and Charlotte had been married for twenty-three years filled with violence – so much so that they had divorced once and remarried, but the second marriage looked to be headed toward divorce as well.

Fred was a huge man standing at six foot four, while Charlotte was petite. During their heated arguments, Fred had no problem using his fists on his tiny wife or his son, Jeff. Things had gotten so bad that Charlotte had instructed Jeff and Jennie to come looking for her if she hadn't returned to the house by the end of each workday.

At forty-two years old, Fred was also a serial philanderer and had a fascination with younger women. Usually having a few girlfriends on the side at any given time, in 1981 Fred was dating a twenty-four-year-old, curly-haired, blonde bartender named Vickie McAllister.

After learning of Fred's latest affair, Charlotte was devastated and filed for divorce. Fred moved out of the family home into a small cabin on the edge of the family's property. Jeff and his wife then moved into the main family house with Charlotte.

It wasn't long after Fred moved into the cabin that Charlotte filed battery charges against him – he had assaulted her when she went to the cabin to take some furniture back to the main house.

Just after sundown on July 24, 1981, Charlotte had not returned to the house after work, and Jeff and Jennie knew something was wrong. She had gone out to the soybean field on her tractor, but when they went looking for her they found the tractor parked inside a machine shed. Her lunch box was still resting on the front tire. Jennie immediately returned home and reported her mother missing to the Clark County Sheriff.

When questioned by the Sheriff, Fred admitted they had quarreled but said that the last time he saw her, she was driving her car toward the interstate highway.

Days later, Charlotte's car was found across the state border in Terre Haute, Indiana, just 16 miles away. Police searched her vehicle and found no blood or signs of foul play, but beneath the seat was a loaded handgun.

Contrary to Fred's story, a friend of Charlotte's came forward and told the Sheriff she saw Fred driving his truck toward Terre Haute with someone following in Charlotte's car – someone other than Charlotte. The witness claimed the person driving Charlotte's car was a young, blonde woman with curly hair.

Investigators found that Charlotte kept a safe deposit box at the local bank. Inside the box, they found notes that she had placed there just ten days before she went missing. In those notes, she wrote that she believed Fred had been stealing farm equipment, and she had doubts that she would live through the divorce. In addition, she wrote that she was afraid of Fred and his business partner, Dale Kessler. The Sheriff questioned Dale Kessler, who claimed Fred had been with him on the evening Charlotte went missing.

At Jeff and Jennie's request, the Sheriff brought Fred and Vickie McAllister before a grand jury – but both refused to talk, invoking their Fifth-Amendment rights. Jennie even asked her father to take a lie detector test to prove he didn't kill her mother, but he refused.

Charlotte's case went cold for three years despite Jennie and her husband offering a $1,000 reward for information. They later raised it to $10,000, then again to $25,000, but still, no one came forward.

Eventually, Jennie hired a private investigator, Charles Pierson. Pierson decided to follow the clue of the curly-haired blonde driving Charlotte's car. Clearly, Pierson believed the woman driving the vehicle was Vickie McAllister and he wanted to talk to her.

Fred and Vickie had since broken up, and she was now living in West Terre Haute, Indiana. Pierson knew that Vickie liked to do two things: drink beer and play pool. He started hanging out in bars in the area and eventually met her and they became friendly.

When Pierson finally admitted who he was and why he had befriended her, she couldn't help but spill the beans. He said the information poured out of her like there was something she desperately needed to get off her chest. She had been holding a secret inside, and it was eating her alive. She was more than willing to finally come clean.

McAllister admitted to Pierson that she was the one driving Charlotte's car that day – but that was just the beginning. Next, she described the gruesome details of what happened that night and the following day.

Vickie McAlister's story made her physically ill each time she told it. Nevertheless, the story would eventually be told to authorities and, later, to two juries.

McAllister recalled that she and Fred Grabbe were in the machine shed that day to get some fifty-five-gallon metal barrels for farm work. As they were loading the barrels into his truck, they heard Charlotte's tractor. Fred told Vickie to hide behind another tractor inside the shed.

Fred went outside the shed to meet Charlotte, where they had a heated argument. The argument escalated as they came back inside the shed, but eventually, Fred couldn't control his rage and began strangling her. Using his bare hands, he choked her until she was almost unconscious. He then released his grip to let her regain consciousness – and then choked her again. He repeated this over and over again until, eventually, he strangled his wife to death.

Once Charlotte was dead, he sodomized her lifeless body while Vickie watched. Fred then grabbed a grease gun from the shed, and he filled all of Charlotte's orifices with grease. He crumpled her body into one of the 55-gallon barrels and loaded the barrel into the back of his pickup truck.

Grabbe instructed Vickie to drive Charlotte's green Ford LTD that was parked outside and follow him as he drove his truck across the state line into Indiana.

That night, they dumped Charlotte's car outside a bar in Terre Haute and drove back to Grabbe's farm, then parked on the bank of the Wabash River. Grabbe took the barrel out of his truck and placed it near a maple tree, where he poured diesel fuel into the barrel until it covered Charlotte's body. He then lit it on fire. Fred and Vickie sat on the riverbank while the barrel burned. The diesel fuel and the grease inside her body burned slowly, all night long.

The following morning, they heard the search party approaching, so they put out the fire and loaded the drum back onto Fred's truck, with Charlotte's charred body still inside. They then headed back to Vickie's home.

At sunset that night, they returned to the river, put the barrel in the same spot, and set it ablaze again. Again, it burned all night. In the morning, Fred rolled the barrel into the river. The only body part remaining was Charlotte's skull. He grabbed the skull, turned to Vickie, said, "This will make good fish bait," and then threw it in the river.

Vickie's confession helped, but it simply wasn't enough. Prosecutors needed some sort of physical evidence to charge Fred Grabbe. With no body, barrel, or murder weapon, investigators need something besides Vickie McAllister's word against Fred's. Officially, Charlotte's case was still just a missing person.

The new Sheriff in Clark County, Dan Crumrin, was curious if the maple tree – which still stood above the burn site – could somehow be used. Crumrin asked the University of Illinois for help, and they sent a plant biologist, Eugene Himelick, and an organic chemist, Donald Dickerson.

During the natural cycle of a tree's life, the seasons will cause a tree to grow in the spring and summer, then go dormant in the winter. This process each year creates the familiar ring in the trunk and branches of every tree. A ring in the tree's branch will show that year's growth.

Diesel fuel is highly toxic to a tree; if it doesn't kill it then it will, at the very least, hamper its growth.

Himelick and Dickerson took samples from the branches of the maple tree. Their findings concluded that three rings deep (meaning three years ago), the tree's growth was much thinner. The tree had gone through some sort of stress the summer that Charlotte had gone missing.

They then shredded the samples into sawdust, which Dickerson analyzed using a gas chromatograph mass spectrometer. A mass spectrometer is a device that identifies the components of a sample, even in very tiny amounts.

In their analysis, they found the presence of hydrocarbons found in diesel products. There were a total of five branches tested: the two branches located on the side of the tree that the barrel was on showed the hydrocarbons, the other three on the opposite side did not.

This forensic evidence was enough to convict Fred Grabbe. One of the prosecutors in the trial was Robert Egan of Chicago. Egan had been the prosecutor for the trial of John Wayne Gacy, a serial killer convicted for the murders of thirty-three young men in 1980.

Fred Grabbe was found guilty of first-degree murder and sentenced to life in prison without the possibility of parole. However, the story was far from over.

During the trial Fred had the support of his latest girlfriend, Barbara Graham, a twice-divorced mother of three from a nearby town. Fred had purchased her a mink coat that she wore in the courthouse during the trial to torment the family members.

A few weeks after Grabbe's conviction, he was being held in the Clark County jail when Barbara Graham attempted to break him out. She showed up at the jail and told Deputy Sheriff Mike Paulson that she wanted to give Fred a love note. When Paulson opened the door she fired five shots, one hitting the deputy in the leg. She hovered over him and said,

 "Don't make me kill you."

Graham's attempt, however, was unsuccessful; she was sentenced to sixteen years in prison for the crime. The judge that sentenced Grabbe to prison was convinced that Fred had somehow planned the breakout attempt from behind bars.

———

Just two months later, with Fred still in prison, both the Grabbe home and the nearby home belonging to Fred's son, Jeff, burned to the ground. Fire marshals determined that both fires were intentionally set. Investigators suspected that Fred had something to do with it from prison, but he was already serving a life sentence; they had no way to prove his involvement.

During Fred's imprisonment, his lawyers filed an appeal of his verdict and got his first conviction overturned on a technicality. By this time, Vickie McAllister was living another life under another name but returned to Clark County to testify against Fred again.

Just a month before the second trial, Fred's son Jeff, who had testified at the first trial, vanished. He was on a business trip in California when all his family members lost contact with him. By the time of the trial date, Jeff was nowhere to be found. The judge allowed his wife, Cindy, to testify in his absence. Despite lacking Jeff's testimony, Fred was again convicted a second time and sentenced to seventy-five years in prison.

One month after the trial, Jeff's body was found floating in the water at Seal Beach in California. Three bullet holes riddled his body, and an anchor was tied around him to keep the body down. To this day, Fred denies having anything to do with his son's murder.

Vickie McAllister received the $25,000 reward that Jennie and her husband had offered, and she relocated under yet another assumed name. She still lives in fear that Fred will somehow find her.

In June 2022, eighty-three-year-old Fred Grabbe was released on parole. He served only thirty-seven years of his sentence.

In yet another strange twist to this family story, years later in 2014, Fred's grandson, Adam Everett Livvix, was indicted on weapons and immigration charges in Netanya, Israel. He was suspected of impersonating a Navy SEAL and plotting bombing attacks on the Dome of the Rock, an iconic mosque in Israel. Livvix was diagnosed as being psychotic and unfit to stand trial. He was held in a mental institution in Israel for a year before he was released back to the US, where he faced charges of stealing farm equipment.

CHAPTER 3
THE MURDER OF ELAINE O'HARA

On the evening of August 22, 2012, Elaine O'Hara went missing near Dublin, Ireland. What happened that day and during the investigation over the next three years proved to be one of the most shocking crimes in Irish history.

On the morning of August 23, Sheila Hawkins planned on taking her partner's daughter, Elaine O'Hara, to the Tall Ships Festival in Dublin before she went to work for the day. Elaine had volunteered to work at the festival weeks before and was quite excited to attend.

When Elaine didn't show up at their meeting point that morning, Sheila contacted Elaine's father, Frank. Frank assured her that Elaine had probably driven herself to the festival and forgot to let her know. He assured her everything was okay and not to worry about it. Regardless, Sheila went to Elaine's house and rang the doorbell – but she left for work when there was no answer.

Frank had spent the previous day with Elaine after she was released from St. Edmonsbury Hospital. Elaine had spent three weeks there for her problems with depression. After leaving the hospital, Elaine and her father had lunch, where she talked about the Tall Ships Festival. Frank recalled that she was clearly excited to be a volunteer. Later, they drove to visit her mother's grave. Frank noticed Elaine texting someone during the drive, but he had no idea who. After an emotional visit to her mother's grave, Elaine went home around 4 p.m. to prepare for the festival the next day.

Later that day, there was still no word from Elaine. Knowing Elaine's history of depression and self-harm, Frank decided to use his key to check on her apartment. Nothing in the apartment seemed out of place, but Frank became worried when he noticed that Elaine's iPhone was there. Still thinking she might have simply forgotten it, he left her apartment and waited.

Elaine had a history of psychological problems dating back to her early teens. During school, she was a bullying victim, and when one of her closest friends died in a car crash, Elaine had attempted to take her own life by slashing her wrists.

Despite her fulfilling work with children, she struggled with her depression throughout the years. It reached a pinnacle when her mother died in March 2002, and Elaine was hospitalized again. By 2003 she seemed back on track, but it was short-lived: the psychiatrist to whom she had grown close, Dr. Anthony Clare, died in 2007. This posed another massive setback for Elaine.

Dr. Clare had diagnosed Elaine with depression and borderline personality disorder. She additionally suffered from asthma, diabetes, and dyslexia. Dr. Clare said Elaine possessed a childlike innocence and was emotionally submissive, with the emotional maturity of a 15-year-old. He also noted that Elaine had developed an obsession with being restrained, imprisoned, and punished, so much so that it had become a sexual fantasy.

Dr. Clare initially diagnosed her with gradually emerging psychosis. He later changed the diagnosis to borderline personality disorder and depression. Elaine was prescribed heavy depression medications and tranquilizers, so much so that her father would notice her falling asleep while eating dinner. Frank recalled that Elaine had lost much of her late teen and early adult life to medication and hospitals.

Throughout the years following her mother's death, Elaine was hospitalized a total of 14 times for depression and suicidal tendencies.

In July 2012, just six weeks before her disappearance, Elaine was once again contemplating suicide when she checked herself into St. Edmonsbury Hospital. During her stay, the hospital staff recalled Elaine constantly talking about the Tall Ships Festival. She planned to volunteer her time for an entire week and was clearly excited to attend.

By the end of her stay at St. Edmonsbury, Elaine's new psychiatrist, Dr. Murphy, had reduced her medications significantly. He said that, despite her struggles, 2012 was a good year for Elaine. She was discharged with no indication of suicidal tendencies.

Frank had agreed with the doctor. Elaine seemed to be doing better, but with her sudden disappearance, he couldn't get the idea out of his head that she may have done something horrible to herself.

Later that evening, there was still no word from Elaine. Frank sent her a text, "Are you still alive?" There was no response to his text message. Elaine's sister called her phone. Again, no answer.

The following morning, Frank and Sheila still hadn't heard from Elaine and decided to recheck her apartment. When they arrived, nothing had changed, but they also noticed that Elaine's handbag was still there. This was something he had missed when he was there before. This was deeply troubling: Elaine would never leave both her phone and handbag. Sheila reached into Elaine's laundry basket and found a latex bondage suit and mask. Out of privacy for Elaine, she initially hid her finding from Frank. He was already upset and this would have just troubled him more, so she decided not to mention it.

Frank and Sheila had known of Elaine's obsession with restraint and bondage since her teenage years, but they had no idea how far her fantasy had gone.

Frank called the hospital to see if Elaine had possibly checked herself back in again. She hadn't. The next logical spot to check was to go back to Shanganagh Cemetery. Elaine's brother-in-law, Mark Charles, drove to the cemetery where Elaine often visited her mother's grave. That's when he spotted her little turquoise Fiat. They contacted roadside assistance to get into her car, where they found two packs of cigarettes, a lighter, her driver's license, a portable satellite navigation system, and a mobile phone charger that wasn't for an iPhone. To the best of their knowledge, the family only knew Elaine to have one phone – an iPhone.

Knowing that Elaine had a history of suicide attempts, and Shanganagh Cemetery was just a short walk to the sea. Frank was distraught at the thought that Elaine had taken her own life.

Now panic-stricken, the family conducted a more extensive search of her apartment. In addition to her iPhone, handbag, and latex suit, they found all her medication for anxiety, depression, diabetes, asthma, vertigo, and cholesterol. She had also printed pages from a hunting website detailing two types of hunting knives, plus maps of Killakee Forest and Vartry Reservoir. Killakee Forest was a large, wooded area located adjacent to Shanganagh Cemetery, where her car was found. Vartry Reservoir was about twenty miles away. In Elaine's desk they found a notebook with website addresses for alt.com and collarme.com. Both were sexual fetish websites.

The following morning on August 24, with still no word from Elaine, Frank O'Hara went to the Garda, the national police force in Ireland. Police headed to the cemetery to investigate the car, the cemetery, and the nearby fields, forests, and shoreline, but they found no clues. They attempted a search by helicopter but bad weather wasn't cooperative.

Police then focused their attention on Elaine's apartment. Her apartment complex had ten security cameras in various spots throughout the property. Elaine was seen leaving her apartment at 5:05 p.m. on the 22nd, just thirty-six minutes after she arrived home from visiting with her father. She wore what seemed to be navy-colored tracksuit bottoms, white running shoes, and a blue hoodie. She was also carrying a telephone which clearly wasn't her regular iPhone. Her friends and family only knew her to have one phone, which was particularly puzzling.

Police again returned to the cemetery and the adjacent park to search further. While in the park, they came across a jogger named Connor Gilfoyle and showed him a photo of Elaine. When asked if he recognized Elaine, he said he had encountered her just a few days ago. Gilfoyle had been trying out an app on his phone called MapMyRun that day, so he was able to use it to give police the exact location and time that he encountered her in the park. He saw her at 5:45 p.m.

Gilfoyle mentioned that Elaine had seemed a bit tense and preoccupied. She'd asked him if he knew the directions to a footbridge that crossed the railroad tracks and led toward the beach. She didn't say thank you when he told her he didn't know, she just walked away. Thirty minutes later, he saw her again on the other side of the footbridge, so he knew she had made it that far.

Police and family members walked the beach for hours but found nothing. Both groups assumed the worst: Elaine had taken her own life. Her case was officially listed as a missing person. One year later, the family laid flowers in her honor at Shanganagh Cemetery, next to her mother.

The summer of 2013 was sweltering hot. A heatwave that swept Ireland that year dropped the water levels in Vartry Reservoir from twenty feet down to almost one foot. On September 10, 2013, William Fegan, his brother, and a friend were fishing from Sally's Bridge when they noticed something shiny beneath the water's surface. When they fished it out of the water, they found handcuffs, clothing, a ball gag, restraints, and leg restraints. At the time, they thought it was amusing and left the items on the bridge. The next day, Fegan was a bit troubled by the items and decided to bring them to the Roundwood Garda station.

Garda officer James O'Donahue treated the BDSM items as evidence, but at the time, he had no idea if a crime had even been committed. He let the items dry out, bagged them, and tagged them. O'Donahue thought, *Why would someone dispose of these in a reservoir? If it's just a couple disposing of their adult toys, why not just throw them in the rubbish? Someone was trying to hide something.*

The following day, O'Donahue went to the spot where Fegan found the items to search the area more thoroughly. Unfortunately, the water was murky due to high winds so he decided to try on another day. On the third trip to the site, Officer O'Donahue searched through the silt and found more handcuffs, an asthma inhaler, and a set of keys. On the keyring were two supermarket loyalty cards, one of which was for the local Dunne Stores.

On September 16, 2013, O'Donahue contacted Dunne Stores to find out the identity of the loyalty card owner. They reported that it belonged to Elaine O'Hara. O'Donahue wasn't familiar with her missing person case until he ran her name through the police computer – and what was happening at the same time just twenty miles away was an unbelievable coincidence.

Magali Vergnet was a professional dog trainer who regularly walked her dogs through Killakee Forest. On August 21, 2013, her dog, Millie, emerged from some dense brush with a bone in her mouth. Magali thought nothing of it, assuming it was an animal bone; she set it on a stack of bricks nearby and continued on her way. Over the next several weeks, Millie went into this same dense brush and emerged with a bone in her mouth. Finally, on September 13, 2013, Millie didn't return from the bushes, and Magali went in to find her. When she found Millie, she also found a ribcage of bones. Magali still assumed they were animal bones until she came across the leg of a tracksuit pant. She touched the pant leg with her foot and realized there was also a running shoe. She immediately left and called the property owner, who then contacted the police.

The police searched the area further and found 65 percent of a human skeleton, including a jawbone and a shovel. When DNA and dental records were searched, it was confirmed that they were the remains of Elaine O'Hara.

It was September 17, 2013 – one day after Officer O'Donahue had positively identified the BDSM items and supermarket loyalty cards. They belonged to Elaine O'Hara.

Police then conducted a much more comprehensive search of the reservoir. They recovered a red and black backpack, a leather mask, multiple knives, various BDSM items, eyeglasses, and two Nokia phones. The phones looked similar to what Elaine O'Hara was seen holding on the security camera footage from her apartment. The eyeglasses had a serial number on them which identified them as having been purchased from a store called Specsavers. Further investigation revealed the prescription was Elaine O'Hara's.

Police had a forensic computer team search Elaine's computer and found that she frequented dating sites that catered to the BDSM world: alt.com and collarme.com. Computer forensic specialists found that she had talked to several users on these sites, but one username in particular stood out - Architect72. The messages between them referenced "cutting myself" and "punishment involving a master's scalpel." Architect72 was also linked to a Gmail account with the username "fetishboy."

Elaine had confided in friends and family members that she had been having a BDSM relationship with an architect, but her friends knew nothing about him other than he was married.

Unbelievably, the two Nokia phones powered on after more than a year submerged in the reservoir. Each phone had only one contact – one with MSTR and the other with SLV, clearly "Master" and "Slave" with the vowels removed. What they found on the phones was quite disturbing. Thousands of text messages spanning several years between the two revealed a very dark relationship.

MSTR: "I'm a sadist. I enjoy others' pain. You should help me inflict pain on you and help me with my fantasies,"

MSTR: "I want to stick my knife in flesh while sexually aroused... blood turns me on and I'd like to stab a girl to death."

MSTR: "If you ever want to die, promise me I can do it"

MSTR: "My urge to rape, stab and kill is huge. You have to help me control or satisfy it"

MSTR: "Every time I stab or strangle you, I want you to think this is it and every time I let you live, you owe me your life and are grateful and worship me,"

MSTR: "Either you let me stab you or you help me do it to someone else.

MSTR: "Lots of people have stabbed and got away with it, why not me?"

SLV replied several times that she was frightened and didn't want to talk of killing or blood anymore.

SLV: "I'm too young to die"

SLV: "you have this hold over me that terrifies me."

SLV: "I'm just so scared. Do you know, sir, that I'm scared of you? You have this hold over me"

SLV: "I know my life is in your hands... every time we meet,"

SLV: "Please don't mention killing for a while, just until I settle back into life"

The phone number for MSTR was cross-referenced with the contacts on Elaine's iPhone, and it matched a contact named David. Investigators called the number, but there was no answer.

Investigators found that the cell phones were "burner phones," disposable phones purchased at a store in Dublin under the fake name Goroon Caisholn. However, they found someone with a very similar name, Gordon Chisholm, and brought him in for questioning. After questioning, police realized he was not their man.

While poring over the text messages, police finally got a potential break.

> SLV: Went well today sir, I take it you are now a daddy again thanks for last night sir, really needed it.
>
> MSTR: Yes, beautiful baby girl (child's name excluded). glad you enjoyed the other night, many more sessions to come, see you sometime over the weekend.

Those texts were from March 31, 2011. Police now knew that MSTR had a newborn baby girl born on that day – and they knew her name.

Another clue they got from the texts was:

> MSTR: "…came fifth in flying"

This one was dated June 11, 2011. Police initially thought he was possibly a pilot or maybe it was a reference to fly fishing. However, after searching for competitions around that time, they soon realized he was referring to model airplanes. He had apparently come fifth in a model airplane flying competition.

Roundwood Model Aeronautical Club had held a competition during that time, and the person that came in fifth was named Graham Dwyer. Coincidentally, when looking further into Dwyer's background, they found that he'd just had a baby born earlier that year.

During this same time, Detective Chief Superintendent Diarmuid O'Sullivan received a tip from a confidential informant who claimed they knew who killed Elaine O'Hara. The tipster pointed to an architect named Dwyer – Graham Dwyer.

Police now knew they had their man.

Superintendent O'Sullivan found Dwyer's house; during the night, he took his garbage from the curb and sifted through his trash. From the contents, investigators were able to put together a DNA profile of Graham Dwyer.

The mattress in Elaine's apartment had puncture marks, possibly from a knife, plus blood and semen stains. Forensic technicians found DNA from the semen stains which didn't match anything in the police database, but it matched the DNA acquired from Graham Dwyer's trash.

On October 17, 2013, police knocked on Graham Dwyer's door. There was no answer, so they went to the side door, and Dwyer answered in his pajama bottoms and no shirt.

Graham Dwyer was a family man: a seemingly respected architect working in Dublin whose hobbies included fast cars and model airplanes. None of his friends, family, or co-workers knew of his double life. Dwyer lived with his wife and two young children in Foxrock, a quiet suburb of Dublin. To the majority of the world he was just an average guy, but it was now apparent that the life he displayed was a charade. To look at him, you would never imagine such a monster could lurk behind his eyes.

Dwyer wrote to his wife from jail and insisted he did not murder "that awful woman." His wife subsequently left him.

The trial was one of the biggest in Ireland's history. The story dominated headlines because of Dwyer's seemingly normal life.

The amount of evidence that piled up after the extensive investigation was overwhelming.

The security cameras from Elaine's apartment showed Dwyer visited the building nine times between January and August 2012. On July 9, the video showed Elaine and Dwyer entering the elevator shortly after 5 p.m., then Dwyer leaving forty minutes later. Footage on August 13 and 15 showed Dwyer carrying a bag similar to the bag found in the reservoir.

Elaine's internet search history revealed searches for "Graham Dwyer Architect."

Gordon Chisholm, the man who was initially suspected because his name resembled the name under which the phones were purchased, Goroon Caisholn, ended up being an old acquaintance of Dwyer.

Even Dwyer's own son pointed him out in the security footage from Elaine's apartment complex.

Dwyer's personal phone was turned off between 5 and 9 p.m. the night Elaine went missing. On Dwyer's computer, there was an online order on August 17, 2012, for a hunting knife delivered to his work address on August 21, the day before Elaine went missing.

Additionally, there was erotic horror found on his computer, and he had shared files with Elaine about stabbing and killing. His computer also had videos he had filmed of himself and four women, where he could be seen stabbing the women during sex acts. Many of the videos featured Elaine O'Hara.

Several of the texts from Dwyer matched the details of and events from his personal life. He often mentioned his children by name, spoke of his daughter's birth, and referenced the Polish embassy he visited for his architectural firm. There were further references to tattoos, car repair bills, purchasing a bicycle ("to get fit for murder"), and the 15 percent pay cut he received at work. Everything from the texts synched perfectly with Dwyer's real life.

Despite the ridiculous amount of evidence against him, Dwyer still insisted he was innocent.

The courtroom was filled on January 22, 2015, when the trial began. The defense tried to argue that all the evidence was circumstantial and called only three witnesses. The prosecution called 194 witnesses, including Dwyer's wife, who testified that the shovel found alongside Elaine's remains was from their garden. Gemma Dwyer recognized the shovel because it had orange paint splatters on it from when they painted the garden fence at their home in Foxrock.

Additional witnesses included Dwyer's former partner and mother of his adult son, Eimear McShea. She described him as controlling and abusive and stated he'd had the desire to stab her during sex. She testified that he had asked to bring a knife into the bedroom. She eventually agreed to his request, as long as he kept it on the side table – but Dwyer couldn't control himself and had to hold it while they had sex.

Darci Day, a young American woman whom Dwyer had chatted with online, testified by video link. Darci testified how he had confided his fantasies of killing Elaine O'Hara.

 "He said he used to cut her… in the stomach area and stuff. That it was mutual and sexual… He basically wanted to go after her, and if she wanted to, he wanted to kill her and come after me."

Photoshopped images on Dwyer's computer showed Darci lying topless with her throat slit and her intestines coming out of her stomach. Police also found a document of fiction titled "Killing Darci," in which he fantasized about stabbing the American woman to death while they had sex.

Still, Dwyer's defense team claimed that because pathologists did not determine a cause of death, there was no evidence that Dwyer was responsible. They argued that Elaine had been released that morning from a psychiatric hospital for having suicidal thoughts and that even her own family believed she had taken her own life. They presented that the text messages the prosecution was using as evidence were nothing more than sexual fantasies.

The prosecution, however, argued that the text messages detailed a very specific plan for Elaine's death and that she had repeatedly asked "not to be stabbed" and "not to be beaten" by Dwyer. They argued that Dwyer knew she was being released from a psychiatric hospital and had lured her to her mother's gravesite and the remote mountain area, knowing that the police and family would believe Elaine had taken her own life.

The trial lasted forty-five days, and on March 27, 2015, the jury of seven men and five women returned with a verdict: guilty. Graham Dwyer was sentenced to life in prison. The judge said he "agreed 110 percent" with the jury's decision. The trial was emotionally taxing on the jury members, and the judge exempted them from further jury duty for the next thirty years.

If it weren't for the strange series of coincidences – the disobedient dog, the summer drought, etc. – Graham Dwyer may not have been caught. It's unknown who Chief Superintendent O'Sullivan's "confidential informant" was, as that evidence was not used in the trial.

The following is the final chain of text messages between SLV and MSTR sent between August 14 and 22, leading up to the death of Elaine O'Hara.

August 14

MSTR: "Am I right in thinking you don't want to die anymore?"

SLV: "I'm sorry I made you so mad."

MSTR: "You'll have to take a punishment. If anything happened to you, who knows about me?"

SLV: "No one knows your name, and no one knows about you really. They know I'm into BSM and that I meet people."

MSTR: "OK, let's keep it that way. If I ever meet your neighbour, I'm your brother, David, ok?"

SLV: "I already told the girl next door that you are a friend."

MSTR: "Would she make a good victim for me?"

SLV: "Too close to home,"

MSTR: "Ok. We will start going on outdoor walks for play and hunting."

SLV: "Sir, do I have to come?"

MSTR: "Yes, help me plan it. You won't be there... but I want to do it this year."

SLV: "Every time I think about it, sir, I want to heave,"

MSTR: "Just think about me being happy doing it. It's what I like. If you were any good, you would help me find her, hold her down while I kill her."

SLV: "Sir, are you going to stab me?"

MSTR: "Yes, I'm going to make you bleed. Nice and deep in your guts,"

August 16

SLV: "I am scared that the punishment will go on for a long time."

MSTR: "No. Swift and brutal. Might even kill you."

August 17

MSTR: "Did a huge walk up the Dublin Mountains yesterday. Plenty of lonely hill walkers up there."

August 20

MSTR: "Morning slave, looking forward to seeing you Wednesday."

SLV: "I'm not being stabbed,"

MSTR: "Ok, but you must take some sort of punishment."

SLV: "I know."

MSTR: "What kind of punishment would you like? Choices are hard anal with stabbing and choking. Whipping till bleeding. Chained overnight in a forest. Choked unconscious. If you don't pick one then it's all four.

SLV: "I don't know sir. Sorry doc came in. Sir u know I can't make choices."

MSTR: "Ok overnight in woods."

SLV: "Sir, I'll take stabbing."

MSTR: "Ok, but I must see blood… And I want to do it outdoors."

SLV: "Please sir, indoors."

MSTR: "Why?"

SLV: "I'm afraid if outdoors, you might kill me."

MSTR: "I won't kill you. If I was, it would be indoors hanging once you are chained up."

SLV: "I know, I mean that's it, nothing else?"

Elaine's next texts explain that she's planning on attending the Tall Ships Festival, so she asks:

SLV: "I was wondering if you could keep the visual marks to a min sir, please?"

MSTR: "That's a big request. But Ok."

SLV: "Thank you sir, I appreciate it. I can cover wrists and arms, it's the neck sir."

MSTR: "Don't worry. I won't stab you in the neck."

SLV: "Maybe not but you want to."

August 21

SLV: "R u mad at me sir?"

MSTR: "No but you must be punished for trying to kill yourself without me and for being unavailable for so long."

SLV: "Yes sir, I know. Master needs to punish slave."

MSTR: "I'm going to get blood on my knife for this a lot of blood then we can move on."

SLV: "Yes sir."

MSTR: "That's my good slave. Master is very horny and needs to put his cock in his slave."

SLV: "Master, may I ask you something?"

MSTR: "Yes, but don't upset me before I am about to cut you."

SLV: "Do you go by the Gorean way and is it just a fantasy? Gorean I mean?"

MSTR: "It's a real lifestyle that people really live by. Yes you are my slave but I need you to be serving me not stuck in a hospital. I wish I could fuck you on my lunch break."

SLV: "How do we do that master?"

MSTR: "You need to get out of hospital and serve me."

SLV: "Yes master im out tomorrow sir. It will be after lunch as the doc wants to see after lunch at 2.30 b4 I go."

Master then turns the conversation again to suicide.

MSTR: "Are u happy going on like this forever?"

SLV: "Sir, please stop. You want me to be in here forever! Can't we just have a normal master slave relationship without this please sir."

MSTR: "Ok but you must promise me next time you fall down that I end you. Hopefully you will be Ok though."

SLV: "Ok, I promise sir."

MSTR: "I mean it now. I will get into trouble if I don't do it at this stage."

SLV: "What do you mean? How could you get into trouble? It's suicide. It's fucking suicide. Don't be troubling yourself. It's suicide! No one will look into it."

MSTR: "I want to watch as well and be there for you so you won't be lonely."

SLV: "Shit. That's shit. I am lonely all the time and you're not there that's how I get like this. You just want a hard on. You're being fucking selfish!"

No reply from Master.

 SLV: "Sir, sorry. Just get angry talking about it. I just want to try again. Be a good person/slave/friend and I want to try and have a normal life without talking and thinking about that. Please let me try."

MSTR: "Ok."

Later that day...

MSTR: It's up to me and you have a big punishment coming up, getting knifed in the guts."

SLV: "I know sir. I better be tied up good sir. Please not outdoors, please."

MSTR: "I know. You will be well bound and gagged and tied to a tree deep in the forest. I have a spot picked out."

SLV: "What if we get caught?"

MSTR: "We won't get caught."

SLV: "I'm not leaving my apartment. You will have to drag me out."

MSTR: "You will do what you are fucking told. I want outdoor play and you are going to follow instructions, or I will double punishment or hang you."

SLV: "How do you know we won't get caught."

MSTR: "I found a really, really remote place. No one will find us."

SLV: "Sir, do I have to be naked!"

MSTR: "It's very deep in the forest and yes you do. I don't want blood over your clothes."

SLV: "Now I'm terrified!"

MSTR: "Trust me it will be exciting."

SLV: "Sure sir. So what time do you want me tomorrow sir? I was going to go see my niece before I went home and they are hols [sic] next two weeks!"

MSTR: "5:30"

SLV: "Do I have to drive, sir?"

MSTR: "A bit, yes."

SLV: "Now, I'm really scared."

MSTR: "Don't be scared."

Elaine reassured Dwyer that she hadn't mentioned him during any of her counseling conversations.

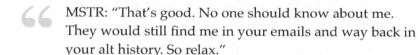

MSTR: "That's good. No one should know about me. They would still find me in your emails and way back in your alt history. So relax."

MSTR: "I'm heading to the spot now to double check."

August 22. The day of the murder.

SLV: "This place, although a pain in the ass at times, is safe because I know what's coming and I don't want to leave. I'm just so scared. Do you know, sir, that I'm scared of you? You have this hold over me."

MSTR: "Do not fear death."

SLV: "Please don't mention killing for a while, just until I settle back into life."

MSTR: "But, tonight's punishment will be like me pretending to do someone for real. It's important to me that you feel it's my right to take my slave's life if I want to. Every time I stab or strangle you, I want you to think this is it and every time I let you live, you owe me your life and are grateful and worship me."

37

SLV: "I know my life is in your hands… every time we meet,"

She texted around midday to say she had gotten out earlier than expected, was on her way home, and to ask if he had any instructions.

 MSTR: "Have a bath, make sure your cunt shaved, no underwear not even a bra. Loose clothes, footwear for mud. Make sure you are fed. Take painkiller,"

SLV: "Can I do what I want until I am needed?"

MSTR: "Like what?"

SLV: "I don't know yet, just anything I want to do."

MSTR: "You will be in a lot of pain later and next few days."

SLV: "It's going to be that bad? I'm going to be busy next few days. Tall Ships please don't make it really sore Please."

MSTR: "You will have stab wounds. You know the drill. The last few didn't bleed. These will."

SLV: "Sir how many?"

MSTR: "As many as I like."

SLV: "Yes Sir.

MSTR: "I want you to park at Shanganagh Cemetery at 5.30. Leave your iPhone at home. Just bring Slave phone and keys. You will get further instructions there."

SLV: "Sir are we doing this if it's raining? Are you coming back to my place? I need to clean, it's dirty."

MSTR: "Yes, if it's raining. No, I won't be back at your place."

SLV: "No offence sir, but do we have to do it in the rain. It's cold."

MSTR: "Don't worry, it's never as bad as u think it's going to be."

SLV: "Yes Sir."

MSTR: "Don't be nervous and enjoy being told what to do."

SLV: "Easier said than done sir."

MSTR: "Empty yourself and become nothing. You are property and a piece of slave meat. Your only job is to serve."

SLV: "Can I wear socks with runners? Can I bring inhaler? Didn't have time to eat, will we be late back?"

MSTR: "Yes to socks. Leave inhaler in car. You should be back at car abt 8. More painful getting stabbed on empty stomach. Suit yourself. See you in a bit. x"

SLV: "Here Sir."

MSTR: "Ok, take only keys and Slave phone. Make your way on foot to park next door and text me in the middle."

SLV: "Please let me take inhaler sir."

MSTR: "Ok."

SLV: "Ok sir is the park with the playing fields in the top part or bottom."

MSTR: "Ok cross railway bridge in the next park near cliffs."

SLV: "I'm lost I'm in the football field now."

MSTR: "Look for railway footbridge near footpath."

SLV: "Here now, where's park?"

MSTR: "Cross bridge and head for opposite end of park near steps to sea."

SLV: "OK on the footpath yes no?"

MSTR: "Yes."

SLV: "Steps here."

She texted him to say she was at the steps. Elaine received the final text at precisely 6 p.m. on August 22, 2012.

 MSTR: "Go down to the shore and wait."

A total of 2,612 texts were sent throughout the years between those two phones; with this final text, Graham Dwyer then achieved his ultimate sexual fantasy of stabbing a woman to death, presumably during sex.

The following is the "Victim's Statement" that was read in the courtroom after the conviction:

 "We know that we are not the only victims of this crime. We recognize that other families are suffering too, and we feel for every other person affected. Words cannot adequately describe how we are feeling, and we would never want any other family to go through what we have endured over the past two and a half years.

We have lost a daughter, a sister, and a friend in the most brutal, traumatic, and horrifying manner. We also have many unanswered questions which we will have to carry with us for the rest of our lives.

Elaine was a very intelligent girl who never fully realized her potential due to her psychological difficulties. She was prescribed a lot of medication and this did have an impact on her ability to be a regular teenager, particularly socially.

She was emotionally immature and very trusting of anyone who showed her kindness. In later years her medication was reduced, hospital stays became less common, and she functioned more effectively. However, she had missed out on those important, formative teenage years.

She had a strong work ethic and loved working with children, as she could relate to them better than to adults. She was always there to help and assist others, giving lifts, covering shifts at work or collecting many of the items for the Christmas Fair at school.

Elaine adored her niece, who was also her goddaughter, and loved reading, painting, and playing with her. For months after she went missing, her goddaughter would point out cars that were like Elaine's saying, "There's Elaine's car."

We smiled and nodded – how can you explain something to a young child that we couldn't understand ourselves? Since she left us, Elaine has two more nieces, but they will never know their aunt.

Elaine's ambition was to be a teacher, and she was studying Montessori. In 2014, we collected a BA in Montessori education, which was awarded to her in St Nicholas Montessori school. She would have been so happy and proud to stand up in her gown and hat to accept that degree herself after overcoming many obstacles to finally get the qualification she longed for, but unfortunately, this was not to be.

When Elaine went missing in August 2012, we were devastated. At that time, she appeared to us to be progressing well in life. She had a new apartment, was studying and working in two jobs.

She had a setback in July of 2012 and was voluntarily admitted to hospital. However, on weekend release, she was in very good form and was looking forward to the future.

The assumed suicide in August 2012 was a surprise to all the family but lack of evidence pointing to any other cause for her disappearance meant we reluctantly needed to accept that she had most likely taken her own life around Shanganagh.

We spent many hours walking the shore from Blackrock to Bray searching for any sign of her. A year after her disappearance we laid flowers in the sea at Shanganagh in her memory and in an effort to find some closure for us as a family.

Our attempt at closure was premature as when in September 2013 Elaine's remains were discovered; the Garda investigation changed from that of a missing person to murder. This led to further anguish for the family as we now faced the imaginable horror of Elaine having been murdered.

The trial has been an incredibly difficult experience. It was distressing to see Elaine's private life laid bare before the nation, despite the fact that she was the victim. Some of the reporting in the print media was insulting to Elaine and deeply upsetting for the family. At times, Elaine's life was relegated to a lurid headline in a newspaper.

It was heartbreaking for us to listen to the texts Elaine received from a depraved and diseased mind. The manipulation of her vulnerability was apparent, and when she tried to resist, she was reined back in.

We can hear her voice in those texts, just wanting to be loved. Hearing the contents of the videos will haunt us forever. We were upset that the credibility of our evidence was questioned, as throughout the two and a half years, all we wanted was the truth and justice for Elaine.

We will probably never know what happened in Killakee on Wednesday, the 22nd of August 2012, but there are questions that trouble us:

When did Elaine realise it was not a game anymore?

When did she realise that the intention was to kill her for real?

Did she try to run?

Was she restrained?

Did she suffer much?

Could she and did she cry out?

Was she left on the mountain to die alone?

This is OUR life sentence. For us, there is no parole."

CHAPTER 4
THE TOOLBOX KILLERS

The 1970s were notorious for serial killers in the Los Angeles area. There was the Night Stalker, the Freeway Killer, the Hillside Strangler, and many others. However, some of the most vile and disgusting killings were perpetrated by the duo Lawrence Bittaker and Roy Norris.

Lawrence Bittaker had experienced trouble with the law since he was twelve years old. By the age of eighteen, he had dropped out of school and spent time in the California Youth Authority for shoplifting, petty theft, auto theft, hit and run, and evading arrest. When he was released, he found that his adoptive parents had disowned him and moved to another state.

Within days of his release, Bittaker was already in trouble with the law again: he was arrested for stealing a car and driving it across state lines. In August 1959, he was sentenced to prison for ten months in Oklahoma and then transferred to Springfield, Missouri, but released the following year.

Bittaker developed a pattern of getting arrested, released, and arrested again. Over the next fourteen years he was arrested at least six times for offenses such as parole violation, theft, leaving the scene of an accident, and burglary.

During his incarceration, he was put through several psychological tests in which he was diagnosed as being borderline psychotic, having a highly manipulative character, and having considerable concealed hostility. He was also found to have quite a high IQ of 138. Further examinations showed he was resistant to acknowledging responsibility: Bittaker confided in his psychiatrists that his criminal activities gave him a sense of self-importance. He was prescribed anti-psychotic medications.

Finally, in 1974, Bittaker was caught stealing a steak from a supermarket. When the store clerk followed him into the parking lot to confront him, Bittaker stabbed him in the chest and only just missed his heart. Bittaker ran but was subdued by two other supermarket employees. The clerk survived, and Bittaker was convicted of assault with a deadly weapon and sent to the California Men's Colony in San Luis Obispo.

Roy Lewis Norris lived only part of his childhood with his birth parents. Still, he was occasionally passed around to various foster homes throughout Colorado, where he was a victim of sexual abuse by a Hispanic family he had been living with. When he was sixteen, he made sexual references to a female relative. Upset that he was punished for it, Norris stole his father's car, drove into the Rocky Mountains, and attempted suicide by injecting air into his artery. He was eventually caught by the police as a runaway and returned home – to the news that his parents were divorcing. They told him they were only married because of him and his younger sister, and they didn't want their children anyway.

At seventeen, Norris dropped out of school and joined the US Navy. At twenty-one, he was sent to Vietnam. While there, he learned to become an electrician and began using heroin and marijuana.

In November 1969, Roy Norris was arrested for rape and attempted rape when he forced his way into a woman's car. However, he didn't spend much time behind bars; just three months after his release, he was caught breaking into another woman's home.

U.S. Navy psychologists diagnosed Norris with a severe schizoid personality, and he was given an administrative discharge for "psychological problems."

In May 1970, on the San Diego State University campus, Norris stalked a female student, attacked her, and struck her in the head with a rock. He pounded her head into the sidewalk while he kneed her in the back. Charged with assault and sentenced to five years at Atascadero State Hospital, he was diagnosed as a mentally disordered sex offender.

After five years of incarceration, authorities determined he was "no further danger to others" and released him into the public. It only took three months for him to revert back to his perverted ways, when he raped a woman in Redondo Beach. Norris was sentenced to California Men's Colony in San Luis Obispo – which was where he met Lawrence Bittaker.

While in prison, Bittaker had saved Norris from attacks by other inmates a few times, and they had become friends. As they grew to know one another, they realized they had many common interests, most of which involved sexual violence toward women. The two discussed how they loved the sight of frightened young women. Bittaker, until this point, had not committed any sexual offenses but expressed his interest to Norris and stated that, if he ever did commit such a crime as rape, he would kill the girl afterward. He said he wouldn't want to leave a witness to the crime.

During their time behind bars, their friendship evolved as did their plots for perversion. Bittaker and Norris discussed at length how, upon their release, they would fulfill their fantasies of raping and murdering young girls – one for each age between thirteen and nineteen years old.

Bittaker was released first in October 1978. He was a skilled machinist earning $4,000 a month, quite a sum for that time and especially so for a convicted felon only a few months out of prison.

He lived in a Burbank motel and was very popular with the local teenagers. It was well-known that he always had beer and pot available.

Norris was released three months later, in January and moved in with his mother in Redondo Beach. He started working as an electrician in Compton, and it wasn't long until he got a letter from his prison buddy, Lawrence Bittaker. The two met in February and planned their mayhem.

The first order of business was to buy a van. If you've heard the term "serial killer van," this is possibly where the term came from. The duo purchased a 1977 GMC cargo van in February 1979 with no side windows and a large sliding door, just like the cliché. They nicknamed their killing machine "Murder Mac."

For three months, the couple cruised up and down the Pacific Coast Highway from Redondo Beach north to Santa Monica. Perfect Southern California weather and beach communities meant plenty of young girls on their way to the beaches. They stopped to talk to girls, offer them pot, offer them a ride, party, have some beer, and take Polaroid photos. It was all just a practice run for their chaos. Norris and Bittaker picked up twenty girls just to practice their routine and get the girls into their van voluntarily.

Once they were confident they could do this, they built a bed in the back of the van. Beneath the bed, they stored a cooler with beer and soda to lure the girls, a toolkit for torture items, and clothes to change into after their victims were soaked with their blood.

Next, they searched for a location. Somewhere secure. Somewhere private. Just beyond the San Gabriel Mountains, they found an old fire road. They broke the lock on the gate and replaced it with their own.

It was go-time. They were on the hunt.

June 24, 1979. Cindy Schaffer was just sixteen years old when her grandmother dropped her off at St. Andrews Church in Redondo Beach for a fellowship meeting. Cindy only stayed for twenty minutes before she decided to walk home.

On her walk home, Bittaker and Norris pulled up to her and asked if she needed a ride. "No, thanks." They tried again and offered her some marijuana. "No, thanks." She kept walking.

They pulled up ahead of her and parked. Norris opened the sliding door to the van and pretended to get something out of the back. As she walked by, Norris grabbed her and threw her into the van. Bittaker cranked the stereo to full volume to muffle the screams while Norris gagged her and bound her feet and legs. This became their modus operandi of acquiring victims.

Bittaker drove the van north on the Pacific Coast Highway to the San Gabriel Mountains and their secret hideout. Once there, Norris told Bittaker he wanted some time alone with Cindy. Bittaker agreed and wandered off into the mountains while Norris raped her. During the night, the two took turns raping and torturing her. Cindy asked if they were going to kill her and Norris replied, "No." She then begged, "If you're going to kill me, please just let me pray." But they declined her request.

Bittaker later recalled that Cindy "displayed a magnificent state of self-control and composed acceptance of the conditions of which she had no control. She shed no tears, offered no resistance, and expressed no great concern for her safety… I guess she knew what was coming."

When it came time to kill her, the two argued about who would do it – both wanting the other one to end her life. Norris lost and was chosen to finish the task. Norris tried to strangle her with his bare hands but, after forty-five seconds, became physically disturbed by the look in her eyes and released his grip. He ran to the front of the van and threw up, false teeth and all.

Bittaker took over. He tried to strangle her as well, but strangling the life out of a person was much more difficult than either of them had imagined. Barely able to breathe, Cindy slumped to the ground and began convulsing. Bittaker grabbed a coat hanger from the van and put it around her neck. With a pair of pliers, he began twisting the ends, twisting and twisting until she died.

Bittaker found a steep cliff, and the two wrapped Cindy's body in a plastic shower curtain, then threw her off. Bittaker assured Norris that the animals would eat any evidence of a body.

Meanwhile, Cindy's grandmother called the police when she didn't arrive home that night. However, without a body and no evidence of foul play, the police were at a loss.

Just two weeks later, on July 8, 1979, Bittaker and Norris were cruising the Pacific Coast Highway looking for their next victim when they spotted eighteen-year-old Andrea Hall hitchhiking in Manhattan Beach. As they slowed to offer her a ride, another car stopped at the same time. Andrea got into the other vehicle but Bittaker and Norris followed close behind. When the first car dropped her off at Redondo Beach, they pulled up next to her and offered her a ride. She accepted.

This time Bittaker was driving while Norris was hiding in the back, ready to strike. Once Andrea got in the van, Bittaker offered her a drink. When she accepted, he told her to get one out of the cooler in the back. Norris lay in wait. Norris grabbed her, and again, Bittaker turned up the volume on the radio while Norris tried to subdue her.

Andrea was a strong girl and put up quite a fight, but eventually, Norris overpowered her, gagged her, and bound her wrists and ankles. All the while, Bittaker drove to their secret location.

Once they arrived, Bittaker raped her twice and Norris once. Norris thought he saw a car's headlights on the secluded fire road, so they decided they would drive further into the mountains and continue. Andrea screamed and pled for her life, but her cries only empowered them.

Bittaker forced her to walk alongside the van, naked and uphill, then perform fellatio and pose for Polaroids. Norris drove back to town to get alcohol; when he returned, Bittaker had already killed her. He told her to give him as many reasons as she could to spare her life, then shoved an ice pick in each of her ears. That wasn't enough to kill her, so he strangled her and threw her over a cliff.

Andrea's sister and brother-in-law reported her missing, but again, the police had nothing to go on. The girl had just disappeared without a trace.

The killers took a two-month break, and on September 3, they spotted fifteen-year-old Jackie Gilliam and thirteen-year-old Leah Lamp sitting on a bus stop bench near Hermosa Beach. The girls had been hitchhiking, and Bittaker and Norris stopped to offer them a ride to the beach. The young girls accepted.

It wasn't long before Leah realized Bittaker was driving away from the beach, not toward it. Bittaker gave the excuse that they were looking for a place to park and smoke pot, but Leah didn't buy their story. She reached for the sliding door and tried to jump out, but Norris had a bag full of ball bearings; he quickly hit her over the head with it and threw her back into the van. When a bystander at the public tennis courts noticed the altercation, Bittaker told the man she was just having a bad LSD trip, and they drove off.

Bittaker drove back to their private location, and the two started their chaos. Neither of them was interested in Leah because they thought she was overweight, so instead, they focused on Jackie. Bittaker took out his cassette recorder because he wanted to record his first rape of a virgin. He commanded Jackie to pretend like she was enjoying it. Norris went one step further when he raped her and told her to pretend he was her cousin.

That night, Norris and Bittaker took turns standing watch while the other slept next to the girls. In the morning, they took Leah up a hill and told her to strip naked. They then took photos of her in sexual positions, tied her up, and left her.

Bittaker again turned his focus back to Jackie. He shoved an icepick into her head and strangled her, just like he did to Andrea.

Leah again tried to escape, but before she had a chance, Bittaker struck her in the head with a short-handle sledgehammer, knocking her out. He then strangled her. To make sure she was dead, Norris beat her in the head.

Both girls were reported missing by their families, but like the girls before them, police had no bodies and nothing to go on.

Another two months had passed. The two men were out on Halloween night when Bittaker saw a girl he knew: sixteen-year-old Lynette Ledford standing outside a gas station. She had left a Halloween party in Sunland-Tujunga, near Los Angeles, after she fought with some boys at the party. She was headed home when Bittaker pulled over and offered her a ride. Since Bittaker was a regular at the McDonald's where she worked, she accepted the ride.

Bittaker was impatient and, rather than drive to their fire road location, decided to do this one on the move. He drove down a deserted suburban street where Norris pulled a knife on the girl, then bound and gagged her with duct tape.

The two men switched places, and Norris drove aimlessly around the streets for over an hour. Bittaker, in the back with Lynette, carried out their most vicious rape yet. Bittaker turned on the tape recorder to record everything while he beat her, raped her, and forced her to fellate him. He forced her to say she liked it through her cries and screams. He then ripped apart her clitoris, rectum, labia, and nipples with a pair of pliers from his toolbox.

By the time it was Norris' turn to rape her, there was nothing left but bleeding orifices. He forced her to fellate him while he beat her elbow over and over again with a sledgehammer. Norris encouraged her to scream louder and louder. He beat her twenty-five times on the elbow, and each blow could be heard on the recording, along with her blood-curdling screams.

They turned the tape recorder off and Norris strangled her to death with a coat hanger, twisting it with a pair of pliers until it was only slightly larger than a silver dollar. Lynette Ledford died with her eyes open.

Roy Norris later recalled the recording of that night,

 "We've all heard women scream in horror films... still, we know that no one is really screaming. Why? Simply because an actress can't produce some sounds that convince us that something vile and heinous is happening. If you ever heard that tape, there is just no possible way that you'd not begin crying and trembling. I doubt you could listen to more than a full sixty seconds of it."

Bittaker believed they were above the law and immune to prosecution. He decided they should dump the body publicly. He drove down a suburban street, chose a random residential front yard, and dumped her body in a bed of ivy on the lawn. He wanted to see the reaction of the public and authorities when the body was found.

A jogger found the body early the next morning, the coat hanger still around her neck. The press, police, and Los Angeles residents were terrified. The murder hunt began, but it would be three weeks before they would get another clue.

The following month, Roy Norris visited an old friend from the California Men's Colony, Joe Jackson. Norris had previously spoken to Jackson about his fantasy of raping young girls and felt comfortable talking to him about his exploits with Bittaker since their release. He included all the graphic details of the most recent victim, Lynette Ledford. At this time, Lynette was still the only body that had been found.

Jackson was an ex-convict, but he was also the father of two young girls. The gruesome details of Norris and Bittaker's killings didn't sit well with him. Jackson contacted his attorney who, in turn, informed the police. The case was assigned to Detective Paul Bynum of the Hermosa Beach Police Department.

The police brought Jackson in for questioning, and he told Detective Bynum about the van Norris had claimed they used during the killings. His description of the van matched a description given by a girl, Robin Roebuck, who had been raped by two men in the area two months prior. Detective Bynum revisited Robin, and she immediately picked out Norris and Bittaker from a photo lineup.

Roy Norris was put under surveillance, then quickly caught when officers saw him through a window of his home weighing marijuana and stuffing it into baggies for sale. Police arrested Norris on parole violations of possessing drugs and dealing marijuana and brought him in for further questioning.

Detectives searched a car that Norris owned and found photos of young women, but Norris claimed none of those girls had been harmed.

That same day, while the police were still at Norris' home, Bittaker called, and an officer answered the phone. The officer was quick to think and pretended to be one of Norris' friends. He tried to lure him in, but Bittaker, with his 138 IQ, didn't fall for it. He immediately drove to a cemetery in the Hollywood Hills where he buried the torture tapes. When he returned to the motel room in Burbank where he was living, police were waiting for him, and he was arrested.

Lawrence Bittaker was surprisingly cooperative when arrested and handed over several Polaroid photographs. Many of the photos were of Andrea Joy Hall and Jackie Gilliam.

Both men initially claimed innocence, but when police found the van, there was just too much evidence to deny. Investigators found over 500 photos of young women, two necklaces from the victims, a book on how to find police broadcasting frequencies, a sledgehammer, a jar of Vaseline, a plastic bag full of lead weights, and – most damning of all – the cassette recording from the final killing of Lynette Ledford. The tape was played for Lynette's mother, Shirley, who confirmed it was her daughter's voice.

In Bittaker's motel room, investigators found seven bottles of acidic liquids. The killers apparently had plans to step up their game with the next victims and attempt to dissolve the bodies.

Detective Bynum and Deputy District Attorney Stephen Kay interrogated Roy Norris. When faced with the mounting evidence, Norris took a plea deal. He confessed to his role in the killings and agreed to testify against Bittaker. In exchange, he was offered a reduced sentence, meaning no death penalty nor life without parole. Bittaker, however, admitted to almost nothing.

Bittaker was charged with five counts of first-degree murder, robbery, kidnapping, forcible rape, sexual perversion, and criminal conspiracy. Norris was charged with the same, except one of the first-degree murders was reduced to a second-degree murder charge.

Norris then led investigators to the fire road in the San Gabriel Mountains. He showed them exactly where each killing took place. During the interrogation, Norris spoke of the murders in a casual, uncoerced manner, like a mechanic would explain a problem with a car. He showed no emotion at all.

Upon searching the San Gabriel Mountains, police recovered the bodies of Jackie Gilliam and Leah Lamp, but the bodies of Cindy Schaefer and Andrea Hall were never found. Jackie's skull still had an ice pick lodged in it, and Leah's skull showed multiple indentations from the blows of a hammer.

During the trial, the most damning evidence was the audiotape of the horrible torture that Lynette Ledford endured. Courtroom attendees were seen running from the courtroom in tears, visibly shaken by the vile recording. Deputy District Attorney Stephen Kay could barely speak to reporters without breaking into tears after the tape was played. Many of the details from the transcription have been left out of this story simply because of its disgusting nature.

On March 18, 1980, Roy Norris pleaded guilty to all four counts of first-degree murder, one count of second-degree murder (Andrea Joy Hall), two counts of rape, and one count of robbery. On May 7, Roy Norris was sentenced to forty-five years to life with parole eligibility in 2010. Norris decided not to attend his parole hearing in 2010 and was denied parole in 2019. He died in prison the following year.

On February 17, 1981, Lawrence Bittaker was convicted of all five murder counts and was sentenced to death. Due to California legal changes, Bittaker was never put to death by the state but died in San Quentin Prison in 2019 of natural causes. He replied to letters from the public during his incarceration, often signing with the nickname "Pliers Bittaker."

Detective Paul Bynum committed suicide in 1987, at the age of thirty-nine. In his ten-page suicide note, he stated that the murders had haunted him and he worried that Bittaker and Norris would one day be released.

The tape of the rape and murder of Lynette Ledford has been used to train and desensitize FBI agents to the horrors of torture and rape.

CHAPTER 5
CHRIS COLEMAN

Chris Coleman grew up in an evangelical Christian family in a small suburban town about an hour south of St. Louis, Missouri. His parents, Ron and Connie Coleman, were co-pastors at the Grace Evangelical Church.

Shortly after high school, Chris joined the Marines and trained in the K9 unit as a dog handler. He also worked in security during his time in the military, including a guard detail for the US President.

Sheri Weiss grew up in Cicero, Illinois, just outside of Chicago; as a young girl, she loved baseball and the Chicago White Sox. When she was ten, her family moved to Tampa Bay, Florida, where she played varsity softball and became a cheerleader. She and her best friend, Tara Lintz, graduated high school in 1995. After working briefly as a waitress, Sheri joined the Air Force and worked as a military police officer.

Chris Coleman and Sheri Weiss met in Quantico, Virginia, while they were both attending a dog training seminar and immediately hit it off. The couple started dating, and not long after, Sheri was unexpectedly pregnant. With Chris coming from such a religious background, it was clear the couple needed to marry.

In their early twenties, Chris and Sheri eloped and married in Chicago outside his parent's church. Afterward, Chris called his parents and told them the news, but they were clearly not thrilled. He had only introduced Sheri to them as a "friend from Chicago." She wasn't a born-again Christian like they were and didn't fit into their evangelical lifestyle.

A few months later, Sheri and Chris had their first son, Garrett. Three years later, in January 2000, his brother, Gavin, arrived.

When Chris was just a small boy, his parents became friends with a woman named Joyce Meyer. Joyce was also an evangelical preacher who had worked her way up to become one of the richest money-making preachers in the world.

Joyce preached what is known as "prosperity theology" – a belief that insists that financial wealth is the will of God and that the more money you give to the church, the more favorably God will look upon you and bring financial riches back to you.

Obviously, this type of belief comes with an ample amount of criticism, especially when it comes from someone who flaunts their wealth as extravagantly as Joyce Meyer.

To this day, Joyce is still one of the more successful evangelical televan-gelists in the world. It was estimated that her businesses were grossing well over $100 million per year while she traveled around the world in her $10 million personal jet, preaching to huge crowds. Her $20 million headquarters in Fenton, Missouri, were adorned with such extravagan-cies as a $23,000 antique marble toilet.

Chris' father, Ron, met with Joyce Meyer at a prayer conference, and Joyce mentioned she needed someone to train a guard dog for her. Ron had the perfect candidate and re-introduced her to his son, Chris.

Chris trained Joyce's guard dog and landed himself a job on her secu-rity detail. Not long after that, he was promoted to Chief of Security, a position that paid over $100,000 per year.

The job application came with a "spiritual requirement" which stipu-
lated that he had to be of the same faith and could not divorce, among
other requirements. Chris, of course, was well-versed in the evangelical movement and had even been "speaking in tongues" since 1996.
Sheri had also become part of the evangelical movement and eventually donated her time to Joyce's ministries in the world outreach
program while she worked as an emergency medical technician.

With Chris' pay raise, the family moved to Columbia Lake, an affluent
suburban family development situated on a small lake. It was a close-
knit neighborhood where Sheri and the kids made friends with the
nearby neighbors.

Although one wouldn't know it from the outside, things started
turning sour for the couple in early 2008. Sheri had three friends that
didn't know one another. If they had, things might have turned out
differently.

On Memorial Day in May 2008, Sheri's neighbor, Vanessa, and her
husband noticed that Sheri had bruises on her upper legs. Vanessa and
her husband were worried that Chris was physically abusing her. Sheri
typically wore long sleeves and pants, so much of the time they
weren't sure if she was bruised or not. Vanessa and her husband hoped
for the best, decided it wasn't abuse, and left well enough alone.

Around the same time, Sheri confided to a different friend, Meegan,
that Chris was beating her. Sheri sent Meegan a text, "Chris is gone
right now, but he just beat me up. I'm ok, though." Meegan and her
husband pleaded with Sheri to come with them but Sheri refused to
leave Chris. Instead, she insisted that Chris was sorry and it wouldn't
happen again.

Sheri's third friend was her best friend from high school, Tara Lintz.
Tara was now divorced and living in Tampa Bay, Florida, working as a
cocktail waitress and jumping from boyfriend to boyfriend. In October
of 2008, Sheri called Tara to tell her that Joyce Meyer was having a
conference in Tampa Bay and that Tara should attend. By then, Sheri
had become quite religious and thought not only that Tara's lifestyle
was reckless but also that Joyce's preaching could help her.

Chris and Tara had already met when Tara visited them in Quantico, back before they were married. Sheri suggested she meet with Chris, since he would be flying in a few days before the conference to make security preparations.

Sheri's suggestion, however, was a mistake. Chris and Tara met for dinner and drinks and didn't waste any time starting an affair. By the time the conference was over, Chris had asked Joyce Meyer if he could spend a few extra days in Tampa Bay.

Immediately after Chris returned from Florida, he got on his laptop and created a document titled "All about Tara." He typed out her birthday, her dog's birthday, her height, weight, clothing sizes, favorite perfume, favorite sports teams, and favorite ice cream flavors. He even wrote down what their daughter's name would be: "Zoey Lynn Coleman." The heading of the document was "November 5, 2008. The day that Tara changed my life."

Almost immediately after Chris arrived home from Florida, he and Joyce received identical email threats. Someone had sent four short emails within five minutes.

 Date: Fri 14 Nov, 2008 20:36:49

From: "Fuck Chris" <destroychris@gmail.com>

To: dmeyer@joycemeyer.org, joycemeyer@joycemeyer.org, davemeyer@joycemeyer.org, danmeyer@joycemeyer.org, davidmeyer@joycemeyer.org, ccoleman@joycemeyer.org

Subject: Fuck Chris's Family. They are dead!!!

Body: I'm sure this will make it to someone in the company. If you jackass's are like any other company this will be someone's account. Pass this on to Chris!! ! Tell Joyce to stop preaching the bullshit or Chris's family will die. If I can't get to Joyce then I will get to someone close to her and if I can't get to him then I will kill his wife and kids. I know Joyce's schedule so then I know Chris's schedule. If Joyce doesn't quit preaching the bullshit then they will die. During the Houston conference I will kill them all as they sleep. If I don't hit there then I will kill them during the book tour or the trip to India. I know where he lives and I know they are alone. Fuck them all and they will die soon! Tell that motherfucker next time to let me talk to Joyce. She needs to hear what I have to say and now she will.

Date: Fri 14 Nov, 2008 20:38:51

From: "Fuck Chris" <destroychris@gmail.com>

To: ccoleman@joycemeyer.org

Subject: Go to Hell!

Body: Your family is done!

Date: Fri 14 Nov, 2008 20:39:37

From: "Fuck Chris" <destroychris@gmail.com>

To: ccoleman@joycemeyer.org

Subject: Houston Death?

Body: They will be done while you are gone at the Houston Conference. I know you will be out of town.

Date: Fri 14 Nov, 2008 20:42:11

From: "Fuck Chris" <destroychris@gmail.com>

To: ccoleman@joycemeyer.org

Subject: Houston Death

Body: Tell Chris his family is dead!! I know his schedule and they will die. Next time that motherfucker will let me talk to Joyce.

Chris immediately reported these threats to the local police. The police force in Columbia was small, but to be safe, they assigned extra patrols to drive by the Colemans' house daily.

Meanwhile, things at the Coleman household were getting worse. Chris had started to direct more hostility toward Sheri. On November 25, just a few days before Thanksgiving, Chris cornered Sheri in the kitchen and said he wanted a divorce. He told her that she and the boys were getting in the way of his career.

Sheri didn't want a divorce. She said she still loved him and asked her friends to pray for her and her marriage.

In mid-December, Chris had to take another business trip to Florida and met up with Tara once again in an Orlando hotel. This time they exchanged promise rings.

On December 21, Sheri called Chris and begged him to come home for the holidays, but he refused. Instead, he told Sheri that she and the kids were keeping him from realizing God's destiny. He eventually came home on December 24.

The following week, on Jan 2, Chris called the local police. He had received another threat letter. This time the threat was typed on plain paper and hand-delivered to their mailbox on his curb. Sheri was terrified.

The letter read:

"Fuck You! Deny your God publically or else! No more oppurtunities. Time is running out for you and your family! Have a goodtime in India MOTHER FUCKER!"

Interestingly, both "publically" and "oppurtunities" were misspelled.

The city of Columbia was just a small town with a small police force and only two detectives. One of the detectives, Justin Barlow, happened to live across the street from the Colemans and was assigned to the case.

Detective Barlow set up a camera from his own house facing the Colemans' house and mailbox and assigned extra patrols in the neighborhood.

That April, Chris had another trip with the Joyce Meyer Ministries. This time was to Maui, Hawaii – and, of course, he invited Tara.

Chris and Tara made sure that none of his co-workers spotted the two of them together. He knew that, because of the "Spiritual Criteria Clause," he would lose his job if he was caught having an affair.

During their time in Maui, Chris and Tara made more plans. Tara gave Chris a deadline for serving divorce papers to Sheri: May 4.

When Chris returned from Maui and checked the mailbox on April 27, he found another threatening letter. This letter read:

"Fuck you. I am giving you the last warning! You have not listened to me and you have not changed your ways. I have warned you to stop traveling and to stop carrying on with this fake religious life of stealing people's money. You think you are so special to do what you do protecting or think you are protecting her. She is a bitch and not worth you doing it. Stop today or else. I know your schedule! You can't hide from me ever. I'm always watching. I know when you leave in the morning and I know when you stay home. I saw you leave this morning. I will be watching. You better stop traveling and doing what you are doing. THIS IS MY LAST WARN-ING! YOUR WORST NIGHTMARE IS ABOUT TO HAPPEN!"

Chris said his security camera caught someone putting the letter into the mailbox, but he didn't have a way of recording it. Strangely, Detective Barlow's camera across the street saw no activity around the mailbox.

When May 4th rolled around, Chris called Tara to tell her that his attorney said there were typos in the divorce papers and he couldn't serve them to Sheri today, but he should be able to serve her the divorce papers the following day.

Of course, there was no attorney and no divorce papers.

That evening, Detective Barlow's camera, aimed at the Coleman mailbox, caught Chris, Gavin, and Garret playing baseball in the front yard just before sunset. The boys asked their father if they could stay the night at neighbor Brandon's house to celebrate his birthday, but Chris refused, telling them it wasn't a good night. Brandon's mother was surprised, since the boys had been staying the night with him for the past several years on that specific night.

On the morning of May 5, 2009, just twelve hours after Chris played catch with his sons in the front yard, Detective Barlow got an early morning phone call that he would never forget. Chris called at 6:43 a.m. while driving home from the St. Louis County gym and asked Detective Barlow to check on his house. Chris had been trying to contact Sheri by phone, but she wasn't answering. He said that Sheri and the kids should have been up by then, and he was worried.

Detective Barlow called for backup, crossed the street, and knocked on the door. No answer. When his backup arrived just a few minutes later, they walked to the back of the house, where they found a window to the basement wide open, the screen sitting next to the house.

The officers called for more backup and crawled through the window with guns drawn. As they climbed the stairs into the house, the smell of spray paint immediately hit them.

What they found as they entered the house was horrific. The scene looked like something that resembled the Manson murders.

The house walls were spray painted with rants similar to the letters and emails Chris had received.

"U have paid"

"I saw you leave"

"Fuck you bitch punished"

"Fuck you I am always watching"

As they walked up the stairs to the second floor, Officer Donjon found thirty-one-year-old Sheri naked on her bed in the master bedroom with a black eye and ligature marks around her neck. He put his hand under her shoulder to lift her and check if she was breathing, but rigor mortis had already set in, and her body was stiff.

Officer Patton entered Gavin's room, where he found the nine-year-old face down in his Spiderman pajamas. His skin was purplish and cold to the touch. Stiff. "Fuck you" was spray painted on the sheets covering him.

Detective Barlow went into eleven-year-old Garret's room. He, too, was cold and stiff. His lips were blue, his skin was grey, and he had ligature marks around his neck.

Chris was only seven minutes away when he called, but it took him almost twenty minutes to arrive at the scene. Several squad cars were parked on the street, and police tape surrounded the house.

When Chris arrived, Detective Barlow told him that his family was dead. He didn't attempt to go upstairs and he didn't ask how they died. He just sat on the driveway and sobbed. He then took out his Blackberry to call his work and his father.

When investigators brought Chris in for his statement, things didn't seem to add up immediately.

Chris claimed he left the house that morning to go to the gym at 5:43 a.m. and claimed his family were alive and well when he left. However, rigor mortis had already set in by the time the bodies were discovered, just over an hour later. A forensic pathologist took liver temperature on the bodies and determined all three died between 11 p.m. and 3 a.m.

During the interrogation, and despite the room being warm, Chris claimed to be very cold and asked for a blanket. However, when investigators gave him a blanket, Chris only covered his arms. That's when the detectives noticed the scratches on his arms.

Investigators asked Chris about his relationship with Sheri, and he admitted to having some communication problems, but nothing that bad. They asked if anything was going on in their relationship that Sheri would not have approved of, and he mentioned that he texted Tara "a ton." However, he insisted he wasn't having an affair and that Tara was just someone to talk to.

What Chris didn't know was that the investigators already knew about Tara. They had already spoken to the St. Petersburg, Florida, police who were interrogating Tara at the same time. Tara was giving a very different story of their relationship.

A Major Case Squad was assigned to the case with twenty-five investigators. When investigators went through his cell phone and computers, the evidence against Chris Coleman began to pile up.

On Chris and Tara's cell phones, police found X-rated photos and videos they had taken and sent back and forth to each other. Investigators found sex videos of the two of them in Hawaii. In fact, Chris had sent one of their sex videos to his father, the evangelical preacher. Their cell phones also revealed that Chris was texting Tara in the interrogation room.

When examining Chris' computer, they found the "All about Tara" document. However, more damning was a further analysis of his computer where the Forensics Team found evidence that the threatening emails had come from Chris' computer. The Forensics Team even recovered proof of the typed letters.

They additionally found that Chris commonly misspelled the word "opportunities" in several other documents – misspelled the same way.

There was also the issue of Detective Barlow's camera. It had been pointed at the house that night and caught no one entering or leaving it besides Chris.

When searching the house, investigators noticed that many windows had been unlocked. It seemed strange that someone who was the head of security for a large company, let alone the recipient of personal death threats just days prior, would leave windows open and unlocked.

Also in the house, they found a hardware store receipt for a can of red spray paint, paid for by Chris.

Even the gym that Chris went to that morning was suspicious. The gym was unusually far away, and Chris had only ever been to that gym two times before. Moreover, he joined the gym just a few days after he started the affair with Tara; it seemed as if he had begun planning the murders immediately.

Investigators traced the route between Chris' home and the gym. They found a latex glove stained with red spray paint and the faceplate from Chris' home security video recorder on the side of the road. They also found a piece of baling twine that had been tied into a noose. The Colemans had bales of hay in their backyard, and one of the bales had a piece missing: the piece they found forensically matched that bale.

Although this seemed a massive amount of evidence, it was still largely circumstantial.

One wonders, why go through all of this trouble? Rather than killing your entire family, why not just get a divorce? The problem was Chris' job. Due to the clause in the contract he'd signed, Chris knew that if he were found to be an adulterer or sought a divorce, he would most likely lose his high-paying job.

Chris Coleman was arrested on May 19, two weeks after the murders. He was charged with three counts of first-degree murder and pleaded not guilty.

Despite previously having a $100,000 per year job, the judge determined that Chris was indigent (poor), and he was assigned two experienced death penalty defense attorneys.

Because of the nature of the murders, the media attention was massive, and the public was outraged – so much so that Chris feared for his life and wore a bullet-proof vest when coming to trial.

The media publicity also meant that jurors were selected from Pinckneyville, Illinois, more than an hour away. They were bussed in for each day of the trial. The trial began on April 25, 2011, almost two years after the murders.

During the trial, prosecutors introduced the X-rated pictures and videos. Tara showed up with bodyguards and, while on the stand, wore the promise ring that Chris had given her.

The prosecution also called Joyce Meyer to testify that indeed, if she had known that he was having an affair, it would have jeopardized his job status.

Several of Sheri's friends testified that she had confided in them that Chris was beating her, that he wanted a divorce, and even that she knew Chris was having an affair with Tara.

However, the most critical piece of evidence was the time of death. Prosecutors showed the jury that Chris' story of the events didn't match the forensic evidence of the time of death.

Jurors began deliberations on May 4, 2011, and returned with a guilty verdict on all three counts. As a result, Chris Coleman was sentenced to life in prison without the possibility of parole.

To this day, Chris Coleman insists he is innocent. His parents still stand by him, and he has unsuccessfully tried to appeal his conviction.

Prosecutors believe Tara had no knowledge of Chris' plans.

CHAPTER 6
DR. JOHN SCHNEEBERGER

K ipling, Saskatchewan, was a tiny Canadian farming town. If someone blinked while driving on Highway 48, they might just miss it. With only about 1,000 residents, life was slow, and pretty much everyone in town knew one another.

On Halloween night in 1992, a twenty-three-year-old single mother named Candice was finishing her shift at the only convenience store in the town. Candice had recently broken up with her boyfriend, Danny. Danny had stopped by to see her at work, but they'd gotten into a heated argument that escalated until she got so angry and upset that she sped off in her car.

Candice couldn't think straight and decided to drive to Kipling Memorial Hospital to visit her friend that worked there.

She arrived at the hospital to find that her friend wasn't working that night. However, the nurses on duty could tell she was distraught and suggested she talk to the doctor.

Dr. John Schneeberger was working the night shift. Dr. Schneeberger had moved to Canada from South Africa and was a well-respected member of the small community, even helping the town build a public swimming pool. The residents of Kipling considered themselves lucky to have such an educated and skilled doctor living in their tiny town.

Candice also knew Dr. Schneeberger, as he had delivered her daughter earlier that year.

She told the doctor about her anxiety, and he quickly suggested a sedative, then left the room. She expected a pill to calm her nerves but was surprised when he returned to the examination room with a syringe filled with liquid.

Immediately after she received the shot, Candice recalled falling back on the table like a piece of jelly. She tried to scream, but only a slow, gurgling sound came from her mouth. Everything afterward was a blur.

Candice was partially unconscious and only vaguely aware of what was going on – but she knew enough to tell that someone was pulling down her jeans and laying her on her side. She was facing the wall when she felt someone inside her. Completely under the effect of the sedative, she was paralyzed and could do nothing.

Hours later, when Candice regained consciousness, she was still too dizzy to drive home, and the nurses working that night suggested she sleep it off in the hospital. The following morning, when she woke with a clear head, she knew something was wrong. She confronted Dr. Schneeberger and asked what drug he had given her. His response gave her an uneasy feeling. He responded, "Why, did it give you crazy dreams?"

Candice knew she had been raped. Before leaving the hospital, she asked the nurses for an air-tight plastic bag, put her panties in it, and then went home and immediately told her parents what had happened.

Kipling was an extremely small town with only one hospital. The next afternoon Candice drove to Regina, a slightly larger town about ninety-five miles away, to find a clinic that could perform a rape test.

In the Regina clinic, Candice gave samples from her panties and jeans, and doctors took a vaginal swab to test for semen. As she suspected, the results of the test were positive. She knew without a doubt that she had indeed been raped.

Before leaving, Candice asked to have her blood tested as well. The results showed that she had a drug called Versed in her system, a pre-anesthetic used to induce anesthesia for procedures such as colono-scopies.

She returned to Kipling and, the following day, filed a formal complaint with the Kipling Police Department. On November 2, Dr. Schneeberger volunteered to give a sample of his blood. However, he was adamant that he was innocent and that his blood DNA would not match the sample from Candice's rape kit.

The doctor voluntarily gave a blood sample from his arm, and he was correct – it didn't match.

After the DNA tested negative, Candice was in disbelief. She spent the next several months insisting to local police that the DNA had been somehow tampered with. Unfortunately, she had no way to prove it. She pressured the Kipling police for almost a year, and in August 1993, Dr. Schneeberger agreed to a second voluntary DNA test.

This time, a Registered Nurse did the test, and police monitored the procedure. They watched as the needle entered his arm and the vials filled with blood. Officers then took the vials directly to police head-quarters.

Again, the second test did not match the DNA sample from Candice's panties. She was devastated.

After two failed DNA tests, residents of the small town of Kipling were not kind to Candice. Dr. Schneeberger was their hero; he was a godsend in such a small town. The citizens of Kipling considered themselves lucky to have such a skilled doctor in their tiny town, whereas Candice was just a high school-educated single mom. Thus, they rallied around the doctor and shunned Candice, believing she was somehow out for financial gain. In addition, some believed she'd had some sort of romantic interest in the doctor and wanted to harm him because he had rejected her.

Residents were also suspicious of Candice because two nurses were on shift the night of her alleged rape, but she said nothing to them at the time.

After the second DNA test and more ridicule from the townspeople, Candice moved from Kipling to Red Deer, Alberta, nine hours away. The Royal Canadian Mounted Police closed the case in 1994, and Dr. Schneeberger continued with his practice, and tried to get on with his life.

In 1995, Candice was still reeling with disbelief that the DNA tests didn't match. Out of ideas, she hired a private investigator named Larry O'Brien. O'Brien was a twenty-five-year veteran of the RCMP (Royal Canadian Mounted Police) who had done undercover and intelligence work in Southern Ontario. Candice tasked him with obtaining yet another DNA sample – but this time in a more covert manner.

On March 3, 1996, O'Brien broke into Dr. Schneeberger's car. Once inside his vehicle, O'Brien collected a hair sample from the car's head-rest. Unfortunately, no roots were attached to the hair, meaning it had no useable DNA. However, he also found a lightly-used tube of Chap-Stick lip balm in the ashtray. The Chapstick contained epithelial (skin) cells that could be used for DNA testing. O'Brien took the ChapStick and rubbed it onto the plastic window of an envelope. He then bagged, timed, and initialed the sample and sent it to an independent forensic lab in British Columbia.

When the results came back, Candice was ecstatic. The DNA sample from the ChapStick matched the DNA from her panties. She had been right all along.

Armed with this new DNA evidence, Candice returned to Kipling and demanded that the police reopen the case. However, since she had obtained this DNA sample without a warrant, the police couldn't use it as evidence. There was also no guarantee that the DNA from the Chap-

Stick was actually Dr. Schneeberger's, so the police wouldn't reopen the case.

Police, however, had their suspicions too, although they were apprehensive about charging him without hard evidence. Still, detectives believed in the science of DNA.

Candice was completely baffled as to why the DNA from his arm didn't match the DNA from the panties and lip balm, so she filed a civil suit against Dr. Schneeberger and brought charges against him within the medical society.

Again, with all the additional pressure, Dr. Schneeberger volunteered to have his blood taken a third time for another DNA test.

This time, to ensure the integrity of the test, the procedure was performed in the police forensics lab and recorded on video.

Not much blood is needed for a DNA test, so it was common for a sample to be taken from a simple pinprick on the finger. However, Dr. Schneeberger claimed he had a condition that caused him to bruise easily on his hands, so he requested that the sample be taken from his left arm. Since this was a voluntary test, and he gave the sample in good faith, the police complied with his request.

On November 20, 1996, inside a police lab, detectives videotaped as they drew the blood from Dr. Schneeberger's arm – but there were problems extracting the doctor's blood. Technician Jean Roney recalled, "The vein appeared larger than I would have expected, and I thought that was a little unusual."

Sometimes, when extracting blood from a patient, there can be an insufficient vacuum in the vein which can cause difficulty getting the blood out. She eventually got a blood sample, but she noticed something strange. "It's a little strange that the blood doesn't look… really… fresh."

The lab attempted to test the blood anyway, but they eventually determined that it wasn't a large enough sample and the blood had been too degraded for an accurate DNA test.

Yet again, Candice was furious. However, just five months later, Candice would finally get a break, but unfortunately, that break came at a high cost.

On the evening of April 25, 1997, just as police were about to ask for a fourth DNA test, Dr. Schneeberger's wife, Lisa, contacted police and accused her husband of raping her thirteen-year-old daughter, his stepdaughter.

The young girl had come to her mother with the accusation and a condom wrapper she found in her bed. The young girl said her step-father, Dr. Schneeberger, had been coming into her room in the middle of the night for years and injecting her with something that would leave her with fleeting memories of sexual incidents with the doctor.

Lisa then searched her husband's home office and found a box with condoms, syringes, and drugs, including Versed. She immediately called the police.

Police didn't hesitate to arrest Dr. Schneeberger and order a warrant for a fourth DNA test. This test, however, was no longer voluntary, and the technician took three samples. Samples were taken from his hair, via a saliva swab from his mouth, and a blood sample from a finger on his right hand – not the left arm, from where they had taken all three of the previous tests.

All three new samples matched the DNA from the ChapStick and the semen in Candice's panties.

Investigators officially charged Dr. John Schneeberger with aggravated assault, which held a maximum penalty of life in prison. He was also charged with two counts of administering a noxious substance with a maximum sentence of life in prison, one count of obstruction of justice with a penalty of ten years, and one count of sexual assault with a maximum penalty of ten years.

Dr. Schneeberger had thwarted police for seven years, but detectives were still puzzled. The nurses, technicians, and police officers had seen the needle physically go into his arm each time. So how did the DNA come up differently? During the trial in November 1999, the world discovered how.

Dr. Schneeberger took the witness stand in his own defense and told the court that the first three times they drew blood, they were drawing someone else's blood. He had taken the blood of one of his male clients and inserted it into a thin rubber tube called a Penrose Drain, along with an anticoagulant to keep it in a liquid state. He then performed surgery on himself. He implanted the tube into his own arm, just beside his vein. Each time they had drawn blood, he had insisted on having it drawn from his left arm. Technicians had no idea they were drawing blood from a tube implanted under his skin.

During one of the videotapes, investigators later saw that he had always worn a long sleeve shirt and didn't pull the sleeves up far enough to see the incision in his upper arm. After watching the video more carefully, they saw the tube protruding from his arm for a split second.

The new revelation explained why, on the third blood sample, the technician thought the blood looked dark and "not fresh." He had removed the tube from his arm after the second test, stored it in a refrigerator, and then replaced it in his arm four years later for the third DNA test.

However, even after explaining how he had faked three DNA tests, Dr. Schneeberger still claimed that none of what Candice said was true. His excuse was that he put the tube of blood into his arm because it was the only way to defend himself, and he didn't trust the police. Furthermore, he claimed that Candice had broken into his house and stolen a used condom from his trash to get the semen sample and frame him.

Judge Ellen Gunn said his defense was "Inventive, fanciful, imaginative. However, one that does not apply is credible" and called his theory "preposterous."

Of course, that defense was not near enough to convince a jury. Schneeberger was convicted of two counts of sexual assault, one count of administering a noxious substance to commit an indictable offense, and one count of obstructing justice.

Amazingly, Dr. Schneeberger was sentenced to only six years in a minimum-security prison.

During Dr. Schneeberger's stay in prison, Lisa Schneeberger divorced him and fought with the legal system for the right to disallow him access to her daughters.

For Lisa Schneeberger, her agony was just getting started. When Schneeberger was arrested, she had four children to support, one of which was only thirteen months old. She sold the house and car to pay the bills, filed for divorce, and took back her maiden name of Dillman.

On the evening before the jury gave his guilty verdict, Lisa refused to let the girls sleepover with him as was required by the visitation agreement. She was ordered to pay a $2,000 fine for contempt of court.

While in jail, John insisted on visitation rights, but Lisa kept fighting. Despite her attempts to persuade judges and politicians, the court ordered her to force the girls to visit him once a month – the man that had repeatedly drugged and raped their half-sister.

When the day finally came of the first forced visitation at the Bowden Institution where he was held, nearly 100 protesters showed up at the gates to the prison and refused to let the car pass. Mad Mothers Against Pedophiles had organized the protesters and claimed the courts were putting sex offenders' rights ahead of children's best interests. However, police eventually forced the crowds back, and the car carrying the girls entered the prison. Upon entering the prison, the girls, aged five and six, were scared to death, crying, and clinging to their mother's legs. A social worker eventually came to the rescue and called off the visitation.

The win, however, was short-lived. Lisa eventually had to bring the girls to see their father on the last Sunday of every month. He eventually dropped his visitation requests after realizing the girls had no interest in visiting him.

In 2002 Bob Mills, a member of the Canadian Parliament, lobbied for a bill called "Lisa's Law." It was an amendment to the Divorce Act to limit the rights of a child's access to sex offenders. However, the bill didn't pass.

During the following months, Lisa continued to fight her now ex-husband. She ensured the Canadian Immigration Department realized that he lied when he applied for citizenship by concealing information (his crimes) and making false representations.

Schneeberger served only four of his six-year sentence, much of it spent in Ferndale Prison in British Columbia, often referred to as "Club Fed." Ferndale was a minimum-security prison with residential-style housing, plenty of open spaces, and even a nine-hole golf course.

Upon his release, Schneeberger was stripped of his medical license and Canadian citizenship and deported back to South Africa. He reportedly lives with his mother in Durban and works for a catering business.

CHAPTER 7
MARY BELL

In the late 1960s, the Scotswood area of Newcastle, England, was a rough neighborhood that was sadly neglected, full of derelict houses and slums. The location was often referred to as "Rat Alley." Many buildings were being torn down to make way for newer high-rise flats. However, despite its roughness and social problems, the community felt safe; children roamed unsupervised, commonly playing in the broken-down homes.

One of the children that wandered the area was ten-year-old Mary Bell. Mary was a well-known bully whom the other children feared. Mary's teachers took note of her as well: though she was a bright and clever girl, she was better known for her sadistic side.

One of her teachers recalled Mary putting out a cigarette on another student's cheek simply because she got a better grade than her. Yet despite Mary having admitted to doing it, school administrators did nothing to address her actions.

On Saturday, May 11, 1968, Mary and her friend Norma Bell (no relation) played with a small, three-year-old boy and told him they were taking him to buy candy. The little boy was later found wandering the streets, dazed and bleeding. The police were called, but again, no action was taken.

The next day, the Newcastle Police received a complaint from a mother that Mary had tried to strangle her daughter in a playground while Norma held the girl down. But again, it was a complaint against a ten-year-old girl, so the police thought nothing of it.

On May 25, the day before Mary's 11th birthday, she noticed four-year-old Martin Brown playing outside with his friends. She told the boy she wanted to play a game with him and took him to one of the nearby derelict houses. Mary took Martin upstairs and told him he had a sore throat. She said she could make it better by massaging his neck. Mary placed her hands around his throat and strangled the life out of the boy.

Hours later, a construction worker found the boy's lifeless body in the building and called for help. A neighbor contacted Martin's mother, who ran to the home to find his skin pale. There were no marks on him, just a trickle of blood coming from the corner of his mouth.

When police investigated the death, they noticed pills lying near his body. Initially, they thought that may have been the cause of death, but later that theory was ruled out, and investigators believed he had died of natural causes. Finally, they thought the boy may have "died of fright" because he had previously fallen down a flight of stairs.

The local newspapers referred to Martin Brown as the "Rat Alley Boy."

Mary showed up at his mother's door following Martin's death. "I've come to see Martin," she said to his mother. Assuming she didn't know Martin had died, Martin's mother told her that Martin had passed. Mary said, "Oh, I know he's dead. I want to see him in his coffin." Martin's mother was shocked and slammed the door.

As the days went by, Mary told family members and other children at school that she had killed Martin Brown, but no one believed her. Then, in her school notebook, she drew a picture of Martin's body the way it was lying in the house and a bottle of pills next to his body. Next to the pills was the word "tablet" and the workman who had found the body.

Mary also wrote in the notebook, "There were crowds of people beside an old house. I asked what was the matter, there has been a boy who just lay down and died." All of this went completely unnoticed by authorities until much later.

Two days after Martin's death, there was a break-in at a nursery. Police found four pieces of paper with scribbles that read, "I murder so that I may come back." Another read, "We murder, watch out." Yet another read, "We did murder Martin Brown. Fuck off you bitch." Police, however, dismissed these notes as a childish prank.

The people of Newcastle blamed Martin's death on the dangers of the "Rat Alley Slums," and protesters marched down the streets, claiming that the city should clear the old buildings properly. Mary Bell participated in the protests on July 31.

Mary's home life was not like the other children's. Mary's mother, Betty Bell, was a well-known prostitute specializing in bondage and sadomasochism. Betty would bring her clients home, where Mary would witness the BDSM acts. Mary was forced to engage in sex acts with the clients from as early as age four.

Betty had repeatedly tried to kill Mary within her first few years of life, giving her drugs as candy and claiming she had accidentally taken her sleeping pills. Other family members became suspicious when Betty claimed Mary had fallen from a window. Betty also attempted to give Mary away to relatives but later changed her mind and took her back.

Betty was well-known for going away for weeks on end, leaving Mary alone and unsupervised. Mary's father, Billy, was no better. He was rarely there; when he was, he was drunk and physically abusive to both Betty and Mary. It was no wonder Mary turned out the way she did.

Two months after Martin's death, Mary struck again, this time with her friend Norma.

The public still had no idea there was a killer amongst them. Instead, they believed Martin's death was the fault of the development companies. As a result, children continued to play unsupervised in the streets, even at the youngest of ages.

Four-year-old Brian Howe was playing by himself and watching the demolition of the houses of Rat Alley when Mary and Norma approached him. They took him to an area referred to as the "Tin Lizzy," a small wasteland.

When Brian was reported missing a few hours later, police found him half naked in a spread-eagle position, with a pair of scissors and a lock of his hair found near his body. Police found that he had been strangled, his legs cut, his calves punctured, and someone had tried to cut his penis off. The letter "M" had been cut into his stomach. It was almost as if Mary Bell wanted to get caught.

Postmortem examinations determined that the cuts were inflicted after his death.

Still, investigators didn't connect the two deaths.

Days later, as Brian's coffin was carried out of his home, a police officer noticed something sinister. While Brian's friends and family wept, Mary Bell was laughing.

 "Mary Bell was standing in front of the Howe's house when the coffin was brought out. I was, of course, watching her. And it was when I saw her there that I knew I did not dare risk another day. She stood there, laughing. Laughing and rubbing her hands. I thought, My God, I've got to bring her in. She'll do another one."
– Detective Chief Inspector James Dobson, Newcastle Police.

When investigators realized that the cuts on Brian's stomach formed an initial, they knew they were looking for a child. They finally realized that the two murders were linked.

Police announced in a press conference that they suspected a child was responsible for the murders, and Mary listened intently at the front. She seemed to want to draw attention to herself.

Word got around to police that Mary Bell had bragged to other children that she had killed Martin, and investigators started looking into her as a suspect.

Detectives spoke to Mary's father, Billy Bell, who initially refused to let them talk to her but eventually allowed their questioning.

Police, by that time, had interviewed a nine-year-old boy who claimed to have witnessed the strangling of Brian Howe. But Mary denied the murder and sarcastically cried,

 "Send for my solicitor!"

The community initially felt sorry for Mary, assuming that, at only ten years old, she had no idea what she had done.

However, the evidence piled up despite Mary's denials. Police made the connection between Mary and the notes that they had found two months earlier.

When investigators spoke to her teachers, they found her school notebook where she had drawn a picture of Martin Brown's body with the word "tablet" next to the body. Police had not informed the public about the tablets (pills) found near the body; they knew then that Mary was the killer.

Mary's friend Norma, when questioned, admitted her involvement in the murder of Brian Howe, but she claimed it was all Mary.

On Aug 8, 1968, Mary Bell was charged with murder.

Detectives were stunned by Mary's intelligence level. She was cunning despite her age, denying accusations and seemingly anticipating the questions before the police asked them.

The local police were as disturbed as anyone over the arrests. They had never encountered offenders of such a young age.

During the trial, Mary was calm, as if she had no idea what she was accused of—dancing near her seat and turning around during proceedings to ask for candy.

Generally, the accused sits alone in a box during trials in England. However, because the defendant was so young, the judge allowed Mary to sit with her lawyers.

The trial lasted nine days, during which Mary and Norma were allowed to state their case. The prosecutor, Rudolph Lyons, started the proceedings by linking the two murders.

Prosecutors then brought in handwriting experts to analyze the confessional notes found in the nursery and the drawings from Mary's school notebooks. They explained how Mary and Norma morbidly taunted the victim's families by asking to see the bodies.

Gray wool fibers from Mary's dress were discovered on both victims' bodies and presented as forensic evidence. Maroon fibers from Norma's skirt were also found around Brian's shoes. The prosecution presented a strong case against both girls.

As the trial progressed, it became clear that Mary was the dominant figure between the two girls, and Norma was simply a follower. Norma was overwhelmed by the trial, and observers took pity on her. Mary, meanwhile, gave quick and witty remarks as if she hadn't a care in the world.

Prosecutors also called on psychiatrists who examined Mary and testified that she suffered from a psychopathic personality disorder, demonstrated a lack of empathy, and was likely to act on impulse.

The jury deliberated for five hours and returned with their verdict. Norma was considered "simple-minded" and acquitted of the charge of manslaughter. Mary was found not guilty of murder but guilty of manslaughter and was sentenced to be detained at Her Majesty's pleasure, which meant an indefinite prison sentence.

The jury and trial observers heard nothing of Mary's home life or how it may have affected her actions.

Because of Mary's young age, authorities wanted to attempt to rehabilitate her rather than punish her, believing Mary didn't truly understand what she had done.

She was too young to go to a mental hospital, so Mary was assigned to a secure school where she could be given constant attention.

The people of Newcastle agreed and felt sympathy for Mary because of her young age and upbringing, despite her horrible crimes.

Mary Bell spent twelve years in detention. She spent six years in Red Bank Juvenile Institution, where she was the only girl with twenty-two boys. During her time there, she continued to blame others for her crimes, never admitting her offenses.

Mary's mother, Betty, visited her in school, but Mary eventually blamed her, too, for the crimes, writing her the following letter:

"Please Mam, put my tiny mind at ease, tell judge and jury on your knees. They will listen to your cry of 'please'. The guilty one is you, not me. I am sorry it has to be this way. We'll both cry and you will go away. Tell them you are guilty, please. So then Mam, I'll be free. Your daughter, May."

Betty Bell gave a TV interview years later, clearly broken and suffering from drug and alcohol addiction.

In 1980, at the age of twenty-three, Mary was released and given a new identity. She had a daughter during her incarceration, and the media eventually tracked that daughter down – who, until then, had known nothing of her mother's crimes. In 2003, Mary and her daughter won a case in the high court which gave them both anonymity for life.

CHAPTER 8
MICHELLE BICA

Michelle and Thomas Bica were ecstatic to learn that thirty-nine-year-old Michelle was pregnant again. The couple had been trying to conceive again ever since the miscarriage she'd suffered the prior year.

They attended birthing classes together, showed friends their sonogram photos, and Michelle shopped for maternity clothes. Thomas had even prepared a nursery for the baby. As time passed, the pregnancy seemed to be coming along normally except for the due date, which was occasionally pushed further and further out.

Thomas and Michelle met in 1994 in jail, of all places. Thomas worked as a county corrections officer, and Michelle was serving a short sentence for receiving stolen property.

In September 2000, Michelle and Thomas were shopping at Walmart when they met Jon and Theresa Andrews. The Andrews' were also expecting a baby, and both couples were shopping for baby supplies. They all discussed their babies' due dates, their genders, and baby-related chit-chat when they discovered they were neighbors who lived only four blocks from each other.

Jon and Theresa Andrews had been high school sweethearts. The couple was married in 1996, and they decided it was time to start a family four years into their marriage.

Just a few days after the chance meeting of the two couples, Michelle announced that she had received a call from her doctor with some news. The doctor had made a mistake when viewing the original sonogram. As a result, she would be giving birth to a baby boy rather than a girl. Still, as long as the baby was healthy, Michelle and Thomas were happy either way.

John Andrews was at work on the morning of September 27, 2000, when he received a call from Theresa. They had been trying to sell their Jeep Wrangler, and Theresa was planning to meet a woman interested in buying it. Later that afternoon, however, when Jon called her to see if she had sold the Jeep, Theresa didn't answer. John tried to reach her several more times before he left work for the day, but the calls went unanswered each time.

When Jon arrived home from work in the early evening, Theresa and the Jeep were gone. He tried calling her once again but felt an instant sense of dread when he heard her cell phone ringing in the hallway. Her handbag and cell phone were still there. She would never have left the house without them.

While Jon was panicking over his missing wife, the Bica household was overflowing with joy just four blocks away.

Thomas Bica received a call from his wife while he was at work. Michelle's water had broken, and she had been rushed to the hospital by ambulance, where she gave birth to a beautiful baby boy. Michelle explained, however, that she and the baby were already home. The hospital had a tuberculosis scare, and they were released immediately after the delivery.

The Bicas named their newborn Michael Thomas Bica and invited friends and family to meet their new baby boy. While Thomas was a thrilled new father, Michelle seemed stressed and saddened. She told her husband she was distraught to hear that Theresa Andrews had disappeared. She explained that, out of respect for the family, she didn't want to put the "New Baby" flag in the front yard as they had planned.

Meanwhile, at the Andrews' house, friends and family were desperately searching for clues to the disappearance of Theresa. It was a week, however, before detectives received their first clue. When they traced Theresa's cell phone records, investigators found that the call she had received about the Jeep they had for sale had come from Michelle Bica's cell phone.

Police immediately questioned Michelle Bica and her husband, Thomas. Thomas seemed confused during questioning, but Michelle was combative and agitated. Still, with no evidence of wrongdoing, both were released.

Investigators quickly began to realize that Michelle's story didn't add up. When they checked with the hospital where she said the baby was delivered, there was no record of a tuberculosis scare and no record of her as a patient. Her story was clearly a lie.

When detectives returned to the Bicas' house to question Michelle further, she quickly disappeared into the bedroom and locked the door. She then put a handgun inside her mouth and pulled the trigger. Detectives found her husband outside the locked bedroom, crying.

Child services immediately took the newborn to the hospital, where they performed DNA tests that eventually proved Jon Andrews was the baby's biological father.

Thomas Bica was taken into custody and questioned. He explained that he had believed everything Michelle had told him about the pregnancy. After twelve hours of polygraph examinations, he was released.

Detectives determined that Thomas had been completely unaware that his wife had faked her pregnancy.

After searching the Bicas' house, investigators found a shallow grave in the garage covered with gravel. Inside was the body of Theresa Andrews – she had a gunshot wound in her back, and her womb was cut open in a makeshift cesarean where Michelle had removed the baby.

Amazingly, the baby, Oscar Gavin Andrews, survived and was returned to his father, Jon Andrews.

TRUE CRIME CASE HISTORIES

VOLUME 2

TRUE CRIME

CASE HISTORIES

VOL. 2

12 Disturbing True Crime Stories

JASON NEAL

INTRODUCTION

As with Volume One, I'll start with a quick word of warning. The stories you are about to read are brutal and gruesome. They represent humanity at its worst. Television crime shows and stories in the news tend to gloss over the horrible parts, but if you've read the first volume of my series, you know I leave out none of the details. This book is no different. Killing can be a pretty messy endeavor. Consider yourself warned.

When I started this volume of True Crime Case Histories, I didn't have a common theme in mind, just random stories that shocked me. However, as I was writing, I realized a few of them have some similarities.

Two stories deal with killers who stole identities or invented an identity out of thin air. Another two involve killers obsessed with taking photos of their victims – both before and after death. In three stories, police, counselors, and other authorities had plenty of warning signs but ignored them. Similar to Volume One, a few stories involve BDSM (bondage and discipline, domination and submission, sadism and masochism). None of these similarities were intentional, it just happened that way.

Trying to understand why killers do what they do can be an exercise in futility. There seems to be no logic other than the fragility of the human mind. Some killers in this book kill out of curiosity. Alyssa Bustamante just wanted to see what taking another person's life was like. Some, like in the case of Myles Fukunaga, killed out of frustration with his own life. Killers who have no control over their anger are probably the most common, like Michael Adams, whose anger was directed toward the one person he loved most. It's a messed up way to show your love if you ask me. Another common trait among killers is mental health issues – murderers like Jamie Reynolds or Robert Napper should have been put away long before they got out of control.

The stories of murder are endless; in this volume, I've added an additional four stories for a total of twelve. I've also added an online appendix for photos, videos, and documents pertaining to the cases. Look for a link to that at the end of the book. I hope you enjoy reading the stories in this volume as much as I've enjoyed researching and writing them.

Lastly, please join my mailing list for discounts, updates, and a free book. You can sign up for that at

TrueCrimeCaseHistories.com

Additional photos, videos, and documents pertaining to the cases in this volume can be found on the accompanying web page:

https://TrueCrimeCaseHistories.com/vol2/

Thank you for reading. I sincerely hope you gain some insight from this volume of True Crime Case Histories.

- Jason

CHAPTER 1
THE GIRL IN THE BARREL

On September 2, 1999, in the suburban town of Jericho, New York, just thirty miles from Midtown Manhattan, Ronald Cohen was preparing to sell his house. He had just found a buyer for the property at $455,000, and the new owner wanted to do a final walkthrough before taking ownership.

During the walkthrough, the buyer was very thorough and wanted to see the crawlspace beneath an addition that had been built onto the back of the house about thirty years earlier.

The crawlspace was only thirty-six inches high, so the two men had to hunch down to get through the large space. At the very back of the crawlspace, they noticed a fifty-five-gallon barrel on its side, wedged beneath the stairs. The buyer asked Mr. Cohen about the barrel, but he said it had been there since he bought the property over ten years ago. He had no idea what was in it or how it got there. He had never used the crawlspace, and it was far too heavy to move by himself, so he had just left it there. However, the new buyer said he wanted it removed before purchasing the property. Mr. Cohen and his real estate agent got some help, rolled the barrel out from underneath the home, and took it to the curb for the trash workers to haul away.

When sanitation workers showed up the next day, they informed Mr. Cohen that, at 355 pounds, the barrel was far too heavy for them to take away. They also had no idea what it contained. He would need to empty it to make sure there was nothing hazardous or toxic inside.

Mr. Cohen and his real estate agent decided to open the barrel and separate whatever was inside so it could be disposed of properly. There was a metal seal around the top of the barrel, so they pried it open with some tools. An overwhelming stench immediately hit the two men—the unmistakable stench of death.

Once they had removed the lid, they saw a curled human hand and a woman's shoe. The barrel was filled with a green gooey fluid surrounded by tiny plastic pellets. Mr. Cohen immediately called the police.

Investigators took the barrel to the forensics lab, where they emptied it onto a large white tarp so they could collect any evidence. Inside the barrel, they found a small, mummified female body. The body had been crumpled over and bent in half to fit into the barrel. Because the barrel was sealed so tightly, her body had been relatively well preserved, with skin the consistency of rubber. However, the body began decaying quickly after the air hit it, and it was immediately taken away for an autopsy.

During the autopsy, they determined that the body was a female of Hispanic descent. She was tiny, only about four foot nine inches tall, with long black hair and some unusual gold bridgework on her teeth. The bridgework was not commonly done in the United States and had most likely been done somewhere in South America. The cause of death was blunt-force trauma to the head. Someone had used a hammer or similar object to smash her head seven to ten times, crushing her skull. She was also eight to nine months pregnant. Police collected DNA from the fetus to see if they could later match it to a father.

When investigators emptied the rest of the barrel, it oozed out a strange, green, gooey liquid, possibly a chemical dye of some sort. They also noticed tiny black-and-white plastic pellets mixed within the goo. The woman's clothes were still intact and seemed to be a style from the sixties. Near the bottom of the barrel, they found a woman's purse with some cosmetic items inside and a badly damaged address book. There was also a green stem from a plastic flower arrangement.

At the bottom of the barrel were three pieces of jewelry: two gold rings, one with an inscription reading "M.H.R. XII 59," as well as a locket that was engraved, "To Patrice Love Uncle Phil."

The pages of the address book were severely damaged and stuck together with the green goo. Detectives weren't hopeful of getting any clues from it, but just in case, it was put inside a forensic drying cabinet for a few days to dry out.

The following day, detectives began researching where the barrel may have come from. The homeowner, Mr. Cohen, explained that it was already there when he bought the house several years earlier. Detectives began going back through the prior owners to find out who built the extension on the house.

After researching four prior owners, they eventually found the homeowner who had built the extension on the home. He was now seventy-one years old and lived in Boca Raton, Florida. His name was Howard Elkins. He sold the house in 1972 and retired when he closed his plastics business in Manhattan. Police wanted to question him, but they needed to collect more information before making the trip south.

As the days went by, the clues started to pour in. On the side of the barrel were printed the letters "GAF," which turned out to be a chemical company based in New Jersey. Detectives took photos of the barrel and brought some of the pellets and a sample of the green dye to them for analysis. GAF confirmed that they used the polyethylene pellets to make many plastic products, one of those products being plastic flowers. The green dye was a unique product called Halogen Green, specifically used to make plastic flower bases in the 1960s. The only customer they had for that product was Melrose Plastics – the same company that Howard Elkins had closed in 1972.

Meanwhile, the forensic documents lab made some progress on the damaged address book. They got it dried enough to separate the pages, but the ink had utterly disintegrated. Using a video spectral comparator device, they could read some of the information using alternative light sources. The first notation in the book was a number preceded by the letter "A." It was a resident alien number. Detectives spoke with immigration officers, but the number was thirty years old, and their systems had changed since then. It would take time for them to come back with a result.

Knowing that the barrel, the plastic, and the dye all came from Howard Elkins' business, coupled with the fact that they'd found the barrel beneath Elkins' former home, detectives now believed they had enough information to take a trip to Florida and question him. Before questioning him, however, they wanted to visit his former business partner in the plastic flower business – Melvin Gantman, who had also retired to Boca Raton.

Gantman confirmed that he and Elkins were once business partners, but he hadn't spoken to him in years. When shown a photo of the barrel, Gantman quickly confirmed that it was one they often used for their company. He also verified the dye color and plastic pellets were what they used in making their plastic flowers. When shown a photo of the plastic stem found in the barrel, he right away knew it was also from their company.

However, the most helpful information Gantman gave was something he recalled from the late sixties. He knew Elkins had an affair with a Hispanic employee at the company and rented her an apartment. He didn't know her name, but he remembered that she had strange gold teeth in the front and long black hair. Gantman recalled receiving a phone call from the landlord of the apartment Elkins had rented for her. The landlord was looking for Elkins. The apartment was now empty, but the girl's belongings were still in the apartment, and the landlord wanted him to get the things moved out so he could rent it again.

Detectives were now more convinced than ever that seventy-one-year-old Elkins was the killer. They went to his home, and Elkins invited them in. Unfortunately, Elkins couldn't recall all the things that Gantman easily remembered from the business. He had no recollection of the barrel, the dye, or the plastic pellets. Nothing.

Surprisingly, when asked if he'd had an affair during that time, he freely admitted he had. However, all he could say was, "Yes, a very short affair. She left." When asked if he knew she was pregnant or even if he knew her name, he seemed not to remember anything about her.

Detectives informed him that the girl was found pregnant and deceased in a barrel beneath his former house. But Elkins seemed completely unfazed. He flatly refused when they asked him for a sample of his DNA.

Just then, his phone rang. It was his wife. After speaking briefly to his wife, Elkins told the detectives they needed to leave. He said his wife was coming home, and they would have much to discuss.

The New York detectives had no jurisdiction in Florida to get a warrant or make an arrest. Still, before they left, they informed Elkins that they would be back with a warrant and put him in prison for the rest of his life.

Early the following morning, the two detectives received a call from the local Palm Beach Police Department. Howard Elkins had disappeared, and his wife had reported him missing.

Friends, family, and the police all searched for Howard Elkins. He was found later that evening in his neighbors' garage in the back seat of their Ford Explorer SUV. That morning, he had gone to Walmart and purchased a 12-gauge Mossberg shotgun. Elkins had sat in the back seat of the SUV, put the butt of the shotgun between his legs, placed the barrel in his mouth, and shot himself in the head.

There wasn't any question of his guilt, but to be sure, detectives collected his DNA from the scene and took it back to New York, where investigators confirmed he was the father of the unborn baby.

As soon as they returned to New York, eight days after they found the barrel, they got word back from Immigration about the victim's identity. Her name was Reyna Angelica Marroquin, and she had immigrated to the U.S. in 1966 from El Salvador.

The forensic document team also got much more information from the address book. They recovered several names, addresses, and phone numbers. Unfortunately, the phone numbers were over thirty years old; detectives didn't have much hope for them, but they tried calling anyway. Amazingly, one phone number still worked. The woman that answered, Kathy Andrade, was a close friend of Reyna and was still living at the same location three decades later.

Kathy identified Reyna from a thirty-year-old immigration photo. She said Reyna immigrated from El Salvador and worked making plastic flowers at Melrose Plastics in the sixties.

In November 1968, Reyna told Kathy that she had been dating her boss at the flower factory and was pregnant with his baby. Kathy didn't know his name, only that it was Reyna's boss. One day Reyna told her that she had made a terrible mistake. She said she'd gotten mad at him and called his wife. Reyna told Mrs. Elkins that she was having an affair with her husband, he had also promised to marry her, and she was pregnant with his baby. Reyna told Kathy she was terrified that he would kill her. It turns out, her assumption was correct. That was the last time Kathy had ever heard from Reyna.

Kathy recalled going to Reyna's apartment one evening and seeing two plates set out for dinner. Dinner was still warm on the stove, but there was no sign of Reyna. She called the police to report her as missing, but the police told her that she couldn't file a missing person report if she wasn't a family member. She tried to call Reyna every day for weeks after that, but she never heard from her and eventually gave up.

———

Oscar Corral, a journalist covering the story for *Newsday*, a daily newspaper in the New York City area, later tracked down Reyna's ninety-five-year-old mother in San Salvador, El Salvador, and flew down to visit her. Her mother said she would speak to Reyna regularly on the phone, and then suddenly, the calls stopped. She had no idea why. She said she would often dream of Reyna trapped inside a barrel.

Reyna's body was transported back to El Salvador for burial. Her mother died one month later and was buried next to her.

CHAPTER 2
THE MURDER OF JAMIE LAIADDEE

I am always amazed when prosecutors go to trial before a body is found. It's an aggressive move. This is one of those cases. In fact, in this case, there wasn't even physical evidence that a murder had occurred. The prosecutor was Juan Martinez, who became famous years later for prosecuting Jodi Arias, arguably one of the most notorious cases in Arizona history. This case was especially intriguing because it happened near my home in an area I'm extremely familiar with.

Jamie Laiaddee grew up in California with her parents, who emigrated from Thailand. Her older sister, Pepper, had graduated from medical school, and Jamie's parents pushed her very hard to do the same. They were obsessively adamant about her getting good grades so she could attend medical school, but Jamie resented the pressure and stress her parents put on her.

When it came time to choose a school, Jamie decided to pursue her degree halfway across the country at the University of Michigan. She created a new life with new friends and excelled in school. Her friends called themselves the "516 Girls," named after the house they shared at

516 Walnut St. in Ann Arbor, Michigan. The girls were diehard fans of their college football team, the University of Michigan Wolverines, and would watch every game together.

After Jamie graduated from college, she got a high-paying job selling medical supplies in Arizona. Her parents pushed and pushed her to go to graduate school, but she was sick of being compared to her sister and cut off contact with her family once she left school.

Arizona was a long way from Michigan, so that meant leaving all her college friends behind and setting out for a new life on her own. She kept in touch with her Michigan friends with phone calls and the occasional wedding, but the girls were now strewn across the world, with some as far away as Germany, Russia, and Australia. In the years after college, it wasn't uncommon to not speak to them for months at a time.

Her new job in Arizona kept her extremely busy with long hours, which also kept her from meeting new people. She decided to join a University of Michigan Alumni group that got together every weekend to watch the Wolverines games at a local bar. It wasn't long before Jamie met a fellow alumnus named Bryan Stewart.

Bryan was good-looking, muscled, charismatic, and just as enthusiastic as Jamie was about Michigan football. He worked as a personal trainer at the local Gold's Gym, and the two hit it off. Within a year, Bryan had moved in with Jamie to the tract home she'd bought in Chandler, a suburb just southeast of Phoenix.

Jamie, of course, made a lot more money than Bryan, but she didn't seem to mind. She covered most of the bills, and from the outside, the two lived a normal life for the next two years.

The economy was hit hard in the Phoenix area during the financial crisis of the mid-2000s. As a result, the house Jamie had purchased earlier was now "upside down," meaning that she owed more to the bank than the property was worth. That was fine until August 2009, when Jamie lost her high-paying job with the medical supplies company. She looked for a new job for several months, but the prospects weren't good during those times.

Her money supply was dwindling – and so was Bryan and Jamie's love affair. Jamie had always been quiet and reserved, but when the money started draining and the job selection grew slim, Jamie became despondent; her affection dropped off.

It didn't help that Bryan had problems with the law. To hear Bryan tell it, he was "wrongfully accused" of trespassing. It was all just a big, silly mistake. But, in reality, he was caught breaking into a Mercedes and was charged with burglary. He missed his court dates several times and was re-arrested a few times. Each time, Jamie would faithfully pay his bail. He had an excuse for her every time. As far as she knew, he didn't have any court dates at all – he only told her that he was "meeting with lawyers."

Bryan decided it was time to end their relationship, so he got his own apartment in nearby Scottsdale. However, he didn't tell Jamie about the apartment until he was ready to move out; on the night of March 17, 2010, he broke the news to her.

But before he had a chance, Jamie had some news of her own. Jamie told Bryan she had been offered a job in Denver, Colorado. She had always told him that she didn't like the Phoenix area, so she was excited to go to Denver and start a new life again. She wanted him to go with her.

However, Bryan didn't like the idea. He wanted nothing to do with Denver and had already decided to break up with her. He told her he thought it was better if she went her way, and he went his. The two argued for a bit, but according to Bryan, they calmed down and went to bed.

Bryan had to be at work early in the morning, so he kissed her goodbye and left at around 3:45 a.m. A few weeks later, Bryan emailed the president of their Michigan Alumni club to tell her that he and Jamie had broken up, and she was moving to Denver to start a new life.

Of course, this whole backstory was just Bryan's distorted truth. It was the story he told Jamie's friends and, later, the police. The actual truth was very different.

Jamie didn't have any close friends other than Bryan in the Phoenix area. The others at the alumni club were more acquaintances than friends. She wasn't on the greatest terms with her parents and hadn't spoken to them in quite a while. Her best friends were her friends from college, but she hadn't kept in regular contact with them either. Thus, it was no wonder nobody noticed when there had been no contact from Jamie for almost three months.

Bryan still attended the alumni meetings, but her friends were getting anxious. They had sent her numerous emails, but she wasn't responding. Even if she had moved to Denver, she would have had the courtesy to return their emails. Finally, the alumni friends pressured Bryan to call her parents. He finally reached her estranged father in California and told him that his daughter was missing.

Jamie's father immediately called the Chandler police, and they stopped by Jamie's home to do a welfare check. Officers looked in the garage windows and saw that her 1999 Honda was parked there, but her 2007 Ford Explorer was missing. When detectives spoke to a neighbor, he told them that there used to be a man and woman living there, but he hadn't seen them in a long time.

The neighbor also mentioned that someone from a local Phoenix company showed up a few days prior and said they had hired Jamie for a job. The man said he gave her a laptop, cell phone, and credit card, but she never showed up for her first day at work. Assuming she had decided not to take the job, the man was there to collect the items.

Police broke into Jamie's house to find it extremely messy, but there was no sign of a struggle, and it didn't seem that anyone had tried to clean up a crime scene. It was just an unkept, cluttered house with mail on the table and clothes thrown about.

Inside the house, they found her passport, clothes, and suitcases, but her driver's license and purse were missing, so it was plausible she'd left somewhere on her own accord.

Knowing that Jamie owned a second vehicle, police put out an alert to watch for it. Many police cars in the Phoenix area had license plate readers – in addition to police cars, they were on traffic cameras, entry gates, toll booths, and many other places. These were scanning devices that continually scanned license plates and stored the data in a massive database. Police were able to track the whereabouts of almost any vehicle very quickly.

The databases tracked Jamie's Ford Escape just eighteen miles away in Scottsdale. The plates were regularly seen entering the gate of a condo complex. Chandler detectives staked out the condo and waited for the SUV to arrive. When it did, Bryan Stewart was driving.

When detectives asked Bryan why he was driving his girlfriend's car, he immediately corrected them, "Ex-girlfriend." He told them he had a perfectly good excuse for driving her car. He claimed she had given it to him as a parting gift before she left for her new life in Denver. But, of course, detectives didn't believe his story.

Bryan had been driving on an expired driver's license, so they arrested him and got a warrant to search his condo. Bryan asked if he could go to the bathroom before they drove back down to Chandler, but the police denied his request. They suspected he wanted to hide something in his condo before they searched it. When they made the thirty-minute drive back to Chandler, he strangely didn't need to use the restroom anymore.

Bryan kept a meticulous home, quite the opposite of Jamie. As investigators searched his condo, they noticed everything was in perfect order to the point of being indicative of OCD. However, one thing seemed out of place: a woman's wallet was sitting on his desk. Inside the wallet were several of Jamie's credit cards. When investigators searched the purchase records they found that Bryan had been using the cards to purchase camping supplies online, shopping at Target,

Costco, and Walmart, and even buying subscriptions to online dating websites.

One of the cards was an American Express business card. The company name was CareFusion. Police later discovered that this was the company that had hired Jamie in Phoenix, not Denver. They had issued her a laptop, cell phone, and credit card.

But even more interesting was a copy of his birth certificate that they found. It was handwritten, whereas most birth certificates are typed. It seemed very suspicious.

They also found an envelope addressed to someone named Rick Wayne Valentini at a different address in Scottsdale. They thought Bryan may have been stealing someone's mail, but they knew something was wrong when they found a divorce decree in his filing cabinet for Rick Wayne Valentini from Michigan.

Police called the wife listed on the divorce decree and quickly realized that Bryan Stewart and Rick Valentini were the same person. The ex-wife explained to police that she'd divorced Rick Valentini several years ago when he had stolen money from her father and fled to Arizona. Rick Valentini told her he planned to change his name so he wouldn't have to pay child support.

She also mentioned to police that Rick was once physically and verbally abusive to her. Police now had enough to bring fraud charges on Bryan and keep him in jail for long enough to investigate whether he had something to do with the disappearance of Jamie Laiaddee.

When detectives confronted him and told him they knew he was Rick Valentini, he freely admitted it. He said he wasn't running from the law but was desperately trying to leave behind a troubled life. He claimed to have had a very traumatic childhood. His mother was only eighteen when she gave birth to him, and his father didn't want anything to do with him. He said his mother forced him to live in the garage for years until she finally sent him to foster care. He said the only love and attention he got as a child was from his aunts and uncles. Police contacted his aunt, who verified his story that he was physically and emotionally abused during his childhood, but detectives didn't have much sympathy for him.

As investigators looked further into Rick Valentini's past, they realized that he actually had three ex-wives. He also had two daughters he never visited nor paid child support for. In addition, the ex-wives all painted him as a pathological liar.

They also found that he was eight years older than he let on. His actual Rick Valentini birth certificate didn't match his Bryan Stewart Arizona driver's license.

The lies just kept piling up. Bryan claimed he'd spent time in the military in Iraq and Afghanistan. He was indeed in the military, but the truth was he'd never been to either of those places. He went AWOL (Absent Without Leave), and when military police arrested him, he stabbed an officer in the hand and leg. He then spent two years in a military prison.

And then there was his University of Michigan story. As expected, despite the diploma for the University of Michigan hanging on his wall and his University of Michigan ID card, Bryan had never attended college. He had forged the diploma and ID, just like he had done with the Bryan Stewart birth certificate. The University of Michigan didn't even offer an "Education Physiology" degree like his diploma stated.

Bryan then revealed that he had an explanation for Jamie's disappearance. He told detectives that Jamie had lost her job and she was about to lose her house. She hated her parents and hated Arizona and wanted to disappear so that she could create another life – a completely new identity. Who better to help her than someone who had experience creating a new identity? He said she wanted him to go with her, but he refused. Instead, he agreed to help her disappear.

He also claimed he had been in contact with her a few times since she left and that she had even been to his Scottsdale condo. He said he had given her a key to his condo, and he sometimes noticed that she had been there while he was gone, claiming she had moved things around inside the condo.

Police still didn't believe his lies but needed more evidence to charge him with anything other than fraud. They wanted to charge him with murder, but there was still no evidence that anything had happened to Jamie.

Further searches of Bryan's condo revealed Jamie's cell phone and a small white envelope in the back of a filing cabinet. Jamie's Arizona driver's license was inside the envelope, cut up into about 30 pieces. Bryan claimed that Jamie cut the license up herself, but the DNA on the flap of the envelope proved that Bryan had licked the envelope and sealed it, not Jamie.

Going through Bryan's bank statements, they noticed a charge to a self-storage facility. Police thought this was their lucky break. Maybe he'd hidden the body or other evidence of a crime. Investigators didn't find a smoking gun, but they did find several weapons, such as hatchets, swords, a sawed-off shotgun, a semi-automatic handgun, a shovel with clumped dirt on it, and a roll of thick, black plastic liner.

In Arizona, there are endless miles of desert. He could have easily used the shovel to dig a grave and the thick plastic liner to wrap her body. But, again, there was no blood evidence or anything that prosecutors could use to get a conviction.

Next were Jamie's credit card statements. They saw Jamie had paid to run an online background check just before her disappearance. Detectives believed she had found out about Bryan's lies. She may have discovered that he had ex-wives, children, never went to the University of Michigan, and that Bryan wasn't even his real name. But still, nothing was solid enough that they were willing to risk going to trial.

Fortunately, the break they needed was coming. While in jail, one of Bryan's cellmates told his defense attorney that he had some information he was willing to share to get his sentence reduced. The informant said that Bryan talked to him about hiding a body.

 "He told me, 'I wish I knew where they were looking.'... he's wondering where you guys are looking for the body. If you guys are getting warm."

The informant also claimed that Bryan told him he shot her with a sawed-off shotgun and got rid of the body where "nobody will ever find it." Then, he said Bryan questioned, "What can they charge me with if they can't find a body?"

It wasn't much, but the jailhouse confession was enough to convince prosecutors to charge him with second-degree murder. The prosecutor assigned was Juan Martinez.

The Bryan Stewart / Rick Valentini trial began in October 2011. The first witness was a personal training client of Bryan's. She testified that Bryan constantly complained about his relationship with Jamie, saying she was his "sugar mama" and calling her a "whining, nagging bitch."

The next witness was from CareFusion, the employer who had offered Jamie a job – not in Denver, as Bryan had claimed, but nearby in Phoenix. Another witness was a friend of Jamie's who testified that he'd seen her covered with bruises just days before she went missing.

The thing that put the nail in Valentini's coffin, though, was when he took the stand in his own defense, despite his lawyer's warnings. On the stand, he told the same old stories he had told the police. It didn't work, and the jury didn't buy it. With only four hours of deliberation, the jury returned with a guilty verdict even without a body or physical evidence that a murder had occurred.

Rick Valentini was sentenced to a total of fifty-four years in prison: twenty-two years for second-degree murder, twenty years for fraud, and twelve more years for other crimes related to the murder.

Eight years after her death, the remains of Jaime Laiaddee were found in a work lot that held large piles of decorative rock for a landscaping supply company. Medical examiners stated her bones were too degraded to determine a cause of death.

CHAPTER 3
THE DEXTER WANNABE

"Drive down the alley and park in the gravel driveway next to the garage. I'll leave the garage door partly open, so you can sneak in underneath. Then close the garage door behind you."

Those aren't exactly the typical instructions you would expect from a girl you're meeting for a first date, but that's similar to what Gilles Tetreault received. Gilles had been chatting on the dating site plentyoffish.com with a girl named Sheena, and it was to be their first meeting.

But Sheena didn't exist. Gilles followed the strange instructions and snuck in underneath the garage door to find himself in a dark garage with a man in a hockey mask and a blue light sparkling in his hand. The blue light was from an 800-volt stun baton the man shoved at Gilles' stomach. He immediately fell to the ground and convulsed as his attacker stuck duct tape over his eyes.

Gilles managed to tear the duct tape off his eyes only to find a handgun pointed straight at his face. He could tell from the eyes peering through the hockey mask that this crazy person intended to end his life. That's when he made the split-second decision to try to grab the gun from his attacker – but the moment he got his hands on the weapon, he had a revelation. The gun was made of plastic. It was a fake. Gilles released his grip from the gun, fell to the floor, and rolled as fast as he could back under the garage door and into the alley.

Once outside the garage, Gilles realized that he couldn't run. The shock from the stun baton had made his legs temporarily useless. He tried to crawl down the gravel alley while his attacker pulled him by the legs back toward the garage. Gilles looked up and saw a man and woman walking their dog and watching the whole ordeal. He called to them for help, but his attacker laughed and said, "Come on, Frank, let's go back in the garage." The attacker was trying to make the couple believe it was all a silly game.

The couple walked away, worried that it was a trick and the two men were trying to rob them. The attacker hid back in the garage, which allowed Gilles the chance to crawl his way into his truck and drive away.

Afraid and embarrassed, Gilles didn't report the attack to the police. Not reporting the crime, however, was a grave mistake. The whole episode would be repeated a week later with a different victim.

Johnny Altinger was a tall, thirty-eight-year-old tech worker looking for love on plentyoffish.com. Johnny had a close group of friends he kept in touch with daily, and he told them he had been chatting with a girl named Jen. He was planning on meeting her that evening.

Johnny had shared his conversations with Jen with several friends until he pulled into the alleyway at 7 p.m. on October 10, 2008. Unfortunately, that was the last time anyone heard from him.

It was a holiday weekend in Canada, and his friends were getting worried when Johnny didn't show up for a motorcycle trip they had planned together.

The following Monday, several of his friends received similar emails from Johnny's email address:

 "Hey there, I've met an extraordinary woman named Jen who has offered to take me on a nice long tropical vacation. We'll be staying in her winter home in Costa Rica. Phone number to follow soon. I won't be back in town until December 10, but I will be checking my email periodically.

See you around the holidays,

-Johnny"

This was clearly out of character for Johnny, and his friends didn't believe he had written the email. Their worry escalated when they called his workplace to find that he hadn't shown up. Concern turned to frustration when they called the police, who refused to do anything.

Johnny's friends took matters into their own hands and broke into his apartment. Once inside, they found his clothes, suitcase, and passport. There was no way he could have gone on a tropical vacation without his passport. With this new information, they went back to the police.

Detective Bill Clark handled the case. He usually dealt with homicide rather than missing person cases, but he knew something was wrong in this instance. Luckily, Johnny's friends had a critical piece of information: they knew the exact directions to the house where the date with Jen was supposed to have taken place.

Police contacted the person renting the home and brought him in for an interview. His name was Mark Twitchell.

Twitchell was an aspiring independent filmmaker. He had produced a low-budget Star Wars fan film and was working on another film inspired by his favorite TV show, Dexter.

During the interview, Twitchell seemed genuinely surprised that someone may have used his garage for an assault. He gladly offered to show them around the garage, which he used as his makeshift movie studio.

When he showed them around, he told the police that the padlock on the garage door wasn't his. It seemed that someone had switched the lock on the door. Once inside, he showed detectives the props he used for his films and even showed the script he was working on called "House of Cards."

The House of Cards storyline featured a serial killer who found his victims on the Internet and lured them back to his "kill room," where he would use a stun baton and a hockey mask to incapacitate his victims.

Police had their suspicions about Twitchell, but without a body or evidence of a murder, they had no reason to hold him. They had to let him go. Afterward, Detective Clark re-watched the video of the initial interview with Twitchell and believed he was being honest and upfront: just a movie geek making low-budget films. They had no idea that Twitchell's movie script matched perfectly with what had happened to Johnny Altinger.

Just after the interview and in a bizarre move, Twitchell sent an email to detectives titled "More info that might be useful." In this email, he claimed that he suddenly remembered that he had bought a car from a man at a gas station. He explained that a random man approached him and said he wanted to sell his car. Twitchell only had $40 on him at the time, and the man accepted it. The car was a red Mazda worth about $20,000. Twitchell claimed the man said he had met a rich "sugar mama" who would buy him a new car when they returned from vacation.

The story was all too bizarre for Detective Clark to believe. He looked up the car Twitchell claimed to have purchased for $40 and discovered it was a red Mazda registered to Johnny Altinger. This information tied Twitchell directly to Johnny and made him their primary – and only – suspect. However, they still had no reason to hold him or even issue a search warrant without evidence that a crime had been committed.

Detective Clark decided to go to the public for help. That was when the couple that had been walking their dog down the alley came forward. When they heard the news, they assumed they had watched the attack of John Altinger and told their story to the police. But police quickly realized that the attack the couple described had happened a week earlier than Johnny's disappearance. Police now realized there may be a second victim out there, with no idea if the person was alive or dead.

A month after his attack, Gilles Tetreault heard the news that Johnny had gone missing from the same garage where he was attacked. He knew it must have been the same attacker. The discovery compelled him to go to the police and finally tell his story.

The news of Gilles Tetreault's attack confirmed detectives' suspicion that a crime had been committed in the garage; they believed Twitchell was responsible. A search warrant was issued for Twitchell's car and the house he was renting. When investigators arrived, they found mountains of evidence.

Upon searching the garage, investigators found the hockey mask, stun baton, garbage bags, duct tape, knives, plastic coveralls, and a pellet pistol, all with traces of blood. Blood was all over the walls, floor, and "kill table." There was even an empty water pitcher with blood residue all over it. Twitchell had claimed that the blood was fake and the other items were movie props, but further testing showed the blood was real. It was human blood and the DNA matched Johnny Altinger.

The trunk of Twitchell's car had a massive pool of dried blood, and in the back seat, they found his laptop covered with Spiderman stickers.

When computer forensic experts got inside the laptop, they found the most damning evidence of all. In the deleted files, they found a file titled "SK Confessions." The text was horrifying. It was a detailed account of his butchering and dismemberment of Johnny Altinger. It even spoke of the previous victim that narrowly escaped.

(A full copy of the "SK Confessions" document and evidence photos are available in the appendix at the end of this book.)

Detectives arrested Mark Twitchell on Halloween. They held him in jail for months while detectives poured through the evidence and built a case against him. They still needed a body to help their case and to offer closure to Johnny's friends and family. Months and months went by, but Twitchell refused to say a word about what he had done with the body.

The text of "SK Confessions" went into graphic detail about how he had dismembered the body and put it down a storm drain. It said nothing, however, about where that storm drain was. Police searched sewers within a one-mile radius of Twitchell's home using snaking cameras but had no luck discovering the remains.

Twitchell still wouldn't speak, so detective Green put him in the back of his police car and drove him around for hours near the murder scene, trying to get him to disclose the location. But his plan didn't work.

Twitchell got a new lawyer several months later, and detectives received a phone call. He finally wanted to tell them where the body was, possibly thinking his cooperation would help his case or reduce his sentence. His lawyer gave police a map printed out from Google maps with exact directions to the storm drain where he claimed to have dumped Johnny Altinger's body. It was only a few blocks from Twitchell's home.

During the trial, Mark Twitchell took the stand in his own defense. His lawyers tried to paint him as a regular guy. Just a young man with Hollywood ambitions. They claimed he planned to lure a few men to the garage, scare them, and let them go, hoping they would tell their story and it would be good publicity for his upcoming movie.

The story was ludicrous, and the jury didn't believe it. After only four hours of deliberation, the jury returned a guilty verdict. On April 12, 2011, Mark Twitchell was sentenced to life in prison with no parole for a minimum of twenty-five years.

CHAPTER 4
THE MURDER OF ELIZABETH OLTEN

It was an ordinary Wednesday evening. Nine-year-old Elizabeth Olten was home with her mother when there was a knock on the door. It was their six-year-old neighbor, Emma. Emma wanted to see if Elizabeth could come out and play at her house.

Elizabeth's mother initially denied their request because she was making dinner and it would be ready soon, but the girls were persistent, and she allowed Elizabeth to go out for just an hour. Dinner was at 6 p.m., so she told her to be home by then. No later.

When Elizabeth didn't come home at 6 p.m., her mother immediately called her cell phone. There was no answer. When her mother called Emma's house, Emma said Elizabeth had started walking home several minutes ago. But they only lived four houses away – she should have had plenty of time for to make it home by 6 p.m. Elizabeth's mother was panic-stricken. She knew Elizabeth was afraid of the dark and would never walk home alone after dark. She immediately called the police.

Word spread quickly of Elizabeth's disappearance, and within a few hours, hundreds of people were involved in the search. The tiny town of St. Martin, Missouri, had only a little over 1,000 people, but more than 300 residents helped in the search. Police jumped into action too.

They had planes, helicopters, dogs, and even emergency divers to search nearby ponds and rivers.

Theories started to spread. Had a child molester abducted her? Had someone kidnapped her? Police set up checkpoints on all roads leaving town and checked in with any registered sex offenders in the area, but there were no clues at all.

By the next day, the FBI was involved, and an extensive investigation began. Using information from Elizabeth's cell phone, they triangulated an approximate position: her cell phone was in the thick, wooded area directly behind their homes. But they had already searched that area and turned up nothing.

In the wooded area, local volunteers found a hole in the ground. It seemed to be a makeshift grave. The FBI processed the hole and the surrounding area, but still, they found nothing to help the investigation.

FBI agents began by looking at the last person who saw Elizabeth, which was six-year-old Emma. This time Emma added to her story. She claimed she was playing outside with Elizabeth, but Emma got stuck in some thorn bushes and ran crying for her older stepsister, Alyssa. She said she left Elizabeth there by herself near the bushes.

The older stepsister, fifteen-year-old Alyssa Bustamante, had skipped school that day. That was different for Alyssa; she was an A and B student who rarely missed school. Alyssa was a normal kid whose friends said she was fun to be around. She attended church at the Church of Jesus Christ of Latter-day Saints and regularly joined in with the youth programs there.

When FBI agents questioned Alyssa, she denied knowing anything about Elizabeth's whereabouts. She explained that she had indeed skipped school that day, but that had nothing to do with the missing girl. She seemed very calm and collected. A normal teenage kid – certainly nothing to raise suspicions with the FBI agents.

During the interview, Alyssa admitted she had dug the hole. "I just like digging holes," she said. Alyssa claimed she would occasionally bury dead animals that she found in the woods behind her home.

While they questioned her, other FBI agents searched the house using their search warrants. Everything throughout the house seemed to be in place, but when they entered Alyssa's room, they found there was a much darker side to the young girl.

The walls of Alyssa's bedroom were covered with writings and drawings. One crude drawing was an outline of a human figure which seemed to have slash marks across its arms. Next to the image was the word "Emma," referring to Alyssa's younger stepsister. Some of the writings on the walls seemed to form poems:

"I cut to focus.

I cut when my brain is racing.

I cut to make physical what I feel inside.

I cut to see blood because I like it.

I don't like to cut, but I can't give it up."

Another said:

"It was written in blood.

IT WAS WRITTEN IN BLOOD!"

Also taped to the walls were cards, photos, and letters from her father, who was currently in prison. In fact, both of Alyssa's parents were incarcerated. Alyssa had a difficult upbringing; when she was six, her mother, Michelle Bustamante, had a drug overdose right in front of her. Her mother had several drug and alcohol convictions, while her father, Caesar Bustamante, was in prison for assault. By 1998, her grandmother, Karen Brooke, gained custody of her and brought Alyssa to the tiny town to give her a somewhat normal life. However, Alyssa had problems – dark psychological problems. She was good at hiding them from the general public, but to her close friends and family, could change from a good girl to a completely different personality. On her fifteenth birthday, a friend recalled Alyssa asking,

 "Have you ever wondered what it would be like to kill someone?"

Her darker persona especially came out online. She posted photos of herself with mascara and lipstick smeared all over her face, with her fingers pointed like a gun to her head. A post on her Twitter feed read: "Bad decisions make great stories." On YouTube and MySpace, she listed her hobbies as "killing people" and "cutting." One of her videos uploaded to YouTube showed her coaching her younger twin brothers to touch an electric fence.

On Labor Day, when Alyssa was thirteen, she tried to kill herself by taking a handful of pills. Her grandmother found her on the bathroom floor. She spent ten days in a psychiatric hospital, bounced from therapist to therapist, and was prescribed anti-depressants.

Finally, just a few weeks before Elizabeth went missing, a panel of psychiatrists determined that Alyssa should be committed, long-term, to a hospital. She was then diagnosed with an antisocial personality disorder. However, instead of hospitalizing her, they decided to double her prescription.

When the FBI agents searched Alyssa's room, they found her diary. The diary had some extremely disturbing entries, with many about self-harm and "cutting." Alyssa was known to be a cutter – a person who physically cuts their own body and inflicts pain upon themselves through self-mutilation. It's believed that many cutters use physical pain to temporarily relieve the pain of depression or anxiety. Alyssa had over 300 cut wounds, burn marks, and bite marks all over her body, all self-inflicted.

Other entries in the diary included talk of burning down a house with the people inside it. Another entry from October 14, one week before Elizabeth went missing, said,

> "If I don't talk about it, I bottle it up, and when I explode, someone's gonna die."

However, the entry that FBI agents were most interested in was from October 21, the day Elizabeth went missing. That day had an entry scribbled through heavily in blue ink; she obviously didn't want anyone to see what she had written. Only one part of the entry was still visible. At the very end, it read,

> "…I gotta go to church now…lol".

Using a bit of simple backlighting, agents made out two additional words: "slit" and "throat." They then knew there was a lot more to this story.

Agents brought Alyssa into the FBI headquarters for more questioning. Meanwhile, the forensics lab went to work on the scribbled-out section of her diary.

As she was only fifteen, Alyssa was accompanied by her grandmother, who was her legal guardian at the time.

Detectives toyed with Alyssa during her interrogation. They knew she was involved but didn't know exactly to what extent. During the interrogation, they built on her stress levels with long periods of silence strictly to make her uncomfortable. It's a tactic that police use to draw out stress in suspects. The tactic worked, and Alyssa started to physically shake.

Detectives told her they had read her diary, even the last entry that she had scribbled out. They actually hadn't, but they wanted her to believe they had. Finally, Alyssa broke down and told the detectives it was an accident. She claimed they were walking in the woods when Elizabeth fell and hit her head on a rock. She said she tried to revive her, but Elizabeth had died.

The police didn't believe her, and they let her know it. They told Alyssa they would recover the body, and it would show the truth. They told her that a throat doesn't get slit by hitting your head on a rock. Detectives then asked her point blank, "Was her throat cut?" and Alyssa replied, "Yes."

Her grandmother couldn't take anymore. She started crying and left the interrogation room. Seeing her grandmother so disgusted with her broke Alyssa, and she told the entire story to the FBI agents.

Alyssa admitted that she sent her little sister, Emma, to Elizabeth's house specifically to get her and then sent Emma back home. She then took Elizabeth's hand and led her into the woods. "I have a surprise for you," she told the little girl. They walked deep into the woods and reached a hole in the ground. It was a grave that Alyssa had dug five days earlier.

Alyssa confessed that she strangled the nine-year-old, stabbed her in the chest seven times, and then slit her throat with a kitchen knife. One thrust to the chest was forceful enough to pierce the chest bone, cut through the top of the heart, and lodge the tip of the knife into her spine. She then rolled the body into the grave. Alyssa covered Elizabeth lightly with dirt and branches and walked home as if nothing had happened. She put the kitchen knife into the dishwasher and went to her bedroom to clean up.

The forensic lab used a blue light device to recover the full text of Alyssa's diary entry from the day of the murder. It showed that Alyssa took pleasure in killing the poor girl.

"I just fucking killed someone. I strangled them and slit their throat and stabbed them. Now they're dead. I don't know how to feel atm [at the moment]."

"It was ahmazing. As soon as you get over the 'ohmygawd I can't do this' feeling, it's pretty enjoyable. I'm kinda nervous and shaky though right now. Kay, I gotta go to church now... lol."

It was clear that the murder of Elizabeth Olten was premeditated. Alyssa had dug two graves five days before the murder and had sent her little sister to Elizabeth's house to get her. She had also spent at least fifteen minutes walking with the little girl – time to consider her actions.

Alyssa led police to the grave she had dug, and they found the body of Elizabeth buried inside, just as she had explained. It was in the same area where they had gotten the cell phone pings and had been searching the entire time.

In Missouri, despite being only fifteen years old at the time, Alyssa's crimes met the requirements for her to be tried as an adult and charged with first-degree murder. That made her eligible for the death penalty. She was charged with two counts of first-degree murder and one count of armed criminal action.

However, in a setback to the prosecution, some tactics used during her interrogation were not allowed on a juvenile in Missouri. The judge then threw out Alyssa's confession.

Additionally, the US Supreme Court was about to pass a law that life sentences without the possibility of parole for juveniles were to be deemed unconstitutional.

Prosecutors then offered the defense a plea deal. If she accepted a charge of second-degree murder, she would serve a life sentence with a chance of parole in ten to thirty years. They took the deal, but Elizabeth's family was livid with the outcome.

During her sentencing, Alyssa addressed Elizabeth's family directly:

"I know words can never be enough, and they can never adequately describe how horribly I feel for all of this. If I could give my life to get her back, I would. I'm sorry."

But the words were too little, too late; the family believed she was only saying that after being coached by her defense team in hopes of getting a lighter sentence.

The prosecution argued for life in prison plus seventy-one years – the years that Elizabeth could have lived. Prosecutor Mark Richardson said, "These sentences are appropriate to fit what happened to Elizabeth at the hands of a truly evil individual who strangled and stabbed an innocent child simply for the thrill of it."

The defense argued that Alyssa's depression and suicide attempts should allow her a reduced sentence, but the prosecution reminded the judge that Alyssa's actions were cold and deliberate. She knew exactly what she was doing and had time to think about it before doing it.

Alyssa was ultimately sentenced to life in prison plus thirty years for armed criminal action. Under Missouri law, Alyssa will serve thirty-five years and five months before she's eligible for parole in 2044.

A year after the conviction, Elizabeth's mother, Patricia Preiss, sued Alyssa for a wrongful death suit and settled the lawsuit for $5 million, but it's doubtful she'll ever see a cent of that money.

She also attempted to sue Pathways Behavior Healthcare and two of its employees, as Alyssa was under their care when she murdered Elizabeth. Patricia believed they knew of Alyssa's tendencies and could have prevented the death by institutionalizing her. However, the judge threw out the lawsuit.

CHAPTER 5
INTERPOL'S MOST WANTED

On July 28, 1996, off the coast of Southwest England, a fishing trawler was having trouble getting their full catch for the day. So the captain decided to sail a little further out to sea, to an area where they rarely ventured. Fishing there for a while, they thought they had struck a big haul when they pulled up the net; the net was much heavier than usual. They initially thought possibly a dolphin had become stuck in the net, but when they pulled it up, they realized they had snagged a human body.

Once on board, they saw it was the body of a fully clothed man. He was wearing a Rolex watch, had a maple leaf tattoo on the back of his hand, and his pants pockets had been turned inside out. He was severely bruised and had a massive gash on the top of his head. The fishermen radioed the police, told them what they had found, and headed back into the harbor.

Devon and Cornwall Police brought the body in for an autopsy. Though his head had a massive wound, his lungs were filled with water. He was alive while in the water and had drowned. The gash on the head could have come from something he hit while in the water. The English Channel area had vast amounts of coastline, and drownings were not uncommon. Investigators assumed the man could have died during a boating accident or even by suicide.

The Rolex Oyster Perpetual watch on his wrist was waterproof and self-winding. Police contacted Rolex and found that Rolex self-winding watches kept the correct time for about forty hours without wrist movement; the watch had stopped at 11:35 a.m. on the 22nd. From the amount of decomposition, they knew the body hadn't been in the water for over a month, so they determined that the watch had stopped on July 22. That made the approximate time of death sometime on July 20.

Rolex also informed them that all Rolex watches had a serial number etched just beneath where the band meets the body of the watch. From the serial number, they could find the owner of the watch from purchase and servicing records. Using the serial number, detectives discovered the Rolex belonged to a man named Ronald Platt, whose address was listed in Chelmsford, Essex, 250 miles east of where the body was found.

In an attempt to contact the next of kin, police first contacted the rental agent of Ronald Platt's flat. The agent only had one contact, which was the reference he listed when renting the flat. The reference was a man named David Davis.

When police contacted Davis, he seemed genuinely sad to hear of Ron's passing. Davis spoke with an American accent and was very personable. He let the detectives know that he was a good friend of Ronald. Ronald had dated a woman that had worked for Davis – they had moved to Canada together but had recently moved back separately. Davis said the last time he talked to Ronald was about six weeks ago when he mentioned he was starting a new business in France.

Dental records confirmed that the body was indeed that of Ronald Platt and detectives now assumed the death was an accident. He had probably fallen off a boat on the way to France.

However, police still needed a signature from a friend or family to add to the coroner's report, so they decided to travel to Devon to the home of David Davis.

The country roads near Davis' home in Devon didn't have house numbers, so when police arrived, they knocked on the first door along the road. The man who answered the door explained they were at the wrong address. The address they were looking for was the next house down the road, but the man was curious and asked why they were looking for his neighbor. The detectives explained they were looking for David Davis, and the man had a perplexed look on his face.

 "There's no David Davis living there. That's the home of Ronald Platt."

The detectives were confused and continued asking the man more questions. The man insisted his neighbor was named Ronald Platt and lived there with his much younger wife, Noel Platt.

Something was obviously wrong here and detectives were very suspicious. They then decided against knocking on David Davis' door and went back to the police station to do some digging.

Davis had mentioned to them that Ronald Platt had been dating a woman named Elaine Boyce. Investigators located Elaine and informed her that Ronald Platt was dead. She explained that she had been in a relationship with Ronald for thirteen years but they had split up two years ago when they returned from Canada. When she heard the news, she immediately assumed Ronald had committed suicide. Ron had always been a very passive, shy, and quiet man.

However, when the police mentioned David Davis, she knew something was terribly wrong. Police told her they had spoken to Davis four weeks ago and told him of Ron's death. However, Elaine had spoken to Davis just two weeks ago, and he had mentioned nothing of it. She knew Davis was hiding something. Elaine also said that she knew Ron had been in the Devon area in the days leading up to his death.

Police decided to look through Davis' phone and financial records around July 20, the time of Ron Platt's death. They found that David Davis owned a yacht in South Devon called The Lady Jane. This information wasn't enough for a conviction of anything, being that they had no proof that Ron's death wasn't an accident, but they decided to risk it and arrest him anyway.

With only suspicion of murder, police arrested David Davis on October 31, 1997. They found fifty-one-year-old Davis there with his twenty-one-year-old wife and two babies. During the arrest, his young wife was packing a diaper bag for the babies, but police noticed the bag seemed extremely heavy.

When officers looked through the diaper bag, they found £4,000 in British currency and two large 1 kg gold bars. During the house raid, they found more currency; British pounds, Swiss francs, French francs, more gold bars, and expensive fine art paintings worth around $290,000.

Detectives were now at a turning point. They still had no evidence of a murder, but it was obvious Davis had stolen Ronald Platt's identity. They just didn't know why. The Crown Prosecution Service gave the detectives a week to come up with some definitive evidence or they would have to release him.

The detectives started by returning to the crime scene to speak to the fishing boat captain. When they questioned the captain, he pointed out a few details the police had missed. Ron Platt's pants pockets had been turned inside-out, so it was apparent someone had gone through his pockets. If someone accidentally drowns, their pants pockets don't automatically turn out. Also, when they hauled up the body in the fishing net, there was a ten-pound anchor in the same haul. When police asked why he hadn't mentioned that initially, the captain simply replied, "You didn't ask." Police then took the ten-pound anchor into evidence.

When investigators raided Davis' house, they found purchase receipts made with credit cards under Ronald Platt's name. One of those receipts was from a nautical shop in Dartmouth, and among the items on that receipt was a ten-pound anchor. They confirmed the anchor Davis had purchased was the same one hauled up by the fishing boat.

When they found Davis' yacht, forensic investigators went over the boat with a fine-tooth comb. In the boat's hull, they found a shopping bag from the same nautical store where they found the receipt for the anchor. Inside the bag, they found all the other items on the receipt – everything but the anchor. Ron Platt's fingerprints were on that bag, proving he was on the boat.

On a seat cushion in the cabin, they found three hairs attached to a chunk of skin. DNA tests proved the hairs were Ron Platt's. Police assumed they were ripped from Ron's head when Davis hit him over the head with the anchor.

The forensic lab also noticed zinc residue inside Ron Platt's leather belt. That zinc proved similar to the zinc on the anchor. Police believe that Davis had tucked the anchor into Platt's belt, like a sword, before he threw him over the edge.

The boat featured new technology at the time, GPS. The global positioning system proved that the boat was in the same general area where the body was pulled up on July 20, the same day that the Rolex confirmed Ronald Platt had died.

The police now believed they had the evidence they needed to secure a murder conviction. However, the one thing they didn't have was a motive. They still didn't know why David Davis had been posing as Ronald Platt in the first place.

It wasn't until they ran Davis' fingerprints through global databases that they realized exactly who they had captured. The man they had arrested was not David Davis; that was also an assumed name. His real name was Albert Johnson Walker. He was number four on Interpol's most-wanted list and was the number one most-wanted person in Canada. When they contacted Canadian police, they got the entire backstory.

Albert Johnson Walker was a seemingly successful Canadian businessman living a normal life in Ontario. He ran a financial consulting firm with six branches and taught Sunday school. Then, in 1990, he took his fifteen-year-old daughter, Sheena, on a skiing trip to Europe and left his wife, Barbara, with their three other children. His wife had no idea, but Albert was running away forever and leaving her with a world of problems.

Even though he hadn't finished high school, Walker was a very skilled con man. He had set up his financial consulting firms in the Cayman Islands and had talked his clients, mostly elderly, into investing their retirement savings in his company. Many of them handed over their entire life savings to him. By 1990, he had $3.2 million in cash from over seventy clients when he fled Canada with his daughter in tow.

Provincial police charged him with thirty-two counts of fraud, and he became Canada's most wanted fugitive and number four on Interpol's most wanted list.

Walker originally ended up in Harrogate, North Yorkshire, where he assumed his new identity of David Davis with his daughter, Sheena, posing as his much younger wife. During this time, Sheena had two children. Authorities never revealed the results of paternity tests on the children, but their birth certificates list David Davis as their father.

During his time in Harrogate, he met Elaine Boyes, who was working for a fine art auction house. Elaine told Davis about her boyfriend, Ronald Platt, and their plans to move to Canada. Ronald had always wanted to move to Canada and even had a Canadian maple leaf tattooed on the back of his hand.

Davis offered the couple a job running his new company – The Cavendish Company. He explained that he would like to put the company in their names because he didn't want his ex-wife back in the United States to find out he was making money.

Elaine and Ron agreed and ran his company, often taking trips to other countries where Davis asked them to convert money from Swiss francs to British pounds.

In 1992, Walker surprised Ronald and Elaine with a generous Christmas present. He had purchased them one-way tickets to Calgary, Canada. He knew how much they wanted to move to Canada and gave them the perfect opportunity.

Amazingly, Walker convinced Ron to leave a rubber stamp of his signature, his driver's license, birth certificate, and a credit card. Walker explained that it was standard operating procedure in those circumstances and that he could continue running the business under their names. With Ron Platt out of the country in Canada, Walker was now free to assume his new identity as Ronald Platt.

His plan worked fine for a few years, but Canada wasn't all Ron had hoped it would be. Finally, he grew tired of the freezing winters and moved back to England. This blew a massive hole in Albert Walker's plan to use Ron's identity, so he decided he would need to get rid of Ron Platt once and for all.

During the trial, Albert Walker pled guilty to defrauding over 70 of his clients of their savings, but he denied killing Ronald Platt.

His daughter, Sheena, testified against her father, claiming she had been "hypnotized" by him. She also admitted the two of them were together in Devon during the time of the murder and had been together every day, except for when he went on the boat with Ronald Platt. After only two hours of deliberation, the jury returned a guilty verdict for both first-degree murder and fraud with a sentence of life in prison.

The clients of Albert Walker could only recover £500,000 of their stolen money; several hundred thousand in gold bars are still missing. After seven years in English prisons, they returned Walker to Canada to face twenty-seven additional fraud, theft, and money laundering charges. In 2021, seventy-five-year-old Walker was denied parole.

CHAPTER 6
PAIGE'S DIRTY LITTLE SECRET

On the afternoon of June 28, 2007, Paige Birgfeld drove two hours from her home in Grand Junction, Colorado, to Eagle, Colorado, for a picnic she had planned with her ex-husband, Howard Beigler. Eagle was the midpoint between Grand Junction and Howard's home in Denver, so it was the perfect meeting point for both of them.

Howard and Paige were high-school sweethearts, but it was a typical story. They fell in love when they were young, and it just didn't work between them, and they divorced after only two years. But now, several years later, there was a lot of water under the bridge. Paige was 34, had three kids, and was divorced for a second time. Nevertheless, she hoped to rekindle some of the romance she and Howard felt when they were young.

Paige's second marriage was to Rob Dixon. Rob came from a very wealthy family that had made their money in the cell phone industry in its infancy, so Rob didn't need to work for a living. Rob had a collection of sports cars including a bright yellow Ferrari and lived in a million-dollar home. When he and Paige first started dating, he showered her with lavish gifts like a $12,000 necklace. So when Rob proposed to her with an $85,000 engagement ring, she couldn't say no.

Rob and Paige had three adorable kids and lived the perfect life, but his demeanor turned when Rob made a string of bad investments, and he showed he had an angry side. During one of their arguments, Paige had to call the police.

> "My husband and I were in a fight, and he was supposed to watch my children while I went to work. He said that I would come home and find them all murdered."

Police filed no charges on that occasion, but the arguments didn't stop. It wasn't long before she called the police again. This time, Rob was arrested for third-degree assault after he had punched and slapped her.

Paige wrote in her blog,

> "My children would ask me if dad was going to kill me. I can't imagine what life would be like for them after he killed me."

When the two divorced after eight years of marriage, Paige gained custody of the kids and kept the house in Grand Junction with its whopping $6,000 per month mortgage payment.

Though stuck with the huge mortgage and not much help from her ex, Paige was determined to make it work. She loved her kids more than anything in the world and turned to her entrepreneurial skills to help support her family. She started a string of dance studios for kids and sold nursing slings for new mothers and cookware through a company called Pampered Chef.

But that Thursday in June, Paige was interested in love. She was hoping there might still be a spark left with her first husband, Howard. The two met for their picnic in Eagle, CO, and that evening, Paige left for the two-hour drive back to Grand Junction.

Paige was due to be home that night, but her kids were terrified when she hadn't arrived by 11 p.m. They got no reply when calling her cell phone. The three children were being watched by their babysitter, who didn't speak English, which only added to the confusion. The poor children, the oldest of which was only eight years old, spent the following day not knowing what had happened and had no idea what to do. The kids finally called Howard in Denver, who told them to have their babysitter take them to the police station and Howard immediately called the Mesa County Sheriff.

Howard told police he had spoken to her around 9 p.m. on Thursday night after their picnic earlier in the day. Paige had called and told him she was just pulling into Grand Junction and had a few people to meet before she went home. However, Howard didn't know whom she was meeting.

That Saturday afternoon, Paige Birgfeld was listed as a missing person, and her family and friends were notified. Of course, the first place to look was with the last person to see Paige, her ex-husband, Howard. He was quickly eliminated as a suspect when phone records showed he spoke with Paige at 9 p.m. that night as she was driving into Grand Junction; he had been on his cell in Denver.

Paige's second ex-husband, Ron, was also an immediate suspect because they'd had such a tumultuous relationship, but he was now living in Pennsylvania and was eliminated as a suspect.

By that evening, over 100 people were searching for her, and police had forensic sniffer dogs were looking for clues. But an ominous clue came that evening from a 911 call to the police. In an empty lot in an industrial part of town, Paige's car was found burning. It was obviously arson. Someone was trying to get rid of evidence.

When police searched the remains of the burned-out car, there were some additional signs of foul play. The driver's side seat was pushed back to its furthest position, yet Paige was only five foot four. With the seat pushed back that far, she wouldn't have even been able to reach the pedals. Someone very tall had been driving her car. Inside the trunk, investigators found Paige's day planner. Though damaged, it had survived the fire and showed that someone had torn out the last four days. Those pages would have shown whom she met that night. Again, someone was destroying evidence.

The forensic dogs tracked a scent at the car and followed it about 500 feet away to a mechanic's shop that serviced RVs, where the scent disappeared.

Despite so many volunteers searching for Paige, the Grand Junction area had vast open spaces. The Colorado River pours into the Gunnison River and twists and turns for hundreds of miles. There were thousands of square miles in which someone could disappear.

Investigators then concentrated their efforts on Paige's last cell phone activity. On the evening that Paige went missing, her last phone call was to Howard. Earlier that day, however, there were calls from another number that wasn't in her contacts. Three calls came in, two went out.

Further investigation of her cell phone revealed that Paige led a secret life that her friends and family didn't know about. There were voice-mails left from men asking to meet her in hotel rooms. Besides teaching dance and selling cookware, Paige was selling sex. No one had any idea that the sweet, loving mother of three was secretly running an escort business she called "Models Inc."

When they did further digging, they found photos of Paige – a beautiful, thin, strawberry blonde – listed on escort websites under the name "Carrie." Paige was working as an escort to pay the bills and bring up her three kids by herself.

The police were particularly interested in the five phone calls on Paige's phone from earlier in the day. One message from that number was from a man called Jim.

 "Hello, yeah, this is Jim. Just calling to see if Carrie was available tonight."

Detectives discovered the phone calls came from a "Tracfone," a disposable prepaid cell phone. Only five calls were made to or from the phone – all to Paige's "Models Inc." number.

Tracfones can be somewhat anonymous, but in this instance, police could tell exactly where and what time it had been purchased. It was purchased two days earlier, on June 26, at the local Walmart. Police contacted Walmart and acquired surveillance video taken during the purchase. The footage showed a large white male in his sixties buying the phone.

Upon further investigation, they found that the man's name was Lester Jones, and he worked at "Bob Scott RV," the same RV repair shop just 500 feet from where they found Paige's car in flames.

Lester Jones had a prior conviction on his record. In 1999, he was convicted of first-degree sexual assault and kidnapping of his ex-wife. Lester Jones was also a very tall man. At six foot five, Jones would have needed to push a car seat all the way back to drive it.

Police obtained a warrant to search the RV shop where Jones worked. There, they found that Lester Jones had his own secret life under the name of "Jim." During the search, they found packets of Viagra, condoms, and men's toupees. They also found handwritten lists with notes about particular escorts, including their appearances, websites, personalities, types of sex they would perform, and bra sizes. But the most damning two pieces of evidence they found were a gas canister and a food scale made by Pampered Chef, the same company that Paige worked for.

Detectives then took the sniffer dogs back to the burned car, where they found the scent of Lester Jones in the vehicle's front seat.

Police brought Jones into the Sheriff's office for interrogation, but he flatly denied everything. He denied ever meeting Paige or even knowing who she was. He denied buying the Tracfone and making the calls. When police showed him the surveillance video, he said it wasn't him. Later, he admitted to being at the Walmart during that time but said he was purchasing a Monster Cable, despite the confirmation of the video, receipt, and the clerk remembering selling him the Tracfone.

When asked his whereabouts on Sunday night when Paige's car was found ablaze, he admitted that he had left the house. He claimed that he went back to the RV shop to turn the shop lights off, just 500 feet from where the car was burning. But he claimed he had nothing to do with the burning car – it was just an amazing coincidence.

Despite the seeming mountain of evidence, police had no crime other than the burning car. There was no body. They had no clue whether Paige was dead, or if she was being held somewhere, or if she had just run off on her own accord. Proving he was guilty of anything beyond a reasonable doubt would be a risk. Detectives had no choice but to set Lester Jones free.

Two weeks later, on July 16, a motorist traveling on Highway 50 stopped to fix a flat tire. While changing their tire, they noticed a checkbook lying on the side of the road. It was Paige Birgfeld's. Police were notified, and an extensive search of Highway 50 began. Spread all along the highway between Grand Junction and Whitewater, Colorado, they found over two dozen personal items belonging to Paige, such as her Blockbuster Video card, clothing, and her children's medical cards. Police speculated that Paige had been kidnapped and was leaving a trail of breadcrumbs by throwing her personal items out the window of a moving vehicle.

Even with this new evidence, it wasn't enough to bring any charges against Jones. The case went cold and nothing happened for another five years.

In the Spring of 2012, about forty miles south of Grand Junction in an area called Wells Gulch, a hiker came across a human skull near the Gunnison River. The flesh around the skull had long since decomposed, but duct tape was still attached to the jawline and back of the head. It was obvious this person had died against their will.

Over the course of almost a year, investigators searched the Gunnison River for more remains. They found bones distributed across a mile of the twisting river. Then, on March 6, 2013, Paige Birgfeld was pronounced dead.

It took another year and a half for prosecutors to put together a case that they believed was strong enough to convict Lester Jones and finally arrested him on November 21, 2014.

Jones' trial started an additional year and a half later in June 2016, but Paige's family was devastated to find that the first trial ended in a mistrial. Nine jurors believed Jones was guilty, but three believed there was reasonable doubt. The prosecuting attorney believed that, because Paige had led a secret life as an escort, some of the jurors may have thought she knew she was putting herself in harm's way and therefore didn't deserve proper justice.

The second trial started the following month. During the trial, Jones' wife testified that he had left the house that Sunday night when the car was found burning. She said that she had often suspected her husband of seeing other women.

As the jury deliberated, they came back with a question. They wanted the prosecution to replay a strange, recorded phone conversation between a police officer and Lester Jones that prosecutors had played earlier.

Sergeant Art Smith had called Jones to return one of his impounded vehicles to him during the investigation when Jones made some odd comments:

> Sgt. Smith: "If you need us to bring one to you or come and pick one of you up; we can do that for you."
>
> Lester Jones: "I don't think so."
>
> Sgt. Smith: "Um, Mr. Jones, I'm not following you."

Lester Jones: "You asked me where I would bury a body."

Sgt. Smith: "I'm sorry?"

Lester Jones: "You asked me where I would bury a body."

Sgt. Smith: "When did I ask you that?"

Almost ten years after Paige Birgfeld went missing, the jury finally returned with a verdict. Lester Jones was found guilty on all counts of kidnapping and murder. He was sentenced to life in prison without the possibility of parole.

CHAPTER 7
THE MURDER OF
GEORGIA WILLIAMS

Jamie Reynolds seemed like an ordinary young man to his neighbors and schoolmates in Wellington, England. But, he liked to play the role of the heartbroken boy who never got the girl. He posted on social media about how he was "cursed" when it came to girls and how he would be "forever alone." Jamie also had a thing for redheads. One girl in particular, Georgia Williams, caught his eye – but in addition to redheads, he also had a much darker obsession.

Twenty-two-year-old Jamie had a crush on a younger high-school girl named Georgia Williams. Georgia was a bright, vibrant seventeen-year-old redhead who was very active in her school and had been voted "Head Girl," a title similar to "Class President" in US schools. Jamie was in the same class as Georgia's older sister.

On Facebook and ask.fm, Jamie made multiple attempts to get Georgia to become his girlfriend and had once tried to kiss her, but she quickly shot him down. Georgia simply wasn't interested, and she made that clear to him. She liked him as a friend but told him she wasn't interested in having a boyfriend at the time. On April 5, however, when Georgia posted on Facebook that she was in a new relationship, it upset Jamie.

He posted, "Whenever I arrange dates, they either never happen, or the girl magically gains a boyfriend … and it's worse when you actually like someone, your stuck, happy their happy but unhappy coz it's not you."

Jamie thought of himself as an aspiring photographer. At least, that's what he told girls. He devised an elaborate plan to lure Georgia to his home while his parents were on vacation in Italy. Jamie told her he was working on an art project and wanted to recreate a "fake hanging" photo shoot; he needed Georgia to be the model. He told her he wanted it to be an "artistic, floating" image. He assured her that several of her friends would be there watching the photo shoot with them, but that was a lie. She was the only one invited.

Georgia checked with her parents to make sure it was okay. Her parents knew Reynolds, as he worked at a nearby gas station and lived only a five-minute walk away. They thought of him as an ordinary boy from the neighborhood and, like Georgia, they believed her other friends would be there too, so they assumed their daughter was safe.

On Sunday, May 26, 2013, Georgia got dressed for the photo shoot in the clothes Reynolds got for her, told her parents goodbye, and left. Just as she headed out the door at 7:30 p.m., she got a text from Jamie:

 "I'm so excited. Please don't be late."

That was the last time Georgia's parents saw her alive.

At 10:30 that night, when Georgia didn't show up at home, her mother sent her a text:

 "Where are you; what are you doing?"

A text reply came back immediately:

> *"I've left with some friends, going to be out for a while. I'll see you later. xxx"*

The "xxx" at the end of her texts was something Georgia typically added to her texts. They represented kisses—one for each of her family members.

At 6 a.m. the following morning, when Georgia still hadn't arrived home, her mother sent her another text. This time, she didn't get a reply for another two hours:

> *"I stayed at friends. I'm fine, but my battery is dying too."*

Reynolds was playing a cruel joke on her parents. By saying that the battery was "dying too," he was leaving a gruesome hint that Georgia was dying or already dead.

Georgia had planned to attend a music festival that Monday, so her parents didn't think much of her being gone most of the day. They assumed she was with her friends enjoying the festival. It wasn't until the evening, when phone calls to Georgia's phone went unanswered, that her parents became concerned. They started calling her friends, but nobody seemed to know where she was.

Georgia's older sister texted Jamie, but he feigned concern, claiming she had left earlier in the day. He even offered to help look for her.

Georgia had been excited to have her first driving lesson, which was scheduled for Tuesday morning. Her parents definitely knew something was wrong when she hadn't arrived by Tuesday morning, and they finally called the police.

The first thing detectives did was pull a background check of the person she was last seen with, Jamie Reynolds. Just a quick look at his background told a dreadful story. They knew right away she hadn't run away: she had been kidnapped. For only a young man of 22, Reynolds had a dark and disturbing past. Without informing her parents, police rushed to Reynolds' house and broke down the door.

Inside, there was no sign of Georgia or Reynolds, but they noticed his parents' van was missing. Police began a nationwide manhunt across the United Kingdom to find Jamie Reynolds and the van.

When police searched Reynolds' home, they found proof that they were too late. Georgia had already died a horrific death.

Investigators found memory cards from his digital camera that he attempted to wipe clean, but using recovery software, they were able to recover photos that Reynolds assumed had been erased.

There were photos of Georgia alive with a noose around her neck. Next, photos of her naked dead body. He had hung her in various rooms throughout the house and photographed her. Then he took photos of himself having sex with her lifeless corpse.

The photos showed he dressed her in the clothes he bought for her and restrained her with handcuffs. He then placed a boat oar over two beams in the loft, slung the noose around the oar, and tied the rope's end to the stairs' railing. He then had her stand on a wooden box and put the rope around her neck. Suddenly, he pulled the noose tight and kicked the box out from underneath her. He took photos and watched, all while she kicked and tried to scream as the life drained out of her.

The photos showed that he then laid her dead body on the bed and sexually assaulted her for over an hour. Next, he dragged her body downstairs and positioned it all over the house, taking pictures of himself in sexual positions with the body for several hours.

In the early morning hours of Wednesday, May 29, police spotted the van parked outside a Premier Inn just outside of Glasgow, Scotland, almost five hours away from his home. Jamie Reynolds was inside his hotel room when police stormed in and took him into custody.

During the interrogation, Reynolds was cold and emotionless. He refused to help the police in any way whatsoever. Despite the incriminating photo evidence, he refused to admit he murdered Georgia. Instead, he claimed he had no idea where Georgia was and had no recollection of anything. It was an excuse he had used before.

It was clear Reynolds would be no help. Investigators continued searching the house and began retracing his steps, from the day he left Wellington in his parents' van until his arrest in Glasgow.

Investigators located security camera footage of him filling the van with gas, while another camera showed he had stopped in Wrexham, Wales, to watch a movie. He calmly spent a few hours watching Fast & Furious 6, a film he had asked Georgia to see with him. He then stopped at a shopping mall to buy a new watch.

After searching his route, they still found no trace of Georgia, so detectives reached out to the media for help. They hoped they could get additional clues if the public knew what they were looking for. They were in luck.

A witness came forward and said they recognized both the van and Jamie Reynolds. They told detectives that Reynolds' van became stuck in the mud on a country road near a wooded area called Nant-y-Garth Pass, and they had stopped to help him.

Just three days after Georgia was reported missing, the people led police to the area where Reynolds' van was stuck. Nearby, Georgia's body was found naked, unburied in the woods. Reynolds was immediately charged with murder.

Investigators now realized that while the surveillance video showed him pumping gas, Georgia was dead inside the back of the van. She was also in the back of the van as he stopped off to watch the movie.

When police finished their search of Jamie Reynolds' house, they found evidence that he had meticulously planned the murder down to the last detail – and he also planned on doing the same to several other girls. He had even taken the time to answer two calls from other potential victims during his murder of Georgia. Reynolds was a serial killer in the making.

Detectives discovered forty stories he had written that read like a script of his plans for the murders. One was titled "Georgia's Surprise."

During the investigation, detectives found that Reynolds had messaged sixteen young women and invited them to his house that same week to participate in similar photo shoots. They believed he intended to schedule backups, just in case his plans with Georgia didn't work.

When police looked into Reynolds' background, they quickly realized none of this should have happened. Jamie Reynolds had a dangerous obsession with sexual violence against women that should have been given more attention by authorities long before.

In 2008, when he was seventeen, Reynolds attacked a sixteen-year-old redhead girl under similar circumstances. Reynolds lured the girl to his home while his parents were away. He told her he wanted her to pose for photographs for an art project he was working on. When the girl refused to go upstairs with him, he attacked. The girl managed to fight him off, bit him, and broke one of his ribs. Once she escaped, she reported the attack to the police. Unfortunately, they only gave him a "final warning" and counseling.

Two weeks after that incident, Reynolds' parents showed police and his psychiatrist images they had found on his computer. Jamie had a strange obsession with "snuff" films and extreme porn that had started when he was fourteen. He liked to watch films of simulated rape, killing, and necrophilia. He had amassed a collection of 16,800 images and seventy movies of women being asphyxiated, hung, raped, and murdered, including sex with their corpses.

Even more disturbing, Jamie had a collection of photos of girls from his school. He had taken their photos from Facebook and photoshopped nooses around their necks, one of which was Georgia Williams. There were more photos of women being attacked, only he had replaced the faces of the women with the faces of girls from his school. He had even pasted a copy of his own face over the face of each attacker. None of these girls were notified that he had done this.

Even after notifying the police, they told his parents to simply restrict his access to porn. The police had put all the burden upon the parents. But this wasn't your everyday vanilla porn; it was much more sadistic. It was violent porn that depicted simulated rape and torture, which ended in death.

His parents put software blocks on his computer, but Jamie could easily get past those. He installed his own routers in their home so he could fulfill his sick fantasies undetected.

A few years later, in August 2011, Reynolds made advances to a girl where he worked. When he persisted after multiple rejections, she confronted him and told him in no uncertain terms that she wasn't interested. He then got in his car and purposely rammed his car into hers in anger. When he was arrested for Georgia's murder, police found images of this girl on his hard drive with a photoshopped noose around her neck.

Just three months before Georgia Williams' murder, Reynolds had lured another young girl to his home. Another redhead. Again, his parents were out of town. He locked the doors to the house and told her he had lost the keys. He tried to persuade her to stay the night, but she could see through his ruse. She screamed and threatened to break the windows and climb out – at which point he miraculously found the keys and let her go. After Georgia's murder, they found notes he had left himself showing that he'd planned to hang the girl.

The police and social services knew about his deviant intentions, yet Jamie Reynolds was only given warning after warning. Six different agencies were aware of Jamie's dangerous obsessions but did nothing to stop him. If police and social services had coordinated information, registered him earlier as a sex offender, and monitored his actions, Georgia Williams may have known of his background, and her life may have been spared.

Over the next six months, Reynolds said nothing and Georgia's family assumed they would have to go through a long and difficult trial. However, just five days before the trial's start date, Reynolds finally submitted a guilty plea. The judge, however, showed no leniency. Due to his potential to become a serial killer, Jamie Reynolds was sentenced to a full-life sentence, meaning he will never be released. This is a very rare sentence in the UK, with only about 100 offenders serving a full-life sentence – Jamie Reynolds is among the youngest.

CHAPTER 8
THE GIRL IN THE BOX

I n 1977, hitchhiking in the United States was a common mode of transportation, even for young girls. Colleen Stan was a free-spirited twenty-year-old girl hitchhiking her way from Eugene, Oregon, to the small Northern California town of Westwood to surprise a friend for her birthday. After accepting rides with truckers traveling south on Interstate 5, she made her way to Red Bluff, California, where she needed to change onto Highway 36.

She turned down a few rides while waiting at the on-ramp to Highway 36. They just looked like they could be trouble. Then, finally, a couple stopped to offer her a ride: Cameron and Janice Hooker. At first glance, they seemed to be a normal enough couple. Safe. Cameron looked a bit nerdy with his big seventies-style eyeglasses, and Janice held a two-month-old baby in her arms. Colleen accepted the ride.

During the drive, there was almost no conversation at all – but Cameron kept glancing at her in the rear-view mirror, which made Colleen a bit uneasy. When they stopped at a gas station, Colleen took the opportunity to use the restroom. Something inside her felt she should find another ride, but she was so close to her destination; she decided to continue riding with the couple.

A bit further down the road, Cameron asked if it was okay if they made a stop to see some ice caves just off the main highway. Colleen said she didn't mind. She wasn't in a hurry.

They drove down a dirt road, stopped, and the couple walked to a creek bed while Colleen remained in the car. She had lost sight of the couple when Cameron suddenly jumped into the car's back seat with her. He grabbed her arms and threw her face down onto the back seat. He handcuffed her wrists, blindfolded her, and shoved a gag into her mouth. He then forced her head into a large wooden box.

The wooden box was a homemade bondage device called a sensory deprivation head box. It was large and heavy, with two sides hinged together at the top like a clamshell. It had a hole at the bottom just big enough to fit around her neck. The inside of the box was coated with carpet to muffle her screams. Colleen was lying helpless in the back seat as they continued driving down Highway 36.

When the car finally stopped, Cameron removed the box from her head and led her into a house, then the basement. He removed her clothes and left her blindfolded. Cameron forced Colleen to stand on a metal ice chest and raise her arms. He bound her wrists with leather restraints connected to hooks on a ceiling beam. He then pulled out the ice chest from beneath her, leaving her suspended from the ceiling by her wrists. He then whipped her back with a leather whip while she dangled, kicking and screaming.

As Cameron whipped her, she could see through a gap in her blind-fold. On a counter nearby, she saw glimpses of a magazine with a photo of a woman strapped up exactly like she was. He was acting out his fantasy from a BDSM magazine. He then let her rest her toes on a box while he and Janice had sex as they looked at her.

Colleen's screams only encouraged him. He howled back at her,

"Go ahead and scream! I'll cut your vocal cords out! I've done it before!"

She believed him, and it may have actually been true. The year prior, a young girl in the area named Marie Spannhake went missing. Janice later revealed that she and Cameron had kidnapped her as well, although Cameron couldn't control himself: he killed her after only one day in captivity.

Colleen's torture continued for hours, until he finally let her sit naked on the ice chest. Cameron then put the wooden sensory deprivation box back on her head, laid her in a larger wooden box about the size of a coffin, chained her wrists together, and tied her feet to the inside corners of the box.

Cameron Hooker had been busy building homemade bondage devices and preparing for his victim. The following day, he put Colleen on another device he called "the rack." He chained her wrists and ankles to the corners of the rack and left her until the next day.

On the third day, Cameron tried to feed Colleen, but she couldn't keep her food down and threw up everything she ate. This only angered him, so he hung her by her wrists and whipped her more. When he finished, he attached her to the rack again.

Later that week, Colleen's roommates were getting worried when they heard she hadn't shown up at her friend's house. They called her family in Riverside, California, and the family began searching for her. They drove 900 miles north to Eugene, stopping at every town along the way to report Colleen missing. Sadly, they found no clues and returned to Riverside.

Cameron kept Colleen naked, chained to the rack, and wearing the head box for the entire first week. Over the next five months, he kept Colleen naked in the box in the basement. She was gagged, blind-folded, bound, and forced to wear the head box. Once every evening Cameron allowed her to urinate, defecate, eat, and drink, but always as he watched.

During these first several months, he allowed her out of the box only for his sadistic pleasures. He whipped her, choked her, shocked her, and burned her genitals with a heat lamp. He also held her head underwater in the bathtub to the edge of drowning. Colleen later recalled that Cameron Hooker hung and whipped her at least 90 times during these first six months – but he was just getting started.

In October 1977, Cameron built another box in which to hold his slave. It was a triangular shape that wedged neatly beneath the stairs, which he called "the workshop." Colleen spent the next six months chained and locked inside the workshop. She was only allowed out for his bondage pleasures and occasionally to do chores around the house.

Cameron built yet another device he called "the stretcher," which pulled Colleen's arms and legs taut and stretched. Unfortunately, over time, this device caused permanent damage to her back and shoulder.

Cameron Hooker's mental manipulation of Colleen really took effect when he told her of an underground organization of slave owners called "The Company." According to Hooker, The Company was a powerful organization that closely watched all her movements. Their members were everywhere. Any slaves caught attempting to escape were taken from their current masters and sold to other masters – masters that could be much crueler than he was being to her. She believed his story, but it was all just a work of fiction that he had read about in one of his bondage porn magazines.

Over the subsequent years, he expanded on The Company story, making her more and more frightened of them. When his wife, Janice, had knee surgery and came home with a bandage on her knee, Cameron explained to Colleen that Janice had once been a slave who had tried to escape. He said The Company had tortured her for trying to escape and permanently damaged her legs.

The truth was that Janice was never a slave; she was Cameron's wife. She had undoubtedly endured his sexual sadism, but not to the extreme that Colleen was currently experiencing.

Janice, however, didn't enjoy his perverted exploits. She wanted some semblance of a normal life and desperately wanted to have another baby. She also didn't want her husband to have sex with another woman. So, Janice and Cameron came to an agreement: she could have a baby, and he could have his slave. But there was one stipulation. He was not to have sex with his slave. He could whip and torture her, but sex was reserved for his wife exclusively.

Colleen's enslavement went through several stages, and in January 1978, a new stage began. It involved a contract. Cameron created a "Slave Contract" that he presented to Colleen. The contract was an official document stating that she was his slave and that he owned her soul. But, again, it was actually something he'd seen in a bondage magazine. Colleen initially refused to sign it, but Cameron explained that a representative of The Company was waiting for the signed contract; she reluctantly agreed.

Once Colleen had signed the contract, he changed her name to her slave name, "Kay." She was to address Hooker as "Sir" or "Master," and she was to call Janice "Ma'am." The contract also required her to bow, kneel, and ask permission before doing anything at all. In addition, a leather collar with a steel ring was placed around her neck to be worn at all times, so she would never forget she was a slave. He also pierced her labia, another symbol of her enslavement.

Although Cameron had agreed with Janice to not have sex with his slave, it was Janice that first suggested he have sex with her. She thought it might excite her if she watched him raping her. It didn't. It only sparked her jealousy. It was also the start of many more rapes to come.

Internally, Colleen retreated to the confines of her mind. She learned that she could do anything and be anywhere in her mind. It was the only way she could cope. Colleen cried every day but never let Cameron see her crying because she knew it would anger him.

In April 1978, the Hookers moved from their small house into a mobile home on an acre of land nearby. This began the third stage of Colleen's enslavement. Cameron built a new box for Colleen in the new mobile home that doubled as the pedestal for their waterbed. Colleen lived in a small box just beneath where they slept and had sex. He only allowed her a bedpan, some toilet paper, and a radio in her new box. She spent most of each day and night in confinement beneath the bed, to be let out only once for a few minutes each night.

In September 1978, Janice gave birth to their second child. The baby was born on the waterbed while Colleen was locked in the box below.

Janice got a night job the following year, while Cameron worked days. In Janice's absence, he let Colleen out of her box in the evenings to do chores and make dinner for her master.

By June 1980, Cameron knew that the fear of The Company was enough to keep Colleen in line – which meant that, when Janice got a daytime job, they allowed Colleen to babysit the two children by herself. This started yet another stage. Out of fear that The Company was always watching, she didn't run. She believed that, if she were caught, she would be tracked down, tortured, and possibly even killed. Cameron had also told her they would kill her family.

During this stage of her enslavement, Colleen was allowed to sleep in the back bathroom while chained to the toilet. The two children had no idea that Colleen even lived in the same house.

By February 1981, Cameron wanted Colleen back in the box he had built under the waterbed, but Janice said she would work from home to watch over Colleen instead. During this time, Colleen was allowed much more freedom. Still, The Company's threat loomed over her, so she stayed compliant and didn't attempt to escape.

Colleen was permitted to work for Janice's employer assembling electronics at home, but the paychecks were all handed over to Cameron. She was also required to help Cameron dig a large hole in the property's yard. The hole was lined with concrete blocks and took two years to build.

Cameron had big plans for the hole that he hadn't told Janice. It was to be "The Dungeon," and he would build a shed over it to house more slaves. He had established his power over Janice and now had plans to abduct four more slaves.

By 1980, three years had passed. Colleen knew Cameron had no intention of killing her, but she also knew that she would never get out of her horrible enslavement. This was now how her life would be – forever. Hoping Cameron may treat her better, Colleen told him she loved him and wrote him love letters:

> "I seem to be falling deeper and deeper in love with you with each passing day."

> "Sometimes, I feel that being your slave has made me more of a woman. But then there are other times when I feel it has made me less of a woman. You know how to make me feel good about myself, and I love you so much for it."

> "My love for you is growing with every changing day. You fill my life with happiness and love. And I pray that that happiness and love will never end."

Colleen begged Cameron several times to allow her to contact her family, just to let them know she was okay. Writing the love letters to him may have actually paid off. After almost four years of confinement, Cameron felt confident in his control over her. He knew she was terrified of The Company and would do what she was told, so he granted her a phone call – but made sure she knew that The Company was listening. Her family would be tortured or killed if she made the slightest mistake or said the wrong thing.

By this time, her family had completely lost hope of ever finding her alive. When she called, her youngest sister, Bonnie, answered the phone. Colleen gave no details but let her know that she was alive and well, then she said her goodbyes.

The family didn't contact the police. Instead, they were happy that she was alive but still left with many unanswered questions. They assumed she had become a member of a cult, which was common in California at that time.

Cameron Hooker enjoyed letting Colleen talk to her family and allowing her bits of freedom. It gave him reassurance that she wouldn't run; it proved that he had ultimate control over her. By February 1981, he told her that he would take her to visit her family the following month. He claimed he had to pay a $30,000 deposit to The Company to cover the extra costs of watching her and her family during the visit.

Before the trip, however, he asked Colleen to prove her obedience. He handed her a gun and told her to put it in her mouth, then pull the trigger. She did as she was told. Luckily, the gun wasn't loaded.

Just as he had promised, Hooker took Colleen to Riverside – but on the drive south, they stopped at "The Company Headquarters." Hooker told Colleen that The Company required her to pass a lie detector test before she could visit her family. She was extremely frightened to meet someone from The Company. Finally, they arrived at a building in Sacramento, and Cameron went inside, while Colleen sat in the car. When he returned, he claimed that he had talked them into waiving the test requirement, and they continued on their drive.

Colleen visited with her family, and Hooker posed as her boyfriend. He told the family that he had a computer seminar in San Diego and would be back later to pick her up.

Now that she was finally alone with her family, she wanted to let them know the whole truth, but she worried for her own safety and that of her family. She knew The Company was always watching. Colleen stayed overnight with her family, and Cameron picked her up the next day.

When Cameron and Colleen returned to Red Bluff, Janice wasn't home. So, he raped her and put her in the box beneath the waterbed.

Cameron often made Janice read the Bible to him. He chose particular passages for her to read that mentioned wives and slaves and how they were required to be submissive. Janice was devoutly religious and deeply feared hell; she believed that if she didn't obey her husband, she would be damned to the eternal torture of hell.

Near the end of 1983, Cameron put Colleen in the hole she had dug in the backyard. She was there day and night and was not to come out despite the heavy rains turning the hole into several inches of mud. She was there for a week, until Cameron suspected a boy from the neighborhood might have wandered into the backyard and seen her. He brought her back inside and put her back in the box under the bed.

Cameron had grown much more trusting of his power over Colleen and gradually allowed her increasingly more freedom. By January 1984, he let Colleen out of the box at night and sometimes slept in the back bedroom. He allowed her to run in the neighborhood for exercise and occasionally ride a bicycle. By May, she began working as a maid at a local hotel in Red Bluff, while Cameron kept all the money she earned. All the while, she knew that The Company was still watching every move she made. Janice had also been attending church regularly and Cameron sometimes allowed Colleen to go with her.

July 1984 marked yet another change. Cameron became much more demanding of both women. He decided he wanted to have sex with Janice while fondling Colleen and vice versa. He broke his agreement with Janice and told her he would have sex with both of them on alternating nights. Neither Janice nor Colleen liked the idea but felt they had to obey.

In August 1984, when Cameron told Janice of his plans to abduct four more slaves, it deeply upset her. She was already agitated that he was having sex with Colleen and didn't like the idea of sharing him even more.

On August 9, Janice dropped Colleen off at work, checked into a hotel, and then went to church to speak with her pastor. She opened up completely to him and told the pastor the horrid story; the pastor advised that she and Colleen run away from her husband. Janice then picked up Colleen and returned to the hotel, where she told her for the first time that there was no such thing as The Company. It was all a lie.

Colleen was distraught that she had believed the threat so whole-heartedly.

The following day, Janice and Colleen took the two children to Janice's parents' house, where Colleen called her family. Her father arranged to wire money for bus fare home. Before she left, Colleen called Cameron and told him she knew there was no such thing as The Company and that he no longer had power over her. Cameron cried on the phone.

Janice tried to stay away, but after only a week, moved back in with Cameron. She took him to church with her and encouraged him to attend counseling. Together, they destroyed many of the bondage items over the next month, but Janice hid some things. For several weeks, Janice suffered debilitating anxiety attacks and was unable to eat or sleep. On September 28, she left her husband again and moved back in with her parents.

In the months after Colleen left, she communicated with Janice and Cameron on the telephone and through letters. Janice begged her not to go to the police, saying she was trying to get help for Cameron. Colleen initially agreed, but her family pressured her to contact the authorities. Nevertheless, Colleen was grateful just to be alive and have her freedom back.

Janice was still terrified of Cameron and worried that he would hurt her or the children. Eventually, at the suggestion of her pastor, Janice contacted the police.

When a woman comes into a police station and claims that she and her husband had kidnapped a young woman, kept her as a slave, and tortured her for seven years, it's a little hard to believe. Initially, detectives didn't know what to think and doubted her story – but after traveling to Riverside to speak to Colleen, they knew her story was true. Police arrested Cameron Hooker for kidnapping with the use of a deadly weapon, three counts of imprisonment, seven counts of forcible rape, two counts of abduction for illicit relations, and single counts of forcible sodomy, forcible oral copulation, and penetration with a foreign object. He brazenly pled not guilty to all charges.

At trial, the prosecution produced over 100 pieces of evidence including the head box, photos that Cameron had taken of Colleen on the rack and in bondage, and a copy of the slavery contract. They rebuilt the entire waterbed pedestal and the stretcher inside the court-room for the jury to see. The prosecution even invited jury members to lie inside the box to see what it was like – and some accepted.

Hooker admitted that he kidnapped Colleen but claimed that, in the later years, she was free to go anytime she liked and had plenty of opportunities to leave. The defense also presented the love letters that Colleen had written to Hooker and a photo of Colleen at her family's house, smiling as she wrapped her arms around Cameron. He also claimed all of their sex was consensual.

Both the prosecution and the defense brought in psychologists. The prosecution's psychologist believed Colleen was coerced by the fear of The Company and was unable to leave. The defense psychologist believed the exact opposite.

The jury found Hooker guilty of ten felony counts – all but one charge. The last charge of rape resulted in a hung jury.

Prosecutors never brought charges for the murder of Marie Spannhake against Hooker due to lack of evidence.

The judge sentenced Cameron Hooker to 95 years in prison and a $50,000 fine. In return for her testimony against Cameron, Janice Hooker wasn't charged and now lives in California under a different name.

Colleen Stan has appeared on several television shows, and a Lifetime movie was made of her story. Watching her on television years later, she seems to have endured the ordeal amazingly well.

CHAPTER 9
THE GREEN CHAIN KILLER

London is known as the greenest city in Europe, with over 3,000 parks covering more than 35,000 acres. The Green Chain Walk was a series of trails that spanned over fifty miles and connected many of the parks on London's south side. Locals used the areas to exercise, walk dogs, and sunbathe, and many young mothers visited with their children.

During the late eighties and early nineties, a string of rapes and murders along the Green Chain terrified London residents. Sadly, the murders were allowed to continue due to blind reliance on a single criminal profile and gross mishandling of police work on several different levels.

In August 1989, a young mother in Southeast London was in her home near Plumstead Common park. It was a warm summer morning, and she had left her back door open to let the air in while she got her kids ready for school. Suddenly, she saw a man standing in her doorway with a knife. The woman was brutally raped in front of her children but escaped with her life. Her children were unharmed.

Three months later, Pauline Lasham called the police and told them that her son, Robert Napper, had confessed to her that he had raped a woman in Plumstead Common, near their home. Police searched their records, however, and found no rapes in the park during that time. The rape in August happened in the woman's home - not on Plumstead Common - so no connection was made, and nothing further was done.

Robert Napper was twenty-three years old, suffered from Asperger's syndrome, and was later diagnosed with paranoid schizophrenia. As a child, he frequently watched his father beat his mother until their divorce, when he was nine years old. After the divorce, he and his siblings were placed in foster care, and Robert received psychiatric treatment for the next six years.

On a camping trip at age twelve, Robert Napper was sexually abused by a family friend. The trauma led to a change in Robert and ignited his journey into violence. In his early teens, he shot his brother in the face with an air gun and secretly watched his sister undressing. In school, Robert was a social outcast to an extreme. In a game of English football, if he headed the ball then the game stopped. None of the other children wanted to play after the ball had touched his head. His first brush with the police was when he was nineteen and caught carrying a loaded handgun in public. His only punishment was a fine of £10.

In March 1992, there were two more rapes along the Green Chain in Southeast London. A third rape, this time of a young mother walking her daughter in a stroller, occurred just months later in the same area.

From witness reports, police developed a composite sketch of the suspect that looked similar to Robert Napper. Several of his neighbors had reported him as a possible suspect in the Green Chain rapes, and police brought him in for questioning.

During questioning, detectives asked Napper to submit his DNA, but twice he didn't show up for his appointment. Police never followed up on his missed appointments, and he was later dismissed as a suspect strictly based on his height. Robert Napper was six foot four; the descriptions of the rapist were of someone shorter, so they promptly crossed him off their list of suspects.

Fifteen miles away in Southwest London was another park called Wimbledon Common. On the morning of July 15, 1992, a young mother named Rachel Nickell was walking with her two-year-old son, Alex, through a wooded area of the park. In broad daylight, with nearly 500 people in the park, Rachel was attacked and raped at knife-point. The attacker stabbed her forty-nine times, slashing her throat to near decapitation. Her son, just shy of his third birthday, watched in horror.

Minutes later, an older man found the little boy trying to wake his mother, but Rachel Nickell was already beyond help. He alerted the police, who immediately closed off the park and questioned everyone they could find.

Colin Stagg was a thirty-year-old man that lived near Wimbledon Common and frequently walked his dog through the park. But that Wednesday morning, police stopped Colin as he entered the park. They informed him that there had been an incident, and they weren't letting people into the park. Colin mentioned that he had already been in the park earlier that morning, so officers took his name and address, and he returned home.

The crime scene was horribly bloody, but the police were left with almost no evidence. There was just a tiny speck on her body that may have contained DNA, but in 1992, DNA evidence was still relatively new. Unfortunately, they weren't able to get any clues from it. A month after the killing, police had interviewed over 100 people but were still no closer to an answer of who killed Rachel Nickell, other than a few sketches of someone that people in the park said looked suspicious.

Police recruited a criminal psychologist named Paul Britton to create a psychological profile of what traits the killer could have. Britton was known for working on other high-profile cases and had already been working on the Green Chain rapes. However, neither Britton nor the police saw any link between the Rachel Nickell murder and the Green Chain rapes on the other side of London.

Paul Britton developed a profile of the killer. He believed the killer was twenty to thirty years old, a loner with isolated hobbies, most likely lived alone near Wimbledon Common, may have an obsession with knives, may have knowledge or interest in the occult, saw women as sexual objects, and was sexually sadistic.

Rachel Nickell was a beautiful, blonde model. Because she was murdered with her young son watching, the media put enormous pressure on the police to find the killer. The profile presented by Britton was released to television stations, and the police received several calls naming one man: Colin Stagg.

When police arrived at Colin's home, he openly welcomed them in. He had no prior arrests, but police believed he fit their psychological profile. He lived alone and near the park, was a bit of a loner, was thirty years old, and they found a book about the occult on his bookshelf.

Colin Stagg was arrested and brought in for further interviews. He had been arrested before for sunbathing nude in the same park, but the area had been a popular spot among nude sunbathers. However, detectives believe he was responsible for the murder of Rachel Nickell. As they had no evidence and only suspicion, they had to release him after three days.

When the news of Colin's arrest reached the media, the police received a call from a woman named Julie Pines. Julie had met Colin through a dating advertisement, and the two exchanged letters. As their letters grew into a sexual nature, Colin told her of his fantasy to have sex in the open air. She still had the letter and presented it to the police. Again, this reaffirmed to the police that Colin was the killer.

Police then went out on a limb and, under Paul Britton's supervision, developed an elaborate plan they code-named "Operation Edzell." Over the next twenty-eight months, detectives enlisted an undercover female police officer named Lizzy James. Lizzy posed as a friend of Julie Pines and sent Colin letters saying she was much more open-minded than her friend Julie.

Colin had never been with a woman at the time and was quite inno-cent in his replies to Lizzy. She wrote raunchy letters laced with sexual innuendo, but his replies were naïve, romantic letters, saying how he would like to sip parsnip wine with her on a veranda. Detectives needed more, so they had Lizzy push him.

She wrote to him,

> "I'm sure your fantasies hold no bounds, and you are as broad-minded and uninhibited as I am."

Colin replied with near-verbatim responses, also saying that his fantasies held no bounds.

Eventually, she escalated the conversation, telling him of relationships she had with other men,

> "The things that happened when I was with this man are not what normal people would like. And even though these things are bad, and I feel guilty, I can never forget how exhilarating they make me feel. I need to feel defenseless and humiliated."

Colin, just wanting to be with a woman for the first time, replied with what he believed she wanted to hear.

Lizzy continued to make the letters more sexual and increasingly violent. Eventually, detectives decided to have Lizzy meet Colin in person while undercover officers watched nearby. They met in a coffee shop where Lizzy told him of her dark secret. She told Colin that her prior boyfriend was into black magic and that the two of them had once murdered a pregnant woman as a human sacrifice. Colin thought she was a bit crazy but played along, listening to her stories and saying nothing incriminating.

By the third meeting, she pushed him to open up. He admitted to her that he had been arrested for the Rachel Nickell murder but told her he didn't do it. That excited her; she said she would have sex with the man that *had* committed that murder. But that was over the limit for Colin, and he told her, "No, I'm sorry, it's not me."

Throughout all the contact with Lizzy, Colin never suggested that he had anything to do with the murder of Rachel Nickell, but that didn't deter the police. They were convinced that the wording of the letters matched the psychological profile developed by Paul Britton. On August 17, 1993, Colin Stagg was arrested again on suspicion of murdering Rachel Nickell. After spending two years with Operation Edzell and £3 million in the process, police wholeheartedly believed they had their man.

Meanwhile, rapes continued along the Green Chain, but detectives and prosecutors still refused to believe the murder of Rachel Nickell and these rapes were linked.

Three months after the arrest, with Colin still sitting in jail awaiting trial, another murder occurred in Plumstead, Southeast London.

Samantha Bissett and her four-year-old daughter, Jazmine Bissett, were brutally murdered in their home. Samantha was butchered with a knife, and parts of her body were cut off and taken as a trophy. Her daughter was raped and smothered to death.

A third investigation team was assigned to this case, separate from the Green Chain investigation team. Again, Paul Britton was brought in as a criminal profiler, but he never once said that he believed any of the crimes were linked.

The Rachel Nickell murder squad was invited to go over the Plumstead murder evidence, but they denied the offer. They were convinced they already had their man behind bars, and there was no need to look any further.

At the Bissett crime scene, investigators found Robert Napper's finger-prints on the outside balcony and a bloody shoe print in the kitchen that matched shoes found at Napper's home.

They had acquired Robert Napper's fingerprints after he was arrested in October 1992 for impersonating a police officer and possessing a firearm. During that arrest, police found a map book in his flat. He had pages meticulously marked and annotated with comments about violent acts and abuse towards women. The marks on the map pointed to several locations along the Green Chain, but investigators still made no links to the Green Chain rapes.

Robert Napper's fingerprints were also found on a knife buried in Wimbledon Common just 100 yards from where Rachel was murdered, but the Rachel Nickell team ignored this evidence.

Colin Stagg, meanwhile, was still sitting in jail awaiting trial. After fourteen months in jail, a judge took one look at how the police had coaxed Stagg into his statements and threw out the case against him. The judge was disgusted with their coercive tactics, calling their under-cover work a "Honey Trap." Although Colin Stagg was released from jail and all charges against him dropped, the court of public opinion had already convicted him. His life would never be the same.

Colin was free in the eyes of the law but not in the eyes of the media and the public, who pegged him as someone who got away with murder rather than someone who was found not guilty. He was met by angry mobs outside the courthouse chanting, "Hang him!" and "Guilty!"

Even Rachel Nickell's father believed they had let a guilty man go. He made a statement to the media,

 "I understand that the police will now keep the files on my daughter's murder open, but they are not looking for

anyone else. The law has been upheld, but where is the justice?"

Investigators in the Rachel Nickell murder had wasted over three years and £3 million chasing an innocent man, but they still refused to admit they were wrong.

In November 1995, Robert Napper pleaded guilty to manslaughter in the Bissett case and admitted guilt in only one rape and two attempted rapes. He admitted nothing regarding the Rachel Nickell murder or the many other rapes along the Green Chain.

Ultimately, Robert Napper claimed "diminished responsibility" and was sentenced to indefinite detention at Broadmoor, a high security hospital for the criminally insane.

For the next seven years, police and Rachel Nickell's family still believed that Colin Stagg had gotten away with murder. In 2002, however, they assigned a case review team to go through the cold case in much more detail. A fresh set of eyes. All witness statements, known offenders, and possible suspects were looked into, including Robert Napper. By that time, there had been considerable advances in DNA research. When they re-examined Rachel's jogging pants, they found a small amount of Robert Napper's DNA. They also found a tiny fleck of red paint in her son's hair that forensically matched a toolbox that Robert Napper owned. This pinned the murder on Robert Napper, who was already serving indefinite detention.

This also finally eliminated Colin Stagg as a suspect, who filed a formal complaint against Paul Britton. Britton was ultimately cleared of seven counts of misconduct, but Colin Stagg was awarded £706,000 for being the victim of a miscarriage of justice. Colin Stagg received a formal public apology from the police, but Paul Britton refused to apologize. Colin says that to this day, some people still think he murdered Rachel Nickell.

Lizzy James was awarded £125,000, claiming that her undercover work on this case ruined her career.

Ultimately, this case led to considerable changes in how investigations are handled in the United Kingdom.

In total, Robert Napper is believed to have been responsible for 106 attacks across London throughout the late eighties and early nineties.

CHAPTER 10
THE MURDER OF NICOLE LEGER

Nicole Leger had some difficulties earlier in life. At seventeen, she was a stunning beauty but unmarried and pregnant. To make ends meet after her son was born, she danced in a few strip clubs around the Dallas area. By the time she was in her thirties, however, things were looking up. Her son was in high school and she was working as an assistant for a stockbroker. She enrolled in nursing school and had just met a wonderful man who treated her like an angel. That man was Mike Adams.

Mike was sixteen years older than Nicole and made his living as a repo man, repossessing cars when people couldn't make their payments. His business did quite well and he owned a lovely new home in the affluent Dallas suburb of Frisco, Texas. When Mike and Nicole first started dating, he was a perfect gentleman who brought her flowers and wrote her love notes.

It wasn't long before Mike asked Nicole and her son, Trey, to move in with him. The bliss, however, didn't last long, and the relationship fell apart quickly.

Mike was obsessive with his personal belongings and his home. He took pride in meticulously maintaining his luxurious house. Items in the closets, cupboards, and refrigerator were all perfectly organized to the point that labels on cans had to be facing the same direction, as if they were on a supermarket display. Even the pool table was strictly a showpiece, never to be used. It was the same with the fancy circular white couch. Worried that it might get dirty, Mike forbade anyone from sitting on it. Order and uniformity were important to Mike; even his extensive handgun collection was sorted by caliber size.

One evening Mike made spaghetti for Nicole, knowing it was her favorite dish. But when Trey spilled a bit of sauce on the tile floor, Mike blew a gasket. A simple spill that was easily cleaned up created a yelling spree that lasted for over a week.

Less than two months after Nicole and her son moved in, they moved out. The yelling was just more than Nicole could handle.

Mike wasn't used to being left by a woman, so he turned the charm back on and asked Nicole if he could treat her to dinner at a nice restaurant. During their meal, he fell over himself apologizing and swore he would never yell at her again. Mike was back to a perfect gentleman.

After dinner and a delightful evening, he took Nicole back to his house and asked her to marry him. Nicole couldn't resist the big diamond ring and, unfortunately, couldn't see through his fake charm. She accepted his proposal, and they decided that she would move back in.

Of course, the arguments started again almost immediately – and they escalated. The yelling got so heated that Mike forcefully ripped the ring from Nicole's finger during an argument, requiring a trip to the hospital for a fractured finger.

Nicole and her son moved out again, got a new apartment across town, and tried to put the past behind them. Unfortunately, life would not return to normal for Nicole.

She came home from work one evening to find the front door wide open and their dog missing. A few days later, they learned a car had hit the dog, and it had died. Another day, Nicole came home to find someone had broken into their home and poured bleach all over her clothes. Finally, her car mysteriously caught fire while parked outside their apartment. Nicole suspected Mike was behind all of these anomalies, but she had no way to prove it.

She couldn't afford a new car on her own, so Mike used the opportunity to come to the rescue and offer to cosign on a loan for a new car. She believed she had no choice and accepted his offer.

In March 2013, Nicole took the car title to Mike's house. She wanted him to sign off on the title so the car would be all hers and she would finally be done with him. She wanted Mike out of her life and also needed to pick up some of the belongings she had left there.

Mike again turned on the charm and offered to make spaghetti for her, knowing she couldn't resist a nice plate of pasta. He claimed he was trying to make peace, but peace was the last thing on his mind.

It didn't take long for the knockout drug to take effect. Mike had spiked the spaghetti sauce, incapacitating her for a few hours.

The drug took some time for full effect, and Nicole remembered being walked into the bedroom and Mike taking her clothes off.

"I'm saying no, but I can't do anything. I can't move my arms or legs," Nicole later told the police.

Mike bent Nicole over and inserted a large sex toy into her. They had never used sex toys when they were a couple. Mike then started taking pictures of her with the dildo inside her. Then she passed out completely.

When Nicole woke up, she was hog-tied in the bedroom, still naked. Her hands were tied behind her back, and her ankles were tied together. She was unable to scream because her mouth was gagged with duct tape.

She managed to get herself untied and ran naked from the house to the nearest neighbor's house, screaming and banging on the door. But Mike heard her screams before the neighbors did, grabbed her, and dragged her back into his garage.

Mike put down a large plastic tarp on the floor in the garage, hand-cuffed her, and bound her ankles with zip ties. His anger consumed him. He tried ripping her hair out, but he couldn't get it to come out – so he cut her hair using a knife.

After being held captive for a full twenty-four hours, Nicole realized the only way she would get out of this alive was to reason with him. She promised she wouldn't press charges if he let her go and vowed they would stay together and go to couple's counseling. It took time, but Mike finally agreed and released her.

Nicole immediately went to the hospital and reported the assault to the police. She pleaded with them to lock him up. They let her know that she would have to testify against him. "He's going to end up killing me," she told the investigators.

Police searched Mike's house and car. He had planned on getting rid of the evidence, but he wasn't quick enough. They found what they were looking for in the trunk of the car —the sex toy, the zip ties, and duct tape with her hair still attached. They even found the near-empty jar of spiked spaghetti sauce.

Detective Scott Greer was in charge of her case. Police arrested Mike on charges of aggravated sexual assault and unlawful restraint, but he quickly made bail and was a free man awaiting trial. Because of his release, Nicole was granted an emergency protective order against him. Mike was to have no contact with her at all.

Nicole and her son moved twenty miles away to Melissa, Texas, in another county. She used a friend's name to rent a home and set up her utilities in hopes it would keep Mike from finding her.

Her hopes were vanquished when Mike sent flowers to her home. She didn't understand how, but he had found her. Nicole filed another police complaint, as this clearly violated her protective order. She told the police,

 "I feel like he will show up at my door or car at any time."

Her complaint to the police only angered Mike more. One day, she came home from work to find a plastic tarp and handcuffs on her front porch. This was obviously a not-so-subtle threat from Mike. He didn't want her to testify against him.

Nicole and her son were terrified. In August 2013, they visited her father in Florida to get away for a while. He pleaded with her to stay with him there and told her there was nothing worth returning to Texas for, but Nicole didn't listen. That was the last time her father saw her.

On September 9, 2013, Nicole's seventeen-year-old son returned home from school to find his mother dead. Nicole's body lay face-down and naked on her bed with two gunshot wounds to her face.

Working for an auto repossession company, Mike had used a GPS tracking device that he attached to her car to track her every move.

Police promptly arrested Mike Adams and charged him with capital murder, a term used only in seven states. It meant the crime was eligible for the death penalty.

Crime scene investigators recovered two used condoms at the scene. Both had DNA that didn't match Mike or anyone in police databases, but the outside of one condom matched Mike's DNA. Clearly, he had tried to plant evidence.

Police also saw on his work computers that he had been tracking her using the GPS and had searched for routes to her home in Melissa, Texas.

The most damning evidence, however, was a storage locker in his ex-wife's name. There they found a massive arsenal of guns, one of which ballistically proved to be the gun that fired the two slugs into Nicole's face.

However, it was revealed during the trial that Nicole and Detective Greer, the officer with whom she filed the first complaint, had exchanged sexual texts. A search of Greer's cell phone showed Nicole had been sending the detective nude photos of herself.

Greer testified in court that their involvement was limited to only photos and no physical involvement, but this information helped Mike's defense. His attorneys claimed that Greer's involvement compromised the case against Mike with Nicole.

Still, none of that affected the trial's outcome and the jury returned a guilty verdict. Mike Adams was convicted of capital murder. In Texas, capital murder carries an automatic sentence of life in prison without the possibility of parole.

CHAPTER 11
THE GLAMOUR GIRL SLAYER

From an early age, Harvey Glatman had a strange fascination with rope. At the tender age of three, Harvey's mother caught him with a string tied around his penis. He had placed the opposite end of the string in a drawer, closed the drawer, and leaned back.

As a toddler, Harvey showed more strange behavior. He laughed or cried for no apparent reason and had no interest in playing games or with his toys. Then, at age four, his mother caught him with a rope tied around his neck; the free end was thrown over a pipe. He was pulling on the rope with one hand and pulling on his penis with the other. Where a boy of only four in the 1930s gets these ideas, we will never know.

In 1937, at age ten, his family moved from The Bronx, NY, to Denver, Colorado. The following year, Harvey's parents noticed he had red rope burns around his neck. Harvey had been masturbating while hanging himself with a rope to the point of blackout. Harvey's father ridiculed him for his odd behavior, telling him masturbating would give him acne and make him "queer."

By the time he entered junior high school, Harvey did indeed have acne, a set of very large ears, and buck teeth. The kids at school bullied him for his looks and his extreme fear of girls. He turned bright red if a girl even spoke to him. As a result, schoolmates nicknamed him "weasel" and "chipmunk."

His fascination with ropes, bondage, and autoerotic asphyxiation continued. Harvey's parents took him to a psychiatrist, where he was prescribed medication.

By the time he reached high school, he had begun breaking into women's homes. He only wanted to steal an item, usually a piece of clothing, but anything would do. He just wanted a trophy of some sort to prove that he had power over the women. However, he seemed more fascinated with the thrill of the act rather than the actual trophy.

Eventually, just breaking in wasn't enough. At twelve, he followed a woman home to find out where she lived. Later, he broke into her home, tied her with rope, and gagged her. He then fondled her breasts through her clothes.

Sometimes, he broke into women's houses, tied them up, sat them on the couch, and fondled and cuddled them while he forced them to watch sitcoms with him. He thrived on their fear.

He continued to break into houses to steal items and acquired a .38 revolver at seventeen. He then used the gun to stop random women on the street and threaten them, taking their money and forcing them to remove their clothes. Occasionally, he'd snatch a woman's purse, run a few steps, and then turn around and throw the bag back at her. This, again, was to show his power over them.

In May 1945, Harvey abducted Noreen Laurel, drove her out of town, and groped her breasts but didn't rape her. Instead, he drove her back home, where she immediately contacted the police. Noreen later identified Harvey from police photos, and he was arrested only for attempted burglary.

Harvey's mother paid $2,000 to bail him out of jail, but he had molested another woman within a month. This time, he was arrested, convicted, and sent to the Colorado State Prison. Although he was still in high school and in the top percentage of his class, Harvey didn't graduate because he was in jail. After serving only eight months, Harvey Glatman was released for good behavior.

Just three weeks after leaving the Colorado State Prison, Glatman mugged a young couple by pulling a cap gun on them. The weapon was just a toy, but the couple had no idea. He tied the man with a rope and pawed at the woman's breasts. When the man tried to escape, Glatman stabbed him in the shoulder and ran.

Just days later, Glatman fled back east to Albany, New York, and continued his mayhem. He mugged and groped several young, unsuspecting women and was again arrested.

By the time he was twenty-one, Harvey Glatman was serving a ten-year sentence in Sing Sing Correctional Facility, where psychologists diagnosed him with a psychopathic personality and a high IQ.

Again, Glatman was a model prisoner and was released early after serving only three years. Police sent him back to Denver to finish his parole while living with his mother.

Harvey Glatman's parole ended in September 1956, and he was no longer required to live in Denver. He quickly packed up and moved to Los Angeles, California. When he arrived in LA, he worked as a television repairman – a trade he had learned while in prison.

Ever since his high school years, Harvey had held a fascination with photography. Once he was set up in the Los Angeles area, he realized that plenty of beautiful women desperately wanted to be movie stars and models. However, once they realized how hard it was to get into the movies, they quickly turned to posing as pin-up girls. Glatman saw an opportunity and placed an ad in a newspaper looking for models. Before long, beautiful young women were calling him and begging for work.

On August 1, 1957, a nineteen-year-old model named Judy Dull answered his ad. Judy was going through a bitter divorce and was trying to get custody of her child. She was an aspiring actress but was desperate for money to pay for a lawyer and so agreed to meet Glatman for a photo shoot.

Harvey's ad claimed he needed photos for a detective magazine, known in the 1950s as "pulp fiction" magazines. When Judy arrived wearing a tight skirt and sweater, as he requested, Glatman bound her with ropes and gagged her mouth. She believed it was all part of the photo shoot. He took photos of her and told her to look frightened, just as she would on the cover of a detective magazine. Then he escalated his sadistic game. Glatman pulled a gun on her to get photos of her *truly* looking frightened. He then untied her legs, left her hands bound, and raped her. At thirty years old, it was the first time Harvey Glatman had ever had intercourse. All the while, he documented the event with photos.

After he finished, he told Judy he would release her. He walked her back to his car but had no intention of driving her home. Instead, he drove east on Interstate 10 toward Indio, California, and into the desert. He then threw her on her stomach with her hands and feet still tied. He tied another rope to the binding on her feet, looped it around her neck, put his knee in the small of her back, and pulled. He strangled Judy Dull to death in the middle of the California desert. Glatman then posed her for a few post-mortem photos and buried her body in a shallow grave.

When Judy's roommate couldn't get in touch with her, she tried to call the phone number she had for the photographer, but it had been disconnected. Her roommate had never met the photographer, so the police had nothing to go on and assumed Judy had just left town.

Seven months later, using the alias George Williams, Glatman met a twenty-four-year-old girl through the Patty Sullivan Lonely Hearts Club. On their first date, he picked up Shirley Ann Bridgeford at her home and met several of her relatives. The two planned an evening of dinner and dancing, but the dancing never happened. After dinner, Glatman drove to the Vallecito Mountains and raped her. He then put flashbulbs on his camera to take photos of his victim on the mountainside at night. After the sun rose, he strangled her, posed her, and took photos of her lifeless body.

Glatman's next victim was a twenty-four-year-old model he had again hired for pin-up photos. Ruth Mercado showed up at his apartment only to be tied up and raped. Then, like with Shirley Ann Bridgeford, Glatman took her to the Vallecito Mountains, raped her again, and strangled her to death. Again, he took photos throughout the entire ordeal.

In October 1958, Glatman got the idea of using a legitimate modeling agency. He realized he could get more beautiful top models that way, so he contacted the Diane Studio who assigned him one of their newest models, Lorraine Vigil.

Lorraine had a bad feeling about Glatman from the very beginning. He showed up at 8 p.m. and informed her they were changing the photo shoot location. As they were driving, Lorraine argued with him, but Glatman had had enough of her whining. He pulled the car over to the side of the road and pointed a gun at her. Lorraine, however, wasn't about to let this man have his way with her. She quickly grabbed the gun's barrel and tried to twist it away from him. The gun accidentally fired and grazed her leg, but that didn't stop her. The two continued fighting over the gun and ended up outside the car, on the side of the road. Glatman was a small man, and eventually, Lorraine overpowered him. She yanked the gun from his hands and pistol-whipped him. In an incredible stroke of luck, a police officer saw the scuffle, pulled his car to the side of the road, and arrested Glatman.

During Glatman's interrogation, he confessed to the murders of Judy Dull, Shirley Ann Bridgeford, and Ruth Mercado. After his confession, Glatman led police to the desert to recover the bodies of Ruth Mercado and Shirley Ann Bridgeford.

During the interrogation, Glatman assumed that police had already found a toolbox he had hidden at his house.

 "You know I killed 'em; there's no way you could've known unless you found the toolbox."

"The toolbox?" The detective asked.

"The one in my house with the pictures… the dead girls… that's where I hid them… the pictures… in my toolbox… You know what I mean? You're just playing with me now."

But until that point, the police hadn't known about the toolbox. When they later found the toolbox in his apartment, it was filled with hundreds of photos he had taken and revealed the methodology of his murders. He had a sequence in which he liked to photograph the girls.

He first photographed them looking very innocent, with an excited look on their face, enjoying the photo shoot. In the second series, their faces had a look of horror. They knew they would soon be sexually abused and most likely killed. The final photos were taken after he had strangled the life out of the girls.

Glatman waived his right to a jury trial. Terrified of spending the rest of his life in jail, Glatman wanted the quickest possible route to end his life. He requested the death penalty several times and asked to remove the automatic appeal given to all death penalty cases.

The trial only lasted three days. The prosecution played recordings of Glatman's four-hour interrogation, where he described the murders with great detail and very little emotion. Harvey Glatman was found guilty of two counts of first-degree murder. When the judge handed down the death sentence, Glatman said,

 "It's better this way… I knew this is the way it would be."

Glatman spent the next nine months at San Quentin State Prison awaiting his execution. Coincidentally, the same prison would later hold Charles Manson and Richard Ramirez. Finally, on September 18, 1959, at the age of thirty-one, Glatman went to the gas chamber. The sodium cyanide took twelve minutes to kill him.

In 1966, parts of Glatman's story were used in a movie called Dragnet 1966. They later made the movie into a weekly prime-time TV show. The movie used actual quotes by Glatman:

 "The reason I killed those girls was 'cause they asked me to. They did… all of them… They said they'd rather be dead than be with me."

It is believed that Glatman may have killed other women during his time in Colorado, before he killed Judy Dull. The body of a woman referred to as "Boulder Jane Doe" was discovered in Boulder, Colorado, in 1954, during the same time that Harvey Glatman lived there. She died after being hit by a car. Glatman drove a 1951 Dodge Coronet, and the police believed the damage to her body was consistent with that model of car. Police, however, could never prove it. Fifty-five years later, in 2009, her identity was finally revealed as eighteen-year-old Dorothy Gay Howard from Phoenix, Arizona.

CHAPTER 12
A WALKING SHADOW

Life in Hawaii in 1929 was much different than today, especially for poor Japanese families. There was a lot of racial tension in Hawaii, mostly between wealthy white people and poor Japanese people. The events in November 1929 would escalate those tensions exponentially.

Myles Fukunaga was the nineteen-year-old eldest son of a Japanese family with seven kids. By all accounts, Myles was a quiet, responsible Japanese boy who stayed out of trouble and worked hard to support his family. However, as the oldest of the large family, much responsibility fell upon Myles.

Myles' father worked long hours, but it wasn't enough for the large family to survive. As a result, Myles had to drop out of high school to work to support the family. He worked eighty-hour weeks at Queen's Hospital, but it still wasn't enough.

The family was several months behind on their rent, and the stress was building in Myles. Twice, he thought he would be better off dead and attempted suicide. He even failed at that task, which added to his humiliation and embarrassment. Myles also suffered from a degenerative dissociative disorder. He had mental issues that were handled differently in those days: they were brushed under the rug.

One morning, there was a knock on the family's front door. When his mother answered the door, Myles could hear her arguing with a representative from the Hawaiian Trust Company. They were there again to collect the back rent, but the family didn't have it. The rent was $35 per month, and when they missed several months' payments, the fees piled on and made the bill unbearable. This fueled the anger inside Myles.

In recent years, Myles had been following two crimes that were in the news. The first was that of Nathan Leopold and Richard Loeb. The two teenage boys had kidnapped and killed a young boy, using a chisel to beat him over the head. They had then sent a ransom letter to his wealthy father. Another kidnapping Myles followed was perpetrated by William Hickman. Hickman had kidnapped a young girl by showing up at her school and posed as an employee of the girl's father. He told the teachers that the girl's father was in a terrible accident; she needed to come with him. Hickman then demanded a ransom from the girl's father and ultimately killed her. Myles thought he could combine these two examples to commit the perfect crime.

Myles called the Punahao School and asked to speak to the registrar. He told the registrar he was calling from Queen's Hospital. He claimed that Gille Jamieson's mother had been in a terrible car accident. They sent a car immediately to pick up the boy.

Using a uniform from the hospital where he worked, Myles posed as a hospital orderly and hired a taxicab to take him to the school of Gille Jamieson, the ten-year-old son of Frederick Jamieson. Frederick Jamieson was Vice President of The Hawaiian Trust Company.

Gille's teacher and the school's principal later told police there was nothing unusual about the young Japanese man who picked up Gilles. Their only description was that he was Japanese, had slicked-back hair, and wore black glasses.

Frederick Jamieson soon received a ransom note from Myles, peppered with strange Shakespeare quotes from Macbeth.

"Life's but a walking shadow, a poor player, that struts and frets his hour upon the stage and then is heard no more."

It seemed that Myles was dramatically referencing his desperation and lack of will to live. The ransom note demanded $10,000 for the safe release of his son.

But Myles had no intention of releasing the young boy. Instead, before the Jamieson family had a chance to respond to the ransom, Myles took Gilles behind the Seaside Hotel – where the International Marketplace now stands on Kalakaua Avenue, just opposite the Royal Hawaiian Hotel – to a grouping of kiawe trees. There, he took a hardened steel chisel, similar to what he had read that Leopold and Loeb used, and beat the boy over the head. He then strangled him to death.

When the media heard about the missing boy, the entire island of Oahu was on alert. Racial tensions flared because the young boy was white, and the kidnapper was said to be Japanese. Japanese businesses had to close because they were getting threats from white people.

Everyone was looking for the boy. The Oahu Schools let out early, and twenty thousand students joined in the search for Gilles across the island. The Jamiesons had a chauffeur they had fired some weeks prior, and he became the first suspect. Harry Kaisan was arrested, brought in for questioning, and put under the influence of a "truth serum." In those days, people believed Hyoscine Hydrobromide would force people to tell the truth. Amazingly, it's still used in some parts of the world today. Kaisan was ultimately found innocent and released.

Frederick Jamieson received a phone call from the kidnapper. The man said to meet him at a band concert on Thomas Square and to bring $4,000, at which point he would give up the boy. No cops. Jamieson did as he was told and didn't tell the police. Myles showed up wearing a black mask, took the money from Jamieson, and disappeared into the crowd without saying a word about the boy.

Jamieson had paid the $4,000 in $5 bills, and as a banker, he had noted the serial numbers. Police alerted local businesses to watch for the bills, and it wasn't long before Myles was caught trying to buy a train ticket with the money. When apprehended, Myles quickly confessed.

About the same time that Myles was arrested, the body of Gilles Jamieson was found in Waikiki. Myles had covered his body with newspapers and a piece of cardboard. On the cardboard, Myles wrote:

> "If you want to die, you have the right to kill others so that you, in turn, will be killed. The devil it is for you to decide."

The arrest of Myles Fukunaga ignited outrage throughout the island. Twenty thousand people gathered outside the jail after his arrest. Police called the fire department to deal with the massive mob and sprayed seven streams of water at the crowds to try and disperse them. The angry mob demanded a swift and powerful punishment.

Swift it was. Police couldn't handle the pressure from the public and wanted the whole ordeal over with as quickly as possible; it seemed that Myles wanted the same. As a result, Myles Fukunaga was arrested, tried, convicted, and sentenced to hang in just three weeks.

Fukunaga was examined quickly by three psychiatrists appointed by the police for only ninety minutes. The examinations typically took several days at that time, but the police felt the pressure and needed to rush to a judgment. Psychiatrists determined that he was competent and ready to stand trial. Myles Fukunaga freely admitted his guilt and asked specifically to be hanged. The prosecution was more than happy to oblige.

In a gross violation of his rights, his two court-appointed public defenders offered no defense and called no witnesses. Though he admitted to killing the boy, Fukunaga was not allowed to enter a guilty plea. Instead, they wanted him hanged and forced him to plead not guilty. A Navy psychiatrist offered to enter his testimony for the defense but was denied.

The jury appointed to the case included members of the search party, the man who dug the boy's grave, and even Frederick Jamieson's personal bodyguard. Despite several attempts for an appeal to show that Fukunaga was mentally unable to stand trial, they denied all requests.

The crime and conviction opened large divisions on Oahu between the whites and the Japanese. Japanese families throughout Hawaii felt a sense of fear and resentment for years after the crime. Fukunaga's family was constantly harassed and even moved to Maui to escape ostracization.

Myles Fukunaga was ultimately convicted of first-degree murder and hanged at Oahu Prison on November 19, 1929, just two months after he kidnapped and killed Gilles Jamieson.

The story of the killing is still told as a ghost story every Halloween to this day in Hawaii.

 "Until we have understood his personality so thoroughly and the circumstances of his life so fully that we can actually feel how he came to act as he did, we have not given him the defense to which he is morally entitled. We cannot discover to what extent society is to blame for this hideous crime or what social changes we should endeavor to bring about."

- University of Hawaii Professor Dr. Lockwood Myrick in a letter to then-Governor Farrington over ninety years ago.

CHAPTER 13
APPENDIX A: "SK CONFESSIONS" BY MARK TWITCHELL

The text that follows is the document *"SK Confessions"* that was found by detectives on Mark Twitchell's computer and used as evidence against him. He had deleted the file, but forensic investigators were able to recover it. Twitchell goes into excruciating detail about his assault of Johnny Altinger and the dismemberment and disposal of his body. It's a jarring look inside the mind of the psychopathic killer.

―――――――――

This story is based on true events. The names and events were altered slightly to protect the guilty.

This is the story of my progression into becoming a serial killer. Like anyone just starting out in a new skill, I had a bit of trial and error in the beginning of my misadventures. Allow me to start from the beginning and I think you'll see what I mean.

I don't remember the exact place and time it was that I decided to become a serial killer but I remember the sensation that hit me when I committed to the decision. It was a rush of pure euphoria. I felt lighter, less stressed if you will at the freedom of the prospect. There was something about urgently exploring my dark side that greatly appealed to me and I'm such a methodical planner and thinker, the very challenge itself was enticing to behold.

This realization was just the last in a series of new discoveries I made about myself.

I just knew I was different somehow from the rest of humanity. I feel no such emotions as empathy or sympathy toward others for example.

Of course when it came to actual one on one conversations with therapists, I had to lie. I mean talk about leaving a trail of bread crumbs. The last thing I needed to do was air out all of my darkest fantasies and half formed plans to someone who is legally obligated to contact the authorities if they think a patient will do harm to themselves or others. I'm not stupid. Nevertheless, deception aside, it was a useful exercise to get to know my label better.

When a man approaches thirty years of age, he tends to question what his ultimate purpose is in this world and where he fits into the picture. And then I remembered something else. A passage I read from a novel by the renowned fantasy writer, David Gemmell in reference to a bronze age assassin. I can't recall the exact wording but it was the philosophy that hit home. The assassin reflected on what he does with his life with guilt (another emotion I am incapable of) and someone imparted a bigger picture wisdom.

He said that the assassin is the hand of fate. Fate has already decided everyone's time to die from the moment they are born. When it's their time, it's their time and if they do not die of old age or sickness, when their time comes other factors are employed by fate to get the job done. I think about that whenever I plan a kill. It's not me who chooses the victims but fate. Oh sure I choose the victim to match my own criteria in the interest of remaining free and at large, but for the most part I am merely following my own nature which was devised by the grand design of the universe.

Now this does not mean I shirk responsibility for my actions. I am very obviously, as you will come to learn, deliberate, level headed and very much in control of my own actions. Although I won't deny that the aforementioned scenario would play well in an insanity plea.

So here I was, armed with this new insight into my inner self and an exhilarating new hobby that I was seeking to undertake. I thought long and hard to come up with a system that would work for me, a method that would ensure I could have my play time and keep from getting caught. It didn't take long before I settled on an M.O.

I would use online dating to rope in my victims. Once I came up with that one clear starting point, all of the other pieces needed to be tended to. I began to ask myself a series of questions designed to get me to consider every possible angle. I wanted to have every step in the process already planned out from start to finish because improvising would be bad and lead to sloppiness. I had to have an order, a plan, something that would bring calm to a chaotic situation.

First question: Who do I want to target? At first I considered married men looking to cheat on their wives. In one way I'd be taking out the trash, doling out justice to those who on some level, deserved what they got. But the logic of the situation denies this possibility. After all people who are expected home at a certain hour tend to get reported as missing and there's other factors that would lead to an investigation I didn't want. No, I had to choose people whose entire lives I could infiltrate and eliminate evidence of my existence from on all levels.

I finally settled on middle-aged single men who lived alone. My reasons were numerous. For one thing, they would be easy to lead by their dicks, easy to manipulate, easy to seduce under my fake female disguises. They were also the most likely targets to have the most expendable money in their bank accounts. A tidbit I would use to my advantage later on. Finally, by living alone, once they were out of the picture I could easily enter their living spaces undetected with no forced entry and remove all sorts of valuable items from the premises.

Oh yes my friend, I am in this for profit. It has always been my attitude that no hobby or venture should ever be done without expected return on investment. For many years I crafted elaborate Halloween costumes, faithful screen accurate recreations of very big blockbuster movie icons. The result of my efforts in these costumes, were various 1st prizes in costume contests that resulted in cash payouts worth at least forty times what I spent to make each outfit. This would be no different.

I had expenses with this new hobby and I would make sure that I generated a profit from it to recoup and eclipse my costs. That was the next step in the process for being fully prepared, a detailed shopping list of all the items I would need to carry out my plans.

First off I needed a location. I scoured listings to find something suitable. I started looking in regular secure storage but the video surveillance and inability to get my victims there smoothly threw that idea out the window quickly. When I finally found my location it could not have been any more perfect.

A double detached garage for rent in the south of the city, tucked away in a quiet neighborhood on a lot with a house occupied by tenants who couldn't even read English, much less speak it, no doubt work program immigrants brought in by a donut chain with supplied housing.

Everything, I decided, would take place here. The approach, the apprehension and the kill as well as preparation for disposal of the body could all be done in relative seclusion from this one building. Total privacy. I immediately went to work removing the address plank from the back, blocking out all the windows with boards and duct tape, replacing locks.

The back driveway wasn't even paved, it was just a bed of gravel with grass growing out of it. The entire surrounding area was blocked out of sight from neighbors with high thick fences and the entire block was dead starting at eight o'clock at night.

My shopping list was very thorough. I went out to several different stores to avoid buying all of my items from one location and I paid cash to avoid a paper trail just in case. A street hockey mask, that I would soon cut the mouth out of and paint gold streaks into for dramatic effect. A basic dark green hoody, something comfortable with pockets that hides distinctive marks, body type and hair. Two sets of disposable overalls for what was sure to be a messy clean up process and I would use the plastic bags all this came in to wrap my shoes for the process.

I bought a hunters game processing kit, which if you think about it is ideal for this scenario. Why not use a whole set of tools designed to take apart large mammals in the forest on the fly? It reduces the spatter caused by power tools, takes the noise level way down too and there's also just something more gratifying about sawing through tendons and bone with your bare hands than using something else that takes the fun out of the work.

My kill knife was different though. I wanted the weapon used for the deed itself to be simple, elegant and beautiful in it's own way so I dropped by a military surplus store and picked up a well crafted hunting knife with an 8 inch blade. I would use this weapon to cleanly and simply slice open a gash in the victims neck allowing them to bleed out quickly and with no pain. I'm not a torture guy. Again, the noise level from the screams is not my thing at all and I only resort to that if they are still alive after apprehension but won't give me the simple information I ask for.

Several rolls of painters plastic sheeting to prep my kill room. At least 6 rolls of packing tape and just as many rolls of duct tape as well as two boxes of contractor grade hefty bags. I picked up a stun baton because I thought that would render my targets without use of their muscles quickly and painlessly and I bought an extra realistic airsoft pistol; something that could very easily be mistaken for the real thing, especially in low light just for that extra edge.

I made sure to acquire construction materials for my custom furniture. I went to town designing and building a rather sturdy four foot by six foot six inch table with stainless steel finish and angle iron edging. I also welded a rather mean looking chair and another table was left there by the realty company, which I used to stay organized on.

Finally I ordered a forty five gallon steel drum which would be the final resting place for the body parts before I incinerated them. I was all set, prepared as I could be. I diligently set up my kill room, creating the plastic bubble I needed to create my nasty mayhem. The trap was set, and now it was time to bait the hook.

I downloaded an IP address blocker first and foremost. I mean it would be rather silly of me to run this whole operation from my home computer without it, just so that if any of my play mates disappearances were ever actually investigated, there would be this electronic trail leading the police directly back to me and my little workshop of horrors.

Once activated, I created all new email addresses and dating site profiles for my dark plan. It was so easy it was almost insulting. But really, who thinks to look outside their pond when they go out fishing? No one. I did a quick search for females that matched what I wanted to represent in other cities around the world and when I found someone I liked, I copied their photos and used them in my new online identity as whoever it was I wanted to be.

I always change things up. I never use the same profile for more than one victim at a time, and I generate new email addresses as well, just in case. After a victim is removed from the world neatly and cleanly, I erase my accounts and every trace they left behind. Sure the mother servers may or may not have an imprinted image, but even if they checked, they wouldn't trace me.

As soon as the profiles go up, within twenty four hours the responses come in like a flood. I review the messages sent and choose my victims based on age, body type, profession, status and living situation. Obviously I'm not going to pursue a 6'4 athletic martial arts instructor who's married with 4 kids. That's just got trouble written all over it. I mean I'm ruthless but I'm not an idiot. I have my own fight training background but I don't have delusions of grandeur.

When I come across a single man in his late thirties to early forties who is self employed, lives alone and stands between 5' 7 and 5' 11 with an average body type weighing in between 150 and 180 lbs, I know I've found my ideal target.

Such was the case with a man I will refer to as Frank. That of course is not his real name and I won't divulge any other sensitive details about the situation but Frank was my very first target ever. I roped him in with a profile I was quite proud of featuring photos of a blonde I would like to bang myself.

I asked him to pick me up from my residence at a prescribed time on a particular night of the week and then gave him detailed instructions on how to find the place. I gave him some song and dance routine about how my landlord had the property setup to where the back gate was broken and padlocked and there was nowhere in front to park because of a no parking zone and a bus stop across the street. So I told him I would leave the garage door open for him to come in through and then to come the back door of the house, all the while realizing of course that he would never make it that far.

So the message was received and confirmed, and I waited.

Generally I was quite pleased with myself. I had a perfectly formulated plan, and I was fully prepared. I adorned my specialty mask, serving the double purpose of facial protection and identity shield to give the victim a false sense of security in thinking they would be let go since I cared about hiding who I was. But without explaining it to them, that thought would not likely cross their mind in the heat of the moment.

I slipped my hoody on and pulled the hood over my head, resting it comfortably over my brow. I slipped the knife holster with the blade in it onto my belt and pulled on my fine leather gloves.

My kill room was perfectly prepped. Plastic sheeting taped together and around my table; a large green cloth screwed into the drywall ceiling to shield view of it from my guests line of sight, and to shield me too of course. I now stood but a few feet away from the front door which I had locked of course. The plan was to wait in the shadow of my curtain until he approached the door and shock him with the stun baton followed by a sleeper hold that would sap away his consciousness so that I could tape him up and set him on my table.

The last thought that crossed my mind before Frank pulled up into the driveway had nothing to do with the event itself, but rather was a mental note that I would need to remember to get a stock of paper towels for miscellaneous clean up in the future.

The cars engine rumbled and its headlights shone bright in the lowering dusk. I thought if his headlights were on a delay self shut off like mine that he would see more than I wanted him to which still wasn't much. Just a few crates of tools and paint cans, normal garage accessories in my opinion. But his headlights turned off as his engine petered out. I heard the sound of the car door opening and closing and then the footsteps that followed.

My head was rushed with adrenaline, my stomach had a half second flutter of butterflies before my resolve strengthened and I stood there, ominous in the dark prepared to strike with my stun baton fully extended and the safety off.

The typical taser guns used by police carry a charge of 50,000 volts and we've seen what they do to the people hit with them. The stun baton boasts 800,000 volts which sounds practically lethal but you have to understand that it isn't the voltage but the amps delivered by the weapon that matter. Either way I was confident in the weapons strength.

My confidence was misplaced.

I took two swift silent steps toward my target and pressing the baton across the back of his neck, pulled the trigger. It shocked and jumped but did little more than merely alert the bastard to what was really going on. It did not render his muscles unusable and the little shit fought back.

I had a distinct advantage. I was taller and outclassed him in tenacity and strength. This was also my environment and he wasn't expecting to run into a psycho in a mask, only a beautiful woman he hoped he would get lucky with. The confusion played to my benefit and I struck him repeatedly. He yelled "what the fuck" at the top of his lungs. The noise was something I had hoped to avoid but I paid it no mind and continued attempting to subdue this defiant little shit.

I dropped the baton and punched him several times in the side of the head but still he would not go down. He broke free and I could tell he would make for the door, for the way he came in so I reached into my pocket and withdrew the gun.

I pointed it straight at him and all of a sudden he took me seriously, his eyes wide. I commanded him to get down on the floor, to which he obeyed quickly. If he lifted his head even the slightest bit I warned him against it. I removed my gloves and went for the duct tape. I tore a piece off and slipped it over his eyes.

It was then that I told him that if he did what I told him to, that I would let him live. I brought one arm down around his back and was reaching for the other arm when he began defying me again.

"No, I can't, I can't do this." He began. Retrospect is of course 20/20 and had I been able to go back to that moment there would have been a hundred things I would have done differently. Obviously overestimating the stun baton is a mistake I would not repeat. The other one was putting up with his bullshit. I should have just pounded him in the back of the head while he was down until he lay unconscious on the floor. I should have shut the big door when I had the chance but everything moved too quickly and I didn't want to take my eyes off him for one second.

He got back to his feet having removed the duct tape and when I pointed the gun at him again, he grabbed it. He gripped down hard, twice and I think I might have seen a gleam in him that indicated he felt the guns construction and realized it was not real but I can't be sure. I still held on for dear life, not willing to give him a blunt object to hit me back with.

Frank made a few feeble attempts to hit me and tried one impotent kick aimed at my groin that I easily deflected. I delivered a head butt to his face and he broke free again. I clutched onto his jacket but he shook himself loose of it and took off for the opening in the door.

He made it into the driveway and that's when I knew I was pooched. I followed him out, not caring anymore who might see me. He was fumbling on the ground. I grabbed him by the leg as if to drag him back into the garage caveman style but my energy was depleting and the human survival instinct is one of the most powerful forces on Earth. He tried to grab at my mask and came quite close to pulling it off. I broke the grasp and he spun away into the alley and sure enough, a couple on an evening stroll saw me coming after him sporting a deer in the headlight look that can only be described as a total lack of comprehension. I stared back at them through my mask for half a moment and then headed back for the cover of my lair.

I don't know why I played it as cool as I did. Maybe it was something Frank said during the skirmish about swearing not to tell anyone if I let him go. Maybe it was my own instincts about reading people and the fear in his eyes that told me deep down, he wouldn't report the incident, but I felt ok.

I still packed any gear up of my own and his stray jacket into a bag. Whatever I felt like keeping I cleaned prints off of and tossed the rest in a dumpster. As a final touch I sent one last warning email to Frank through the dating site telling him I had traced his IP address through his messages and that if he did report me, I would hunt him down where he lives when he least expects it and finish what I started. I threw in a line about having cased the garage, that it wasn't even mine and that I never use the same location twice. My last lie was to tell him he was lucky number eighteen on my spree.

I wasn't sure if I should believe it worked. I walked calmly out to my car, got in and drove away, across the entire city back to my home where my wife and child waited for me. During the entire trip I kept thinking surely this douche bag would call the police. Not that it mattered if he did. I covered my tracks well.

You see in my day life I'm an independent film-maker and everything in that garage could be easily explained away as props for filming a psychological thriller. How I could be on one side of the city scrapping with a potential kill up until 7:20 pm and be home less than an hour later would have been a stretch at best.

Still, I couldn't shake the foreboding feeling. I kept thinking any moment I'd see flashing lights behind me asking me to pull over, despite my perfect adherence to posted speed limits and cautious observance of the safety belt law. Surely the arresting officer would wonder why I was so sweaty and why there was a bag with a hoody, a jacket, a prohibited stun weapon and a set of handcuffs in my trunk.

But those lights never showed up in my rear view mirror.

I checked my voicemail messages and had two; very unusual this time of night. One from my wife wondering if I could be home by 8:30 so that she could pick up a package before 9:00 and one from my prop guy asking if he could borrow my airsoft pistol. Paranoia set in. My wife wouldn't care about picking up a package this late, she'd wait until tomorrow. Could the cops have gotten to her and convinced her to pretend to get me home quicker so they could arrest me?

But I had to stop and think clearly. This was all happening way too fast. There's no way that was possible, this wasn't a movie, this was real life. Even if the police were contacted, their response time to the location would be in the neighborhood of twenty minutes to two hours and there'd be no way for them to verify who rented the garage that quickly.

My fear subsided and I drove home. I practiced my entire behavior pattern should I come home to police cruisers parked along my front yard. I would rush the door in a panic and upon entering or being stopped by patrolmen I would appear utterly surprised and beg them to know if anything had happened to my precious wife and/or daughter. My genuine shock of their presence would start me on the innocent path in their eyes, and then my cover story of being at a therapy appointment would become my short term alibi until I could confess to the cops later that therapy was a cover story I gave my wife so I could have just one night a week to myself.

Between that and the total lack of hard evidence I'd be free regardless and yet still the nervousness set in.

It's pretty fucking hard to concentrate on anything when you live in constant expectation of the police arriving at your doorstep. It turns out my wife did need to pick up a package, a pilates chair that she wanted me to assemble. The directions couldn't be any more complicated than the directions for making mac and cheese but I had a really hard time because the apprehension was always there.

Every time I heard a car drive by I'd feel compelled to look out the window. I heard a massive group of sirens get closer, and closer and closer. My heart leaped into my chest until I realized there was a house fire somewhere close to the area.

Seeing a police cruiser slowly and deliberately pull around my block was the worst part. But then I remembered our across the street neighbor had an itchy trigger finger for calling the cops when the rowdy teenagers next door partied too loudly and it subsided.

A day passed. I spent that day with my 8 month old daughter as my wife ran errands and kept appointments. Then the day turned to night and once again I was suspicious but nothing happened. That was the night I was totally convinced I had gotten off on this one pretty much scot free.

No patrol car would come to take me away bound in handcuffs to be brought up on assault charges, forever ending my serial killing career before it began and bringing down my marriage with it when my wife finds out what I really am.

That first time experience was the basis for my revised method of operandi.

Previously I wanted my victims alive and conscious after I had subdued them. I wanted to get information from them like their email and dating site passwords as well as the pin codes to their debit cards and credit cards. But this priority is now a distant second to making sure I don't get caught. I got lucky that first time and I wasn't going to assume that would ever happen again if anyone else got loose.

So I had to revise my apprehension system in order for it to go more smoothly. I decided to ramp up the savagery of my attack, leaving no margin for error in rendering a target unconscious within the first ten seconds. I dropped the stun baton for the favor of two 24 inch lengths of galvanized steel piping. I was confident that swinging for the fences to the back of the head would do the trick. I would go on a shopping trip the next day to make it happen.

Chapter break

Oh my sweet Laci. Just in case you are wondering, Laci is not my wife, or my daughter. Laci is my ex girlfriend. On paper she's the complete opposite of everything that should be my perfect match. She has two small dogs that she treats like human children and those people usually drive me up the wall.

She's also periodically depressed and suffers from frequent anxiety attacks whereas I usually prefer a much more together woman. All these things exist but I love her uncontrollably and always will.

Laci and I met in my first year of college. I was 19 at the time and unbeknownst to me at the time she was 24. I've always been into older women. The first time I met her I was waiting outside the door of an English class I didn't need to take since the school had just dropped the required grade for my program the night before. Still, I thought it couldn't hurt to ride the class out since I had already paid for it and would possibly use the higher mark for something else in the future.

I sat on the floor writing a story. Laci sat down across from me and simply said "Hi." I said hi back and that was the beginning of the end for us.

Our relationship is always and forever on unstable ground. When we first met she was just trying to be friendly but she had a boyfriend. A very stiff, unemotional, dependable long term boyfriend. I was too young and naive to know where this was headed.

I lied to her from the onset. I lied to her about my heritage and my age. Stupid basic life things that are completely pointless to lie about but I did it anyway. Part of me was insecure about just being myself but part of me also didn't think this relationship would go anywhere since she was taken.

I was wrong. It went somewhere very quickly. We became fast friends, she wanted to be in the story I was writing. We began hanging out on a regular basis. I had lied to her about having a girlfriend myself so as not to appear single and therefore, pathetic. So it was really rather easy for me to show up to class one day pretending to be distraught over my girlfriend having dumped me. That day our friendship grew into something stronger.

We spent more time together, very often curling up on a couch as just friends, while we watched TV and nuzzled. Friends rubbed their faces together affectionately didn't they? These ones did, at least until one night when we couldn't take it anymore and made out like a couple of teenagers, which technically speaking I still was.

It was a long hard complicated battle over the next several months as she hummed and hawed over what to do. She was a serial dater to my future serial killer and had never taken down time between relationships, always afraid to be alone. Eventually she did in fact dump her boyfriend for me but the fast transition left damage. She would act out in inappropriate ways, kiss another guy and then say she had to in order to see if what we had was real.

It was no worse than what I had done to her of course. Toward the end of our relationship she also began to find religion and I knew the end was nigh. It's not that I have a problem with religious people per se, I have some very good friends who are quite religious. It's just that I could see major issues down the line with butting heads over what to teach our kids or how to live our lives. Not to mention the fact that killing people isn't exactly welcomed in the kingdom of the man made, 'make me feel better about myself through guilt' system of the faithful.

I didn't need to wait for any of these issues to wreck our relationship. Eventually one lie after another began to unravel. First at my birthday party when my age was revealed to be a year younger than I told her, and then the death blow when she flat out asked my parents about the family origins in the car one day.

Dishonesty had taken its toll and Laci decided to end the relationship. I was absolutely devastated. Crushed beyond all reckoning. I lost my soul mate, the one true love of my life and would never get over it. I told her as I left that night that I love her more than anyone I've ever loved, that I will never love anyone the same way again and that no one she ever meets will love her with the same intensity, passion and commitment that I do.

Laci tried to tell me I cared for women too much and that I would find someone else. It was remarkable how right I was and how wrong she was about the entire situation.

For eight years I thought about her constantly. Several times I tried to touch base with her to see how she was doing. At one point I made brief contact after I found her in a hotmail member search but she cut things off sharply and quickly, said she was getting engaged and that was it.

I would soon come to find out she hadn't written those responses, but her friend did on her behalf and two weeks later, Laci had changed her mind and wanted to get together but she never reconnected with me.

I went through one failed marriage in the meantime, and so did she. When Laci and I reconnected through a social networking website, she was just in the process of getting divorced, ironically from a total sociopath who drained her of all her self worth. Years of neglect and mistreatment at the hands of a negative, unaffectionate douchebag who would rather play a video game than be intimate with her had taken its toll.

By the time I found her again, Laci had forgotten what it had been like to be in a caring loving relationship. Her self esteem had been torn to shreds and she had turn to the unconditional love of her animals to keep her going.

By this time I was already married for the second time, to a wonderful woman. Tess was everything I needed to balance my life out. She kept me on my toes and organized. She was a very high stress person with a lot of tension and I mellowed her out too. We had hit it off from the beginning, found what I thought was love and gone on to be married and have our daughter together, beautiful Zoe.

I even gave Tess the Laci test. I coined this after years of finding the way to figure out if a relationship was worth keeping or not. I would simply ask myself "If Laci walked into my life and asked me to run away with her, would I do it?"

If the answer was yes, then I should end my relationship. If the answer was no, I finally found true love. With Tess, I answered no so the next logical choice was to ask her to marry me. What I didn't count on was finding Laci again... through Facebook.

It started out as a congratulations on each others happiness, which led to a meeting, which led to feelings which then led to an intense make out session in a local restaurant. Every feeling I had for Laci came flooding back to me. The strength of love, the adoration, all of it; it was like a tidal wave crashing through me.

Tess was 3 months pregnant with Zoe at the time and I had a panic attack. A huge conflict of motivation, obligation and sense of duty overcame me and I actually felt guilt. Like an idiot I confessed everything to Tess the next day thereby destroying the trust in our relationship. Trust is all anyone has in a relationship and it's the one pillar everything else is based around. Mess with that and you end your world.

This did not happen amazingly. Tess is a very strong, independent person with very strong opinions on morals and ethics. I was certain she'd dump me, pregnant or not but she didn't. She made a conscious choice to forgive me, accept my temporary insanity plea and trust me again.

Ending things with Laci after promising her I would leave Tess for her resulted badly. There was anger, frustration and heartache. I was blocked on Facebook for a long time. A year in fact. I had all but lost any hope of ever hearing from Laci again. And then I got the strangest email.

Laci sent me a message on Facebook asking to be friends again. She was engaged again to some other sociopathic douche and just like last time, she was on the verge of ending it. He was just another neglectful, self serving, immature limp fish who had disappointed her for the last time with his philandering and mistreatment of her.

We quickly began a dialogue and although I told my wife Laci had emailed me, I also told her that I deleted the message and ignored her. That was obviously a lie. Tables had turned. Laci knew more about me and my situation than Tess did. It wasn't fair to her but she was also in the dark, which was better for her all around.

I started seeing Laci again. First it was innocent little coffee dates and movies. We went to see a horror film, something low budget and shot entirely hand held as was the Hollywood fad at the time and we maybe caught 20 minutes of a 90 minute movie between all the intense kissing we were doing.

It was the first week of October and I had always done something very elaborate for Halloween. Laci wanted to join me for Halloween, get a hotel and spend the entire day having sex. I was all about it but I knew there was no way I could wait that long. The engine in the back of my head that makes things happen started planning and plotting immediately on how to make this happen. Only problem was, she lived about an hour out of town and logistics were difficult to manage.

I would come back to this problem later, right now I had someone to kill and some new methods to try out.

I went to my neighborhood Home Depot to find what I needed and sure enough, in the plumbing section there they were; two galvanized steel pipes. I thought it might do to pick up some hockey tape while I was there in order to create a better grip on one side.

I rounded the aisle just in time to see a daddy daughter team shopping for plumbing accessories, no doubt for their original intended use. The

211

little girl couldn't have been any older than five and had found the stick portion of a toilet plunger without its companion on the end. She wielded it like a sword and held a defensive pose, quite expertly I might add.

Ordinarily I'm somewhat irritated by children but when they do something stunningly mature for their age or endearing to my heart I can't help but smile and smile I did at this feisty little sweetheart who I hoped would be Zoe in 4 years.

The girl grinned sheepishly back at me. Her smile revealed her thoughts. She was smiling with a face that said "I'm a little embarrassed that you caught me but you seem to think it's cool so I'll return the devilish grin you're giving me." I think the young lady and I shared a moment just then.

I strolled out into the parking lot and got back into the comfy me shaped indent in the front seat of my maroon sedan. I wrapped the pipe ends in hockey tape for optimal gripping. Satisfied with this, I went home to relax and to set up my next victim.

The cool thing about a seven month old is that you can openly tell them anything and they can't rat you out. I needed that from my daughter, since anyone else I could spill to would be dialing nine one one before I finished. I knew I only had a limited amount of time before Zoes comprehension got to the level where that wouldn't fly so I got in as much talk time as possible in her early development when the words were just soothing sounds to get her used to the English language.

---

break.

I'm a huge fan of the Showtime series Dexter, as you may have guessed if you're at all familiar with the show. Dexter enjoys the sweet dark alone time of his own apartment since his TV girlfriend Rita and her two kids, Astor and Cody are not as tangled into his life as my family is with mine. I had to do with the sweet dark alone time of my basement computer office.

Once the child was snugly tucked away in her crib and my wife was sleeping peacefully, it sufficed perfectly for what I needed to do. My wife is certainly no sound sleeper, requiring ear plugs just to conk out and getting up several times during the night but we sleep apart so my disturbing her from getting up was never an issue.

Some people think that sleeping apart is detrimental to the relationship. I don't see how. I mean I'm only a serial killer, seeing my ex girlfriend on the side and my wife has no clue about it. But neither of those things has to do with the sleeping arrangements in our household. I sleep in the basement because I often stay up later than my wife and when we do sleep together, there's never enough room in a queen bed for two. Eventually the kicking and blanket hogging had us re-evaluate the importance of sharing a mattress.

I fired up my IP address blocker and launched two windows for my dual purpose. Keeping to my rules of never using the same account twice for anything, I opened a brand new email account. I stuck to the majors. Hotmail, Yahoo, Gmail. Something generic. When choosing a username it always reflected my new alias in some way. If I was an immigrant from Ireland looking for guys with a thing for redheads I'd use a username to the effect of Irishfirecream or something else just as apt.

Once the account had been created I used the second window to launch the dating site of choice. I switched that up to keep it interesting as well. Sometimes I would use a basic free service, and sometime I would use an elaborate pay service. It never mattered because women never have to pay to use those sites anyways. It's the homy retards on the other end who let their dicks dreams open their wallets.

On this night, a Thursday, I decided on a free site. Now photos are important. A photo of a girl that looks too professional gets overlooked because it reeks of spam bot. It also causes the guys to ask for more photos, which I would, of course, not have and would be forced to start from scratch.

A handy trick I use is to steal other women's photos from the same site, but in a different city. So if I posted my profile originating from say Portland, I would do a quick search in Nashville first and find a woman who I would genuinely be attracted to. Someone who doesn't come off as a total slut, but who also doesn't exude prude either. In this case I went ahead and chose the redhead from Ireland going out of country entirely for the photos.

Writing a woman's dating profile is very simple. You read enough and they all start to sound the same after awhile. I wrote delicately, sweetly, as a woman would write. I listed a few of the things my new persona was not interested in and made a few kind comments at the end and an invitation to message me.

This profile was listed looking for 'dating', which is much more manageable than 'intimate encounter'. When looking for dating I only had to sift through less than thirty emails throughout the day. But when putting 'intimate encounter' it's more like thirty messages per hour, sometimes more. That can be good or bad depending on what you're looking for.

I was looking for someone to match my needs for a new victim. I wanted a man who was financially stable, lived alone, didn't answer to too many people and might have some time off coming up. I got exactly what I was looking for.

Amongst the smart assed punks and the creepy old fellas who frankly, would be more suspicious of me if I gave them the time of day than not based on their appearances, was my target. A six foot'ish seem-ingly nice man who appeared clean cut, not overly good looking but not an ogre either and most importantly, fit for the profile.

We exchanged messages back and forth but when it came time to move in for the invite, another curve ball came my way. He wasn't available Friday, only Saturday. I had put in too much time with this asshole to start over and my mind began to race about how to fit it in.

I chose Fridays because I had a fake appointment with an imaginary psychiatrist who I told my wife I was seeing to sort out some of my issues, although I had already done that some time before. It was a very convenient and perfectly credible cover story though and I saw the merit in keeping the illusion going for the purpose of my late night freedom.

So every Friday I would leave the house, and prep for a kill while my wife was convinced my shrink was working his magic. I even added the special performance of seeming lighter and more relaxed when I walked back into the house. It was only partially an act since I did in fact feel good about my evening, just not in the way Tess quite expected.

Starting a kill on a Friday works on so many levels. For one thing, most people are not hard and fast expected to be anywhere on the weekend which gives me three days to clean up and tie up the loose ends. For another, I ordinarily need to skulk around doing my dirty work in the dead of night after Tess and Zoe are fast asleep. With all that night activity I get pretty bagged during the day so it's nice to not have career obligations on top of a lack of sleep.

I wasn't quite sure how to deal with my new friends schedule change. I thought to myself that starting over and slamming on the gas with a different profile entirely in order to stick to plan would have been the best idea. But I had already groomed this guy and felt profile mattered more than time of day.

I decided to leave it open and sleep on it, deciding what to do in the morning.

Friday morning came and my decision was made. I would scrap yesterdays escapade and start over fresh. I found some new photos of a girl from L.A. and whipped up an intimate encounter profile. Something quick and dirty and to the point. She was on the prowl and looking to hook up that very night, my chosen night.

Then something happened I did not expect; a pleasant surprise among the scads of emails from young douchebags with no appeal at all and some flaming rude comments at the ready. I got a message from Mr. Thursday.

It seemed that he was not only a liar but a wannabe player as well. He lied to my other dummy account about being tied up Friday and was seeking something with more immediate gratification for the time being. It was all I needed to see.

I flirted back and forth like it was an art form. Finally when enough messages had been exchanged and I felt comfortable with his comfort level I invited him in. It crossed my mind to use my other account to message him and entice him into this night as well just to watch him squirm but I would watch him squirm plenty in person.

I gave him step by step directions to my kill room without revealing an address and making sure to include the general excuses about the bus stop in front of the place and the lack of parking. He bought it hook line and sinker. The time was set. 7:00 pm.

My kill room was still perfectly set up from the last time, plastic sheeting hanging from the walls, on the floor and of course around my glorious table, duct tape sealing the seams to create a bubble to work within. I put that useless stun baton away and stretched my body out to limber up. I donned my mask, pulled my hood up and waited. The lights were still on inside the garage. It was 6:47 and I had a little time yet so I got myself psyched up for the main event.

Suddenly I heard the rumble of a car engine and sharply turned to see the wheel base of a Mazda slow and then continue. My adrenaline soared. That was him. The bastard was early and I know he had to have seen my feet at the very least. I decided to stick to the pattern anyway. I shut the lights all down and waited behind the curtain I had rigged up to shield me from sight; my two pipes in hand.

I ran entirely on sounds now. The cars engine silencing. The brief pause where all I could hear was the distant sound of main drag traffic lightly dancing in the background. Then the door opened, footsteps followed and then the car door slammed shut.

Another pause.

I could hear the crinkle of his clothing as he crouched to get under the door. He stood up and said "Hello?"

I froze. This was new. I've never heard anyone call out hello to a black empty room before. He assumed I was still here, and he was right. After all I had told him under my alias that there would be a guy using the garage for the weekend as a workshop.

I quickly took the mask off setting it on the weaker secondary table I used for my laptop. And without any other plan I began acting again.

"Hello?" I called back in a cheerful tone. I moved to the light switches and illuminated the room. "I'm Harry" I said pointedly, not sure what else to say exactly. "I'm a local film maker, preparing a set that's supposed to look like a serial killers little area here. You might have heard of my stuff. I'm the guy who put together the comedy feature at our local film festival."

"l haven't heard of that." replied the man who I will refer to from now on as Jim.

I went into super friendly mode, showed him my prop gun and how it wasn't real. I quickly mentioned that his date was running a little late and would be back in about twenty minutes. He said he would come back.

For twenty minutes I paced back and forth considering what to do, weighing the risks and the benefits. He could be on the phone to one of his friends revealing the address and telling them all about my set up. On the other hand he knows me so now I have an advantage over him and simultaneously, an obligation to use that advantage to remove him from the picture.

Still when my twenty minutes were up, I chickened out. As his car pulled up for the second time I whipped out my cell phone and in another grand performance pretended to talk to my alias over the phone. I delivered the bad news that tragically it looked like she wasn't going to be able to make it.

"I'm sorry bud, I don't know how long you had to drive to get here (27 blocks total, 10 minutes tops including lights) but it sounds like she's stuck in traffic and has no idea how long she'll be."

And with that, my victim left. He walked right out the door that should've been closing on his doom right then. I took stock of my situation. I was standing in the middle of a perfectly prepped kill room and was actually going to let this go down as strike 2. I already had the room set up and the whole night was mine to do with as I pleased so I jumped back online to find someone who was willing to drop everything and head over right away.

My new account which I had just created that morning had clear over 200 messages from all sorts of people. After twenty five minutes of perusing I still had nothing when my twice escaped victim sent me a message. My immediate reply was a huge apology and an offer to reschedule for the next day.

His reply was to come over again that very night. He didn't live far and didn't want to waste his night any more than I wanted to waste mine. I stared at the laptop screen, unmoving for half an hour deciding. Humming and hawing over the details. Finally I went for it. I typed a message back with a quick apology for the delay and an invitation to come back. I meant business.

Crouched, poised, I had a whole new plan. No mask needed this time. Just pretending to be poking around at the back of the set and then WHAM! I would slam him unconscious and his survival would be a bonus, but not necessary. He played into it perfectly. He reappeared through the garage door and I soon followed.

"I guess I'm just a glutton for punishment" he shrugged.

"You have no idea."

The room filled with the echo of the pipe crashing into the back of his skull as I could feel my predator self take over. That one single motion was the end all be all. I had committed now and there was no going back. The jig was up and it was kill or get arrested for aggravated assault with a deadly weapon, maybe even attempted murder.

I won't go to jail for an almost. But the son of a bitch didn't drop like the sack of potatoes I was expecting. Are you serious? I asked myself. I continued thwacking Jim over the head repeatedly but it only seemed to fuel his adrenaline too.

He began screaming at the top of his lungs. "Police! Police! Police!" and I just about shat my pants. My fury doubled and I blasted him so hard blood spattered everywhere, but primarily on me. He hit the floor but was still conscious.

Just like they all do, he offered money immediately. I always find this a little degrading for both my victim and myself. Like I couldn't just kill them and take it anyway. No please Mr. victim, give me some petty cash from your wallet and run along to the cops only to lead them back here. Ridiculous.

I paused for a minute. "You promise?" I said.

"Yes just please stop hitting me, Oh my skull." Was his reply. And then in the instant he had to think about it I wailed on him again. Despite receiving several mortal blows to the head, the shock and adrenaline of the situation gave him the fire to fight back a little.

"I've had enough of this." He said as he feebly and dizzily tried to grab the pipe away from me. My anger resurged, I wrestled it from him and that was the last straw for me. I pulled my hunting knife from it's sheath and watching the shock on his face as he saw the blade, I thrust it into his gut. His reaction was pure Hollywood. The lurch forward with the grunt was dead on TV movie of the week.

I didn't even notice the garage door was still part open. Wasn't I suppose to close that? Will I never learn?

No one came. No one rustled, not even from across the alley. My little notices that I sent out to the neighbors about shooting thrillers here did their job and no one paid attention, assuming it was a scene or some-thing. Oh it was a scene alright.

Jim moaned and groaned. I plunged the knife deep into his neck. Days after the event I would reflect on this and wish I had tricked him by offering to call an ambulance if he just gave me his debit pin code before I sliced open his jugular. Maybe I'll save that for the next victim since they never seem to just fall the fuck asleep like they're supposed to.

I let him bleed out right there on the floor, away from the plastic sheeting specifically put up to avoid that sort of thing. But hey I had bigger problems. I had no real idea if a jogger, a dog walker, an unconvinced neighbor or some other random individual had actually called the cops, just as a precaution.

I was standing there covered in blood. It was all over my face, my hoody, my coat and my jeans. I was holding the murder weapon in my hand standing over what would be in moments, a corpse and not nearly enough time to make it go away.

I got my things ready and did the only thing I could do. I waited. I waited for a sign on what to do next. I waited for the fast approach of sirens as a cue to leave and come up with a damn good story for later. I waited and I was rewarded with silence. Sweet sweet silence. I got lucky. No one freaked out, no one reacted, no one inadvertently witnessed it and no one called the boys in blue. I was home free.

I assessed my situation and went to town on my improvised solution. I had a dead guy that needed processing so that's what I did. I processed him.

I remember thinking as I hoisted this giant up onto my table that I should really stick to smaller guys from now on. This guy was at least 2 inches taller than I was and maybe a couple of pounds heavier, and I'm no shrimp.

But I got his dead carcass up on that table and I figured that since I went through all this trouble and made all this mess that I would have to clean up, I got my game processing kit out which contained a butcher knife for the hefty meat, a fillet knife for smaller works, a skinner which might come in handy for scalping the skull, and a serrated saw for the bones. A pair of scissors there was also and a cutting board. I had the cleaver there from another order I had placed.

I decided the best course would be to go from the feet up. First things first, I pulled out his wallet and keys and placed them on my computer table. Then I used the scissors to cut his pants apart and pull them away. I had my 45 gallon steel drum host to a contractor grade hefty bag where I was putting all the items. I cut the shirt off too but left the underwear. I don't need to see my kills dead junk hanging out while I'm trying to work.

I poked and prodded the joints to find the path of least resistance. I began cutting the legs off at the knees, all in one piece. I didn't even bother to take his shoes or socks off. The knife went through flesh like it was nothing. I was surprised at how utterly non resilient human tissue can be. Even the tendons and ligaments separated cleanly.

There was almost no blood. Not surprising since the grand majority of it was pooled on the floor, thankfully soaked up primarily by Jims jacket which had come off during our struggle.

I put the severed leg in the trash and moved on to the thigh which was essentially the same routine, only thicker, more fatty. I noticed that it wasn't nearly as horrendous as the media made it look on TV or in movies. Dismembering a human body was a relatively unexciting event. But I had my ways of making it more fun. I sang to myself as I worked, talked to myself, reflected on the new tools I would get to make the next one easier.

I took the arms off at the elbow joint and used the scissors to cut off fingertips for added confusion in identifying the body. This man was very common with no special internal additions to speak of.

Severing the head was also a simple matter and going through the vertebrae in the back of the neck didn't take much at all by going through connective tissue.

The torso was surprisingly heavy all by itself and I cut that in two across the diaphragm. Human intestines just look like one long roll of uncooked sausage as opposed to the gruesome millage of stringy nastiness they appear to be on film. I was surprised. Funny sounds and pressure releases took place on my table as the torso sank.

Once the body was in bags, I started my cleanup process. I took down the plastic walls from my bubble which surprisingly had almost no spatter on them. Then I started to roll the plastic on the table up and to my chagrin, noticed it had very little effect in keeping the blood off the tables steel surface. I soldiered on, cleaning up all of the plastic. I tore my green cloth backdrop down and placed it over the larger blood pools on the floor after I picked up the soaked coat and trashed it.

The green backdrops went into the trash next and then I began my stain removal process. I had two bottles of pure ammonia that I dabbed into paper towels to wipe away small stains. The spatter was every-where. There were dozens of small spots on the floor and tiny streaks on the walls and big door. I wiped them all away. The great thing about ammonia is that even if the stain won't completely wipe away, it destroys the sample so that no DNA can be processed. It also eats fingerprints like acid. It's only downside is the fumes, which I didn't smell so much as feel like a cold winter breeze shooting its way through my sinuses.

I kept away from it and wore masks whenever possible. I wiped my table clean, scrubbed the areas on the floor that needed it, wiped my computer table down and noticed a few tiny spots had made it onto my laptop. I was not impressed but knew they would be easy to spot clean.

Next time, the whole room gets bubbled, not just the half for my kill room. I had used a plastic sheeting normally chosen to cover living room furniture when painting walls, but it obviously didn't suffice. This time I used a single layer of mid grade quality stuff. Next time I would double layer the high grade material for sure.

When I got finished I looked down in horror at the sheer level of blood staining my clothes from head to toe. I couldn't walk back into the house like this. I mean I had extra clothes in my car I could change into, that wasn't the point. But surely there would be a smell and I couldn't get all the blood off my face, not all of it.

My phone rang. The familiar buzzing of it's vibrate setting going off. The caller ID showed it was Tess calling. What could I do? I answered.

"Hi baby, what's up?"

Not much. Where are you?"

"I'm just leaving the gym hun."

"The gym closes at nine."

I checked my watch hurriedly, it showed 9:57 pm. My mind raced. I couldn't get caught in a lie. Not again.

"What are you talking about babe? It closes at ten."

"The big gym by our place?"

And there was my window. I had switched gyms when we moved to our new house so it sorted itself out as I jumped back in to play the game. "No, my old gym babe."

"I thought you cancelled that membership a month ago."

'I procrastinated…" as I do tend to do quite often. "and did it a few weeks ago but I still have a couple weeks this month that are paid for so I figured I'd take advantage since it takes an hour to cross town anyway."

My wife is not stupid. It takes a lot to convince her of an elaborate lie. When she caught me surfing internet dating sites, I spun this quick tale of how I was just research an article on online dating I got through a free lance website. Fortunately for me, I really was a member of the free lance site already and could prove that part.

The next part was much harder. She wanted proof upon proof. I had to manufacture an entire person which is a lot more hassle than it sounds. I created a fake employer, ran out to get a prepaid cell phone and then hired an actor to do a role play on the phone with me, on speaker so Tess could hear it. Then I had him leave a voicemail message as this person so that if she called the number it would sound legit.

I went through great lengths to bring my wife over to the comfortable belief I wasn't cheating on her, but me hiding anything was the problem. Even safely believing in my fidelity didn't matter next to the dishonesty of hiding the article from her in the first place. And so our trust issues flared up again. Now every conversation was an interrogation. Not just a simple question where she could take my answer at my word. There had to be back checking involved. So I waited for her response to my explanation and after a short breath…

"Ok, well listen on your way home can you pick up a case of ready made baby formula at Shoppers?"

"Will do. Anything else?" In my mind I begged for her not to ask me to get her a late night latte. That's all I needed was to walk into a Starbucks in mismatching attire, dried blood across my face and hands. That sort of thing people notice, even if they feel too awkward to ask questions.

'No, but I'll probably be in bed by the time you get home. I'm so tired." She said with a yawn. Finally a break. A dark silent home to come to where I can go straight into the basement, throw my coat, hoody, pants, shoes, socks and shirt straight into the laundry and shower any remnants off of me.

"Fantastic. I'll see you tomorrow then."

"Kay, bye."

I packed up my laptop bag and then opened the garage door, half expecting a team of police cruisers to be waiting outside, but the alley was empty and silent save for the Mazda parked in the driveway. I took the keys and got in. A fucking manual transmission. I had never learned how to drive them but necessity is the mother of invention after all. I probably stalled the damn thing a good ten times before enough trial and error got me to the point where I could manage to get the stupid thing inside the garage.

I laid a plastic sheet across the hatchback floor and put the body bags in the trunk. At least the car was clean and empty. After a quick search I found Jims cell phone, turned it off to avoid pings sent from the police to track it and made sure there was no GPS turned on either. I locked up the garage, went out to my car under cover of night and changed clothes, stuffing the blood soaked ones into my duffle bag. I changed shoes as well. Another glance at my watch gave me the realization the store would be closed by the time I got there and sure enough, by the time I reached the other side of town I was way too late to buy formula. It was the last of my worries.

I decided to wake up early and run out to the store to grab the formula before the baby woke up but I was so bagged from the events of the night before that I overslept and had to make up something to the warden about them being out of stock last night when I went which allowed me to make the trip Saturday morning.

I had a pretty normal Saturday. Watching the kid so Tess could get some personal stuff tended to, having a bit of a break from the constant supervision of a young infant, cute as she was.

Zoe had always been exceptionally adorable and it wasn't just us biased parents who thought so. Everyone at the hospital was of the same opinion and every time Tess ran errands, the ladies at the bank would swoon over Zoe like she was the second coming of Christ in a female package. She charmed everyone who met her. She softened the hardened selfish prick that was Tess' father, and won over several others who until meeting Zoe, had not been "kid people" at all. The final confirmation of that was when mother and daughter had gone to get her first professional pictures taken and even the people at the photo studio who dealt with children all day every day noted how exceptionally happy and easy going she was.

Zoe was born mellow. When other kids are throwing tantrums in public she stares at them with a questioning as to what the hell could be wrong with them. She loves going places and was very early to alertness. When other babies were dough eyed or utterly confused, she was looking around, tracking everything and looking at people directly with curiosity.

She's a wonderful baby, an angel that we were spoiled to have with such an easy disposition. I really hope she doesn't end up like me. I watched an episode of Dexter where the flashback showed his father showing Dexter CAT scans of a human brain. He identified the differences between a serial killers brain and a normal persons brain.

Up until I saw that I was convinced that what I was, was my own decision, my own path but now I truly wondered if I had little choice at all, and if genetics play a bigger role than I thought.

Logically then it should have occurred to me that those traits have a possibility of being passed to my offspring. I do have hope for Zoe though. My parents are certainly not like me so there's no guarantee on generational transition, and she is also half Tess and I've never seen such empathy, moral code or ethical sturdiness as I have in her.

Quite the odd couple Tess and I. On a couple of occasions we even discussed my apparent total lack of empathy and it troubled her greatly. She asked me a long series of probing and somewhat leading questions to see if I would give her the answer she desired but I never did.

"When you see news stories of people going through tremendous grief or strife, do you feel bad for them?"

"No.'

'Do you ever think about what it would be like if that were your family in that situation?"

"It's never crossed my mind." was my answer and it continued like this until Tess was satisfied her husband couldn't feel much of anything at all I imagine. I did calm her fears though by at least reassuring her that I did care very much about her and Zoe and that neither of them would ever feel unloved.

I do love my daughter very much. She brings me great joy, and I love playing games with her. If anyone ever threatened her happy innocent existence in any way I would kill them, cut the body up and make it disappear. Most people say that about their children, only I actually mean it literally.

Sunday was all set up for more family merriment, much like the Saturday before it. I began to get itchy though and wanted to move on to the next part of my overall plan for Jim. I woke up at the crack of dawn, 5:00 am and left the house. Neither of the ladies would be up for another three hours and I had a person to erase.

I drove across town to the South side, not for the kill room this time, but for the home of my victim. I found his place without pause, parked in front of the building, careful to examine surroundings and make sure that there was no video surveillance. It was still early morning and comings and goings were common in the area.

I wore my hoody to cover my head and face, and my gloves to leave prints out of the situation entirely. My shoes had just come out of the dryer and were spotless. They would leave no imprints anywhere inside the apartment. I used his keys to enter the building, cautiously watching for video surveillance and strolled down the hallway until I found the door I needed.

I paused for a moment, better not to take chances. I knocked first, just in case for whatever reason, there was someone inside. There wasn't and slowly I entered the place closing and locking the door behind me. A simple one bedroom apartment. Somewhat clean save for a few dishes left out. It represented a single man perfectly. Motor cycle gear, a big screen TV, a computer desk, a nice barbecue and some online gaming machinery.

I found cash on the dresser which quickly found its way into my wallet. I searched drawers and shelves for anything else of interest, putting everything back as it was. Then I sat down at the computer desk. I wasn't sure what I would find. I was hoping some basic searches would yield passwords or something but Jim had done me one better. He left himself signed in to everything. Messenger, outlook express, his online dating profile and his facebook all had the passwords auto saved.

I couldn't have had an easier time. I changed the auto response on his email to say he had decided to run away with the woman he hooked up with on Friday to go on a two month vacation to the Caribbean. I changed the status on his facebook account to reflect the change and then I proceeded to delete his online dating profile. Judging by his email content it seemed he was on several sites at once so that trail would go cold real quickly.

My phone rang. It was Tess again asking where I was. I said I had gone to my parents to pick up a few tools for working on the downstairs bathroom and that I would be back in an hour. Conversation over. I had an after thought. What if the police ever did track this back to me and checked my cell phone records? They would see the towers my phone picked its signal up from and notice I was in the area. If the garage I rented wasn't already a few streets away that might be a problem.

I packed Jims laptop up and took it with me. I also took his multifunction printer and threw it into a dumpster because the email I sent him with directions to my kill room had been printed on it and it wouldn't do to have that be recoverable by the police. But I did find something in the printer that would help. A letter to his insurance company with a clear unmarked signature on white background.

It was one last gift from the dead. I could easily use that to forge a bill of sale for the car. If the authorities ever questioned me about it I could corroborate my own story. "Yeah officer it was the strangest thing. This guy approaches me on the street and tells me he met this phenomenal woman, a real sugar mamma who is going to take care of him and that he doesn't need his car anymore. So he asks me how much I have on me and when I tell him I've only got twenty three bucks, he says 'Ok deal' and I end up with a free car."

Armed with my new toys and info I headed home. My next problem was what to do with the body. I mean it's not like I had an ocean to dump it in, or a boat for that matter. What did that leave? When you live in a land locked city what are your options for making two hundred and thirty pounds of dead human go away?

Incineration. I had looked into buying an actual batch incinerator. Something with the pressure and heat needed to get the job done. The problem with those are that they cost upwards of five thousand dollars to acquire and I wouldn't be in a position to make that purchase for another month or two. I had a jerry can of gasoline in my trunk and a steel drum though. Close enough.

Monday morning and I had some free time to myself, at least until about 4:30 in the afternoon when the wife expected me to be back home. To keep the illusion of my day job up, I would leave earlier on Mondays to pretend I had to be in a Monday morning meeting.

I went straight to my kill room. I lined my trunk with plastic sheeting and stuffed the body bags in. I laid the drum across the back seat and stuffed my garbage bags into it to save space and extra trips. I took everything to my parents house. They were gone during the day and had a nice fenced back yard for privacy.

My arms were very sore. Maybe the athletic event leading into the weekend had been quite jarring but I was experiencing shooting pain that was clearly the result of pinched nerves in my back. I didn't have the time or money to see a chiropractor but I would use the massage chair I gave my wife for Christmas one year several times later that night.

In the meantime though, everything was a chore. Lifting the barrel, lifting the bags out of the trunk; they were all accompanied by soreness and agitation. At some points my arms would recoil sharply in exhaustion from pushing them no further than what felt like an average hoisting.

I doused the first bag which contained the torso pieces in gasoline after dropping it into the barrel. I lit a match and tossed it in. The instant whoosh of flames consuming flammable liquid exploded from the top and the burn began. I had placed the barrel squarely in the center of the yard. It was broad daylight but everything was sealed in bags so no one could see anything, especially not the burning process.

I've heard that there is no smell like that of a burning fleshy person. If I had a sense of smell I may have taken note but I lack that particular member of the five sense group so you won't get any dramatic descriptions from me.

I imagine it smells like barbecue steak mixed with singed hair. When you cut up a person you realize we are really no different than animals. We're just sacks of meat at the end of the day. The internal muscles and tissues of the human body look a whole lot like steak actually. In fact, if properly trimmed and packaged, I believe most people would have a hard time telling them apart.

Maybe they taste different but I never felt the compulsion to cross that line. I could see the curiosity that Dahmer had and I understand the mentality behind why he did it, I just don't think that way and I'm not about to eat any meat that's been dead and sitting out for days, regardless of the source. It tends to change how one views a sirloin when it comes to the table though.

I checked on my burning waste and added more gas. Not straight out of the jerry can of course, I'm not up for any Darwin awards. I poured some into a coffee cup and dumped accordingly. I repeated that three times when I realized it wasn't doing anything. The pain in my arms became merely the start of my problems. My biggest issue now was the complete lack of effectiveness this method of disposal had.

As if that weren't bad enough I heard sirens. Now in my kill rooms neighborhood sirens are customary and you know it's time to worry when you don't hear them on a nightly basis. But in this nice sweet little schoolyard area, sirens mean something significant. Someone spotted the smoke and called the fire department. I now had two very big reasons to put the fire out.

I doused the fire in water extinguishing it immediately. The smoke dissipated and almost as if the fire crew knew exactly what was happening, the sirens stopped. It could have been a massive coincidence but I heavily doubted it. All I knew was that having the fire crew pull up to the house and start poking around was not an option. Granted a charred and cut up torso looks somewhat similar to a couple pieces of big beef but any closer inspection would expose me and that wouldn't do.

When the smoke cleared I found that the bag had melted and some of the edges were charred but for the most part, the body was still in tact, some of the skin hadn't even been cooked. I knew there was no way the organs were affected. It would take a week to burn the waste unrecognizable at this pace and use more gas than I could afford. So I re-bagged everything, loaded it back into the car and took it back to the kill room.

Realizing that incineration was out completely I had to change strategies. I decided to cut the body into smaller pieces and dump it in the river that ran straight through middle of the city creating an impromptu border between the North and South sides of town. I didn't have time for that the same afternoon, it would have to wait a day or two.

After the days activities were complete I headed home a little earlier. I played with Zoe, watching her while Tess took a shower and relaxed. I fed the child dinner, gave her a bath and then it would be time for her to go to sleep. Zoe slept straight through the night only a week after she was born. The kid loves sleeping and by seven months on the planet she was out for twelve straight hours every night starting at 7:30 pm. Like I said, lucky.

As Tess settled in on the living room couch to watch her evening programs I jumped on the computer. Laci was online and I began chatting with her. At first it was cordial, loosely discussing plans to get together again. I was looking forward to having her again and I know she felt the same way. We were both getting impatient and it was showing in our conversations.

Neither one of us had experienced sex nearly as good as each others in the eight years we had been apart. Her relationships were with pathetic losers who preferred playing online games over actual human affection and when they did get in the mood, they lasted for only a couple minutes at a time. I never understood how a guy can cum so easily with so little self control lasting less than ten minutes in a session. I always loved taking my time and Laci felt the same way.

My first marriage was heated all the way through but this meant the fighting was just as intense as the love making and it became too much to handle. Besides I got married for all the wrong reasons the first time, getting into a relationship just because I thought I was ready. I was very young, only twenty one at the time and too stupid to realize the truth. My wife was less attractive than me, and a little overweight but cute.

At any rate it didn't last. The second best sexual experience I ever had was with a Laotian girl I was essentially using for my rebound, but of course she didn't see it that way. She was under the impression we were a long term thing and we might have been if I wasn't so screwed up. She could hold her own in the marathons and would actually say (almost out of breath) after we were done "How can anyone go for three hours straight?"

So when Laci popped up on the instant messenger inviting me to her place for a late night rendezvous I did everything in my power to make it happen. I knew I would need to wait until Tess was in bed so I could safely sneak out. I could easily spend the night at Laci's house since I could pass off not being there in the morning as getting an early start.

But even though Tess was tired and wanting to go to bed early, it just didn't happen. She stayed up, delaying my departure and I knew there was a solid hour and a half drive time to get to Laci's. As Tess was going to bed I took my computer bag into the living room telling her I was going to stay up and write for awhile. She accepted that with no reserve and went to bed.

In two minutes I was out the door. I jumped into the car and headed out to Laci's as fast as I could. Too fast in fact. I was pulled over for speeding on the freeway. I did another round of top notch acting pretending to give a shit about breaking the posting limit and begged for him to go easy on me. He gave me a ticket anyway but at least it was less than half the price it could have been and I also appreciated how quick he was about it. I was back on the road in five minutes flat.

I remember thinking how hilarious and dramatically ironic it was that the cop had pulled over a cold blooded murderer who had a dismembered body in his rented garage not too far away and had no clue what was going on. He just did his duty and took off. Now every time I pass a police car on the road I chuckle to myself.

I got to Laci's without further incident. She let me inside dressed in her pajamas and no sooner had I dropped my bag on the floor than we were making out intensely. We moved to her bedroom and shut the door to keep her dogs out. We kissed passionately in juicy anticipation of what was coming next. She lay on her bed and opened the pajamas to reveal a sexy set of white lingerie style underwear. The bottoms were a thong which always gets me insanely turned on.

Laci looked better than I had ever remembered her. A decade ago at the tender age of twenty four she was gorgeous but still not as fine as she looked this very night in question. She had been hitting the gym, gone tanning to prepare for her vacation and had taken up the hobby of belly dancing. I have never been a fan of scrawny girls. In my opinion if you can see ribs poking through the skin the woman needs a hefty helping of cheeseburgers very badly. Laci was beautiful, sensual with curves in all the right places. Now she was the ideal textbook form of what a woman should look like with the added skill of how to rotate her hips in ways most women only dream they could.

Her large deep green eyes stared seductively into mine and I couldn't resist her even if I tried, not that I would want to try. Being with her took on the pace of quickly catching up to how we used to be.

Laci and I explored each other for a good two hours that night trying several positions, all of them making both of us crazy. I was free to suck on various parts of her body and go down on her for as long as she could take it before needing me inside her again. The way she felt, the way she tasted, all so familiar and so amazing to have again. She came to orgasm four times before I let myself get to the same place and when we were done there was no describing the contentment we experienced.

I laid there next to her gently stroking her hair and back. I examined the tattoo on her left shoulder blade, the one I had designed for her in college. It was a celtic knot style cross with vines intertwined within it; a beautiful piece, inked by a real master. Her second;

placed on the back of her neck acquired at the same location, was done by someone clearly less experienced since its lines were not perfect and the shading slightly out of balance. It still looked good from a few feet away but this close up it didn't compete with the first.

She remembered mine too. The one on my left shoulder I had gotten while dating her all those years ago. It had since been retouched and I was physically much bigger from filling out as an adult and frequent trips to the gym. Maybe it was me being of a larger stature than my thin teenage self of the past, but she seemed smaller this time. My other two tattoos were more recent and new additions to her.

Some of our past together was as clear as day to Laci. Other elements were lost to her. She had gone on a vacation to a third world tropical country and brought back with her a virus that attacked her brain. She had been ill for two years as a result and it could have ended much worse with some sort of organic brain dementia or even death coming for her. She escaped with her health and her faculties, as well as this smoking hot new body.

I fell asleep next to her and when I awoke in the morning, she had to be at work in the city, whereas I had nowhere to be. So I slept in, she left me a spare key and when I was ready I got ready to leave. Her dogs woke up to greet me. They are small annoying little things that she treats as if they were human children, which I never understood but could easily respect since for years they were the only constant source of unconditional love and acceptance in her world.

In my opinion, a dog is something roughly the size of a German shepherd that you can actually wrestle with and take on walks without fear that a bird of prey will snatch it up like a squirrel and run it off to feed it to its young, but that's just me. These two uppity things would bark at any average Joe walking down the street and I couldn't wait to get out of there.

Laci had left the TV on so I turned it off, thinking that it would obviously be a tremendous waste of energy since I highly doubted a dog could get anything out of watching The View. I packed up my things, and left her spare key under a statue on her front porch before I took off for the day. I had work to do.

---

break.

It was time to assess the situation again. I had a hatchback with body parts in the trunk locked inside a garage I still had to sweep clean. I had waste to dispose of and tracks to erase. I had no idea who this guy had talked to in the interim periods between his first arrival at my lair and his last, so for all I knew some friend of his out there could even have the exact address or at the very least detailed descriptions of how to get there.

If I ever figured out a safe, quick way of rendering my victims unconscious at another location without witnesses or forensic evidence left behind, I would do that. But for now this system was fine as long as I stuck to strict adherence of the plan. I headed straight for my kill room to deal with my mess.

First things first, I grabbed breakfast from a Dennys that was just up the street from my sanctuary. My moons-over-my-hammy was especially delicious and I just had to stop by a 7-11 to pick up a chocolate milk and a large French vanilla latte. This meal would keep me satisfied for at least a couple hours. I made sure to pick up some snacks for the day as well.

When I arrived on the street of my kill room I approached cautiously, as always just in case. As each time prior there was no fanfare of police and ambulance gathered around the front or the back. No one had accidentally found anything and called it in. No weird smells were emitting from the place and very well shouldn't be considering everything was sealed and still fresh.

I got inside and prepped for what my day would be like. The nights rest had numbed the great majority of my nerve pain and I felt fine to continue. I began by taking the bags out of the Mazda and placing them on the floor next to my butcher table. I double sheeted the table this time, placed my processing kit, my cleaver and the galvanized pipe at one end, my ammonia cleaning supplies and paper towels on the other. I placed plastic sheeting around the table on the floor as well and moved the steel drum over within leaning distance with a brand new empty hefty bag in it to catch the waste.

The next step was to prep myself. I wouldn't allow any blood and guts to get on me today. I used some of my plastic sheeting and duct tape to fashion a makeshift apron for myself. I picked up new much higher grade plastic abrasive cleaner resistant gloves and then duct taped two grocery bags around my shoes to keep them clean also. I wore a basic white painters mask to keep fumes away from me and take some of the edge off the ammonia smell.

I picked up the first bag and set it on the table. I put my cutting board on the table, to prevent my knives from accidentally puncturing or tearing holes in my plastic sheeting which I suspected may have played a role in drenching my table surface last time. I had previously closed the bags by twisting the ends and wrapping the tightest part with duct tape so this time I just cut them open with the short knife.

I took out one of the arms. It was stiff and cold, rigor mortis having set in by now. It was also quite brisk outside today since it was fall heading into winter. I was grateful for the temperature though since my outfit was warm and I would be doing quite a bit of physical activity today.

I chose the butcher knife to start out with and simply shaved the meat from the bone in a downward motion. I didn't bother getting every single shred, since I knew that once dumped in the river, it would rot off in a timely fashion anyway. When it was cleared, each slab looked like a cutlet sitting on the table.

I put each chunk on the cutting board and used the fillet knife to slice them into even smaller pieces. When I was satisfied with my medallion sized portions, I tossed them into the garbage bag. Very little mess was made at first.

I repeated the process with the legs, thighs and upper arms. Routinely shaving the meat off them, placing the bones in a pile and filleting the meat into small pieces before tossing them into the bag. When the bag got somewhat heavy to lift easily, I closed it off in the same fashion as the originals and got a new one.

Once in a while I would take a break, check my email, answer a few phone calls, check the status of my ebay page and have a bag of chips. I got a message from Laci on Facebook commenting on how hot the night was and how she was looking forward to the next time. I fantasized about the night before and how Laci had been a total porn star in the sack. I was incredibly lucky. When I realized two hours had passed I decided to get the rest of the waste dealt with as soon as possible so I could take as much of the afternoon off as possible.

Every couple of body parts, I would need to clean and sharpen my knives since they were doing a lot of work going through so much material. I decided to do the head next. I sliced the face off in several different pieces, cut the ears and lips up so that again, they couldn't be visually identified. This way if someone did see it floating in a river, they would think nothing of it anyway.

Once the flesh was removed, I used the pipe to knock out the teeth, eliminating dental records as a form of ID. I broke the jaw after that and used the scissors to cut the ligaments, ripping the jaw clean from the head in it's multiple pieces held together only by the tissue at this point. I used the knife to destroy the eyes as well and then rammed the pipe into the side of the skull to bust it open. At this point it was fueled only by a curiosity to see the human brain live and in person since I had never seen it before.

I realized I was spending too much time on the head and tossed it into a new hefty bag to move on. Next came the two heavy torso pieces. My arm pain flared up hoisting them to the table and then subsided by simply mentally pushing it out of the way. I began with the lower portion. I removed the intestines first, carved out the reproductive organs and anything else taking up space. Then I shaved the meat off the hip bones for as much would come off.

Removing the skin and flesh in the back was easy. These were the chunks I tried to burn the first time around so the skin was charred in some places making it more stiff in some places and easy to cut. I hacked off the ass cheeks and marveled at how fatty they were for such a slim person. I immediately thought of the movie Alive and how well the rugby team must have feasted on this part of the human body while trapped in the Andes. But the freezer burn from the bodies being in the snow and frozen solid might have ruined the experience. Well that and the trauma of realizing you're eating a dead person but that never entered my thinking at all. Meat is meat after all. It all tastes like beef or chicken.

Once that was processed, I moved on to my final piece, the upper torso. I started with shaving the outside, taking all of the skin, muscle and fat in single passes, like I was carving a turkey. In fact once everything else had been removed, I was surprised at how closely the chest cavity resembles the overall shape of a turkey.

This was the messy portion. All of the blood that hadn't come out was inside this piece, trapped in the lungs, still close to the heart. It dumped out onto the table, not quite enough to overflow to the floor or anything but messy nonetheless. I used a knife to cut all the tissue around the inside edge of the rib cage in order to free any remaining organs. The lungs, the heart and the liver all came out. I cut those up too before trashing them.

It reminded me of emptying a pumpkin for Halloween. Somehow every single event in life would have a whole new level of perspective to it. Carving a pumpkin and spilling its guts would now carry a double meaning. So would slicing up a steak, carving a Thanksgiving turkey or laying plastic down to prepare for painting the family room.

This experience changed my sense of place in the world forever. I felt stronger, somehow above other people. I felt like the proud owner of a very dark secret that no one would ever be in on. Things that I said to people would carry double entendres like they hadn't before. "Oh honey work was murder today." would be more literal than Tess would ever know.

When the body was dealt with I used paper towels to soak up much of the blood spill on the table so it wouldn't flow onto unprotected floor in the clean up process. My makeshift outfit went into a separate trash bag, one designated for secondary waste, not body parts. All table plastic and surrounding plastic got rolled up and tossed accordingly. At first it appeared my double sheeting on the table did its job but upon final reveal, it turned out I needed to scrub with the stain remover again. High grade stuff next time, for sure

I felt good about this. My plan now involved simply waiting for dark to come so I could visit a bridge. I opened the garage door, satisfied that nothing conspicuous was showing to the outside and unlocked my car, which I had parked closer to the back door this time for easy transfer. I laid new plastic in my car trunk and placed the new bags in one at a time. I closed up shop and headed for home.

It's an interesting feeling, driving around town with what used to be a human body bagged up in your trunk. No one has any idea they are stopped at a light right next to a serial killer with what could very well be one of their friends now sacks of meat parts in a hidden compartment. It made me wonder, in all my ten years of driving around, had I ever unknowingly passed a vehicle or sat parked at a red light next to someone just like I would be one day? It blew my mind.

I stuck to the posted speed limits, signaled when I changed lanes and didn't push any yellow lights whatsoever. I'm convinced that car insurance companies would get exceedingly rich from not paying claims and hospital traffic would slow to a crawl on major holidays if everyone drove as if they had a dead man in their trunk and a mortal fear of going to jail for twenty to life in the event they ever got pulled over and a police man decided to check their cars contents.

I got home without incident and went through my evening routine with ease. I hopped on the instant messenger to find Laci online. Only this conversation was not a happy one at all, it had taken a terrible turn for the worse. She was horribly depressed from reflecting on her past relationship situations and behaving erratically. She said she couldn't continue to see me because she was messed up and didn't want to put that on me, even though I expressly said to her that her and I could take things at whatever pace she felt comfortable with.

But it was more than that. Laci had discovered her ex husband met the clinical definition of a sociopath. The epiphany didn't come from consulting a psychiatrist, it came from finding a detailed article on the internet that outlined what male sociopaths do to the women they shack up with. In it she found all of his most redeeming qualities. Chronic pathological lying, using and abusing his partner, scamming everyone around him, treating other people with a total lack of respect or regard for their well being. What really pushed her over the edge was reading all the traits of women who usually fall for people like this and brought the problem onto herself. She was certain there were several things terribly wrong with her and tonight that had spiraled into contemplating suicide.

I was completely taken by surprise and had no idea what to do. This wasn't her usual bummed out attitude when reflecting on the years wasted with the idiots who couldn't appreciate her: both her ex husband and the boyfriend she had shortly after whom she had recently dumped for neglecting her and mistreating her much the same way. This was different. She was repeating back to me something I had said about how those who threaten suicide usually don't mean it unless they have a specific plan laid out.

That's when I panicked. She talked about pills, wondering what four would do and I remember thinking it depended entirely on what the pill was, the difference between sickness and death. I couldn't take chances. I begged her not to do it and used every phrase to dissuade her, until the words "too late" popped onto my screen.

I did the only thing I could think of that was left. I picked up my phone and dialed 911.

"911 emergency."

"Hi, I've just been chatting online to a friend who has threatened suicide."

"Ok what's your name sir?"

"Darren Ascot." It was obviously not my real name but that was irrelevant.

"And your friends name?"

'Laci Barret."

"And where are you sir?"

"I'm in Bloomington heights."

"And where is she?"

"She lives in Whetstone."

'How long have you known her?"

"Ten years.'

'Did she say why she's doing this or how?"

"She didn't specify why." which was true. She didn't say and my guesses were still only assumptions. "She talked about pills."

"Do you have her address?" I answered with the exact numbered address of where she lived. "Ok we're sending people out right now."

"Thank you." Just in case Laci was still awake I got back on the instant messenger and typed in 'I just called 911 .' She responded shocked and appalled. She said I was being ridiculous and I asked her what else she could possibly expect me to do under the circumstances. The next message was hilarious.

'You are adding to my stress level' to which I could only reply…

'YOUR stress level?' She was emotional and crashing and it was completely understandable. Her ex husband fit the sociopath profile draining her of all her self esteem, leaving her wondering if she was an alien or something. To follow it up her most recent boyfriend was in his early thirties still living at home with his mother and had abused and neglected her in the same way, blowing her off throughout their entire relationship and regularly cheating on her.

But that wasn't enough for this clown. When she finally mustered the courage to dump him once and for all, he had the sickening gall to prey on her compassionate nature by sending her countless messages begging to get her back. He didn't do it because he genuinely cared about her needs or health, only to control and manipulate her using her bleeding heart to her own detriment.

Laci showed me his messages and they instantly reminded me of a four year old throwing a temper tantrum to get what he wants from parents who haven't established clear rules and consequences. Everything was 'I need, I want, you need to give me' rather than any of it being about her. With my consolation and step by step coaching and translation of his true meaning and intentions, I helped her decode his bullshit.

While she was with him her sleep patterns were horribly disrupted. She woke up at all times during the night in cold sweats, had to wear mouth guards to stop her teeth from being worn away by grinding and she was on anti depressants which weren't even appropriate for her bodies chemistry. This guy did a real number on her and he was ever so close to being next on my short list.

Getting his personal information from her had been exceedingly easy. I would email her questions like 'what's his street address?', 'What's his full name?' and 'What's his email address?' I expected a tiny amount of screening from her like asking me why I wanted to know but all I got was direct answers, almost like she was encouraging me. I doubt the information would have been so readily available if she knew the intimate details of my new hobby.

I don't copy cat the style of Dexter Morgan. I don't have steady access to high power tranquilizers or the free time to stalk someone to get to know their routine well enough. I also don't keep souvenirs or trophies so I don't own a rosewood box with blood slides or anything quaint like that. My butchering tools are also more hands on rather than going powered since high speed spinning devices tend to make more spatter mess and I'd like to avoid a total blood bath if I can.

Laci sent me an email the next morning apologizing for the hurtful things she said to me when I had called the response units. She regaled me with her tales of how the night went, the psych pro they sent and the adventures of being poked prodded, examined and so forth. I was just glad to hear she still had a pulse. I told her she could repay me for saving her life by never doing that ever again.

Laci has people in her life besides me who love her and depend on her. Even those two runt mutts would lose their spoiled lifestyle with her gone. I just couldn't stand the thought that a pig like Evan would be the reason she took her own life. He was so much lower than scum on the food chain that it would be nothing short of tragic to pay him any kind of compliment by making him think he was that important or had that much impact on anyone's life. And he was messed up enough to take it as a compliment too.

The night had taken a lot out of me so far and I just wasn't up to dumping a body out in the middle of nowhere. I was blasted so I decided to hit the sack and get up early to do it in the morning. It was halfway through fall anyway and it would stay dark until 8:00 am. If I got up at five, I'd have more than enough time to get the job done.

My alarm clock woke me up gently to the soft sounds of the easy rock station. That beeping noise all alarm clocks have drives aggravation and annoyance into my bone marrow when I hear it. Even when they use it in commercials I want to throw a brick at my television and that's just no way to start the day. Maybe Rod Stewart and a couple of DJ's who are mistaken about how funny they are isn't much better but it's a lot easier on the brain pan.

I geared up, got everything I needed to get going including a simple steak knife to cut the bags open quickly and silently moved through the house and out the door. It's moments like that that made me glad I had done little home improvement tasks like spraying WD40 in the hinges to eliminate the creaking. I got into my car and took off. There were two bridges over the same river I knew how to get to off the top of my head that would make suitable locations for the dump.

I got to the freeway bridge at the stroke of five thirty. It was still pitch black with no sun in sight. Right away I knew I couldn't do this from the bridge itself. There wasn't enough shoulder to stop without turning on my hazard lights and that would have attracted a cop car like a moth to a flame. There just wasn't anywhere to hide.

Coming off the bridge though there was a path marked by a sign that showed me a potential boat dock. Although it was a lie with no boat dock visible, it could get me to the water. Upon closer inspection of the area though I realized it just wasn't suitable. The only way to get to the waters edge was by traversing a very steep slope covered in loose rocks and I would have bet money that lugging heavy hefty bags down it would have me slipping to serious injury without fail.

I also wasn't comfortable with the layout under the bridge. It was too dark to tell but there boxes everywhere that I couldn't identify and if I wasn't sure it wasn't a surveillance camera, I didn't want to take the chance. I left the same way I came in and moved on to my next choice.

This one was more rural, further out of town between two farming communities and would have been ideal except that by the time I got there my timing was no longer optimal. The early birds had come out to play and the commuters were getting an early start to beat the morning rush hour traffic. I was pooched, having chosen sleep over peak timing and had to consider waiting yet again to get rid of this thing. I decided to head back to my parents place and recoup.

On the forty five minute drive I tried to search for a solution. I asked myself If burning wouldn't work and bridge drop was out, what other way could I dump these parts in a safe unseen way? Once again necessity is the mother of invention and my need to get rid of this evidence brought the solution to me like a child showing a parent their latest pencil crayon drawing.

The sewer. Of course, how obvious. No one ever goes down there. The body would rot away completely before anyone ever discovered the bones and by then it would be way too late to identify the person.

Once again everything got lighter. I grabbed breakfast at a coffee donut place and ate it in the car on the way to my destination. A banana nut muffin, a double chocolate donut and a café mocha. I love caffeinated beverages but I can't stand the taste of black coffee so as long as it can be dressed up not to taste like coffee, I'm all about it.

I chose the Eastern suburb of the city to dump my waste. It would be practically a ghost town with most of its residents either having commuted to work in the city or otherwise occupied and away from their homes. The housing in this part of my world was also older, done back in the sixties and seventies when neighborhoods were not so congested so there were back alleys to be had. Newer neighborhoods have the homes grouped so close together with attached garages facing the street that alleys don't exist in the new city plans anymore.

Within a few moments I found exactly what I was looking for; a manhole cover placed off to the side behind a power pole. I parked in an empty driveway and popped the trunk. Although it was broad daylight I wasn't worried. No one appeared to be around and I was checking throughout the entire process. Lifting the cover was a piece of cake and my arms gave me no complaint, the pain gone finally. I removed the hefty bags one at a time from the trunk and walked them over the three paces it took to reach the sewer.

With each bag I sliced the tops off and turned them upside down letting the pieces fall into the sewer hearing the splashing sounds as they touched down. I crumpled the bags up, put them back in the trunk and then closed it. I got back in the car, fired her up and took off. My total time there could not have been longer than three minutes max.

I drove back to the kill room to finish destroying evidence. Once there, I packed my trunk remnants into a garbage bag and put everything else in there that needed to burn. Documents from Jims car, receipts, even my empty chip bags. I had five full hefty bags full of garbage that actually would burn, this I knew for a fact. Plastic sheeting, cloth back-drops and paper towels. It may not have been good for the environment but one less person creating pollution for whatever forty some odd more years he would have walked the Earth more than evens that out.

It was funny. This time I burned garbage for a solid three hours making sure nothing was left and did not hear a single siren in a neighborhood where sirens are as common as the sound of a bus stopping and going again. I suppose if my shit hole of an unheated rented detached garage goes up in smoke, no one gives a rats ass, and I was sure there had to be the areas fair share of unemployed people or passersby to call it in if they really wanted to.

To be fair though, plastic burns a lot more colorless than attempted flesh and the smoke was barely visible. The only irritant I had to contend with were the garbage trucks making their rounds up and down the alleys. Every time they would come past I'd have to lid my drum, snuff out my fire, drag it back into the garage and close the door to avoid unwanted attention and then drag it back out and start the process over again.

I used the gas from my jerry can again, soaked all the garbage

---

The available text of Mark Twitchell's "SK Confessions" ends there, mid-sentence.

TRUE CRIME CASE HISTORIES

VOLUME 3

TRUE CRIME
CASE HISTORIES

12 Disturbing True Crime Stories
JASON NEAL

INTRODUCTION

As with the two prior volumes of True Crime Case Histories, I want to
start with a quick word of warning. Most news articles and television
true crime shows skim over the sticky details of truly gruesome crimes.
I don't gloss over the facts in my books, regardless of how horrible
they may be. I try to give my readers a clear and accurate description
of just how demented the killers really were. I do my best not to leave
anything out. The stories included in these books are not for the
squeamish.

I had read about some stories in this volume in the past, but it wasn't
until I thoroughly researched the cases, reading through court documents and searching old newspaper articles, that I fully realized how
disturbing they were.

I didn't intend to give this volume a theme, but it coincidentally turned
out that six murders in this book involved dismemberment. In five of
those murders, investigators never found some of the body parts.

There's the story of the psychopath that cut off the hands, feet, and
heads of his girlfriends and dumped them in the canals of London and
Rotterdam. Then, there's the drug kingpin that chopped off the head of
one of his dealers and carried it around in a Home Depot bucket.

Another drug dealer butchered an entire family so he could take over a man's fruit shipping business and transform it into a drug shipping business.

There's also the story of the young woman, jealous of her wealthy socialite friend, that poisoned her by lacing her coffee with cyanide.

That's just a small sample of the twelve stories included in this book. Also, I've included a bonus chapter from a previous volume of True Crime Case Histories at the end of this book.

In many cases, I like to include what happened after the sentencing. Most of the time, the killer is caught, locked up for life, and that's the end. However, sometimes there's more to the story – whether it be something that happened while they were in prison or additional murders they're suspected of. But I'm particularly amazed at how many killers are released early, despite their horrible crimes.

In one story in this volume, I write about a woman that shot her husband, froze his body, hacked him up with a jigsaw, and was caught dumping his torso in a trash dumpster. She was released fourteen years after her conviction and is now living in France.

Another story recounts the case of a young man who strangled his girlfriend and crammed her body into an eight-inch crawlspace beneath the stairs. After serving only eleven years in jail, he was released... only to strangle his next girlfriend.

If there's any common thread between these cases, it would be that many of them happened near places I've lived throughout my life.

Three stories took place in the London area, one of which happened just a five-minute walk from my home. Two other stories took place in Scottsdale, Arizona, where I've lived a large part of my life. Another took place in Maui, Hawaii, while I was living there, and finally, another took place in Oxford, UK, very close to where I've been working over the past year.

The stories in this volume are dark and disturbing, took place all over the world, and range from the 1940s to 2018.

The stories are a bit longer this time than in the previous volumes. As usual, I've added an online appendix with more photos, videos, and documents about the cases. Look for the link at the end of the book.

Lastly, please join my mailing list for discounts, updates, and a free book. You can sign up for that at

TrueCrimeCaseHistories.com

Additional photos, videos, and documents pertaining to the cases in this volume can be found on the accompanying web page:

https://TrueCrimeCaseHistories.com/vol3/

Thank you for reading. I sincerely hope you gain some insight from this volume of True Crime Case Histories.

- Jason

CHAPTER 1
THE COFFEE KILLER

The Billy Blue College of Design was nestled beneath the Harbor Bridge in Sydney, Australia. Sydney was a long way from Indonesia, which was perhaps why Mirna Salihin and Jessica Wongso became such close friends. They had both started their first year at the prestigious school for graphic design, and they had both come from Jakarta, Indonesia, specifically to attend the school.

The young girls were like two peas in a pod. Both came from wealthy Indonesian families, had a passion for graphic design, and were eager to start their careers. They were inseparable.

After graduation from college, however, Mirna took a job in Jakarta, where her family still lived, while Jessica stayed in Sydney. Jessica loved Sydney so much that her parents and two siblings also immigrated there in 2008.

As the years went by, Jessica and Mirna kept in touch. Both had secured well-paying jobs doing graphic design and had fallen in love with young men: Mirna with a young Indonesian man, and Jessica with a young Australian man. However, the men differed significantly from each other.

In 2014, when Mirna took a vacation back to Sydney, the two girls met to catch up. During their time together, Mirna and Jessica discussed their lives, work, and boyfriends. During the discussion of boyfriends, however, Mirna was surprised to learn that Jessica's boyfriend, Patrick O'Connor, was a bit of a bad boy. When the girls were friends at college, they were pretty conservative and had concentrated on their studies, but now Jessica was dating a young man with a completely different way of life. O'Connor was involved in drugs and alcohol, and his habits seemed to be rubbing off on Jessica.

Despite their solid friendship for many years, the two girls argued about Jessica's boyfriend. It was clear that Mirna disapproved of her dating a man that was such a bad influence on her and told her in no uncertain terms that she should get away from him. Mirna told her that this guy was messing up her future, and if she didn't change her path, it would change her life forever.

Jessica didn't take the advice well and told Mirna that she loved Patrick despite his faults and would stick with him. She became furious with Mirna to the point that Mirna was uncomfortable being alone with her. The rest of her Sydney trip became awkward, and Mirna ensured that there was always another friend with them whenever they went out.

Despite her initial objections, Jessica reluctantly took Mirna's advice and dumped her boyfriend. Still, Jessica secretly harbored deep resentment toward Mirna for suggesting that she leave the man she loved. Leaving him didn't stop her problems, though. They were only getting started.

After breaking up with Patrick, Jessica developed a drinking problem, and her attitude toward friends and co-workers began to change. Over the next two years, Jessica drank more and more until one night in August 2015 when, while driving drunk, she plowed her car over a curb, across a grassy area, and through the wall of a busy nursing home. Her vehicle landed within meters of the bedrooms of elderly residents. The fiasco landed her a DUI, a cracked rib, some time in jail, and an embarrassing video of her on the nightly news. Despite potentially killing residents of the nursing home, Jessica was angry rather than apologetic.

Throughout 2014 and 2015, Jessica attempted suicide five times. She was admitted to Royal Prince Alfred Hospital each time, and when she returned to work, she told her boss,

"Those bastards in the hospital didn't allow me to go home, and they treated me like a murderer. If I want to kill someone, I know exactly the right dose."

In October 2015, during one of her failed suicide attempts, Jessica tried to poison herself. Police found her unconscious, with a bottle of whiskey and three handwritten letters next to her bed. One letter blamed her ex-boyfriend, Patrick O'Connor, for her death. She addressed two other letters to her family and work friends, saying her goodbyes.

Jessica's anger and alcohol problems were affecting her work. She worked as a graphic designer at a firm called New South Wales Ambulance, but despite working there for less than a year, she developed deep-seated anger toward her boss, Kristie Carter. At one point, Jessica threatened Kristie because she wouldn't help Jessica find a place to stay after crashing her car into the nursing home, telling her, "You must die, and your mother must die." Kristie reported the threat to the local police.

Jessica regretted her breakup with Patrick and sent him countless text messages and voicemails. She threatened to hurt herself, him, and his friends if he didn't take her back. Patrick, however, wanted nothing to do with her. She was clearly unstable, and in December 2015, Australian police issued an urgent restraining order against her.

Back in Jakarta, Mirna was having the time of her life. Her picture-perfect life was that of a wealthy socialite: she had a well-paying job that she loved and was planning her dream wedding. But due to Jessica's continuing problems and their uncomfortable discussion, Mirna decided not to invite her to the wedding.

In her mind, Jessica already thought Mirna was to blame for her problems. Her downward spiral was all a result of Mirna's bad advice. As a result, her anger and resentment escalated when she wasn't invited to Mirna's wedding.

Mirna and Arief Soemarko had an island wedding in Bali in late 2015. The wedding ceremony was elaborate and straight out of a fairy tale. They had plans to honeymoon in Korea and wanted to start a family as soon as possible.

A few days after the wedding, Jessica continued her downward spiral and was fired from her graphic design job at New South Wales Ambulance. Now jobless, Jessica took some time to return to Jakarta and visit friends. She wanted to get together with Mirna, let her know that there were no hard feelings, and congratulate her on her wedding.

The two girls agreed to meet for coffee at 5:15 p.m. on January 6, 2016, but Mirna was apprehensive despite Jessica's assurance of good intentions. Mirna didn't want to visit with Jessica alone, so she asked their mutual friend, Hani, to accompany her. Hani had also attended Billy Blue College with them in Sydney.

Jessica arrived oddly early at Olivier, a trendy restaurant in the posh Grand Indonesia Shopping Mall in central Jakarta. Mirna thought it was unusual when Jessica texted her at 1 p.m., insisting she would pre-order the coffee for the three girls. Mirna assured her there was no need for that and that she would order when they arrived later that afternoon.

Jessica arrived at Olivier at 3:30 p.m., more than ninety minutes before Mirna and Hani were scheduled to arrive. She walked around the restaurant looking for the perfect table, then left the restaurant to do some shopping. She wanted to buy gifts for her friends, so she stopped at Bath & Body Works. Jessica purchased three small bottles of bath soap for the three of them and arrived back at Olivier at 4:14 p.m. with three large gift bags. The gift bags were unusually large for only having a single, small bottle of bath soap in them.

Security cameras showed Jessica walking around the entire restaurant, still looking for the perfect table and occasionally glancing directly at the cameras. After a few minutes of searching, she chose a half-circle booth on the side of the restaurant with large palm trees behind it. The palm trees behind the booth conveniently obscured the security camera behind them, leaving only a single security camera across the restaurant pointing directly at the table.

Jessica then placed the large gift bags on the table, waited a few moments, and then moved the bags toward the center of the table. Almost an hour before Mirna and Hani were due to arrive at the restaurant, Jessica ordered a Vietnamese iced coffee for Mirna and two additional coffee drinks for herself and Hani. When the drinks arrived at 4:24, Jessica was seen on the security camera doing something with the glasses, but the cameras didn't pick up the details because of the gift bags blocking the view.

The drinks then sat on the table for fifty-two minutes until Mirna and Hani arrived at 5:16. Within a few seconds of sitting down, Mirna took a big gulp of the Vietnamese iced coffee Jessica had ordered for her and immediately knew something was wrong. She began rapidly waving her arm in front of her mouth and told the girls something was wrong with the coffee. She pushed the glass away from her and continued frantically waving her hand. In less than sixty seconds, Mirna's head fell back against the top of the padded booth. Her eyes rolled back in her head, her body began to convulse violently, and she started foaming from her mouth.

Restaurant staff and other patrons of the restaurant started to gather around. Their first assumption was that Mirna had epilepsy and she was having a seizure. Hani, crying and panicking, called Mirna's husband. Jessica, however, showed no signs of stress at all.

Mirna was unresponsive, and emergency medical workers carried her out of the restaurant in a wheelchair, rushing her to the hospital. She died shortly afterward.

Jessica was the first person to make accusations. When people started gathering around at the restaurant, Jessica immediately said to the restaurant manager, Devi Siagian, "What did you put inside the drinks?!" Because of this accusation, Devi had the foresight to collect the three coffee glasses and save them in the back of the restaurant until the police arrived.

In the days after her death, it was assumed Mirna had died of an epileptic seizure, and Jessica and Hani were not questioned at the scene. However, three days after Mirna's death, when police analyzed the contents of the Vietnamese iced coffee, they realized she didn't die of an epileptic seizure at all. Mirna's drink had contained a lethal dose of cyanide; the case was now considered a homicide.

Mirna's family initially objected to an autopsy. Indonesia is a predominantly Muslim country, and it wasn't common for autopsies to be conducted as the procedure mutilates the body. However, the police assured the process would be brief. Finally Mirna's family agreed to an autopsy, and on January 10, the medical examiner found that there was bleeding in Mirna's stomach consistent with that of a corrosive substance. Traces of cyanide were found in her stomach but not in her other internal organs.

When police analyzed the security camera footage from the restaurant, they noticed Jessica awkwardly backing away from the scene while Mirna was convulsing. She made an odd movement with her hands, but exactly what she was doing was unclear. Speculation was that she was moving something from one hand to the other, while another theory was that she was scratching her finger because she had just stirred poison into Mirna's drink using that finger.

(A link to the security camera footage can be found in the online appendix at the end of this book.)

When the Grand Indonesian Police heard about the relationship problems between Jessica and Mirna, they turned to the authorities in Sydney to look into Jessica's background. While Australia had abolished the death penalty in the 1980s, it was still in effect in Indonesia and was carried out by firing squad. The Australian Federal Police only agreed to help investigate the case after assurances from the

Indonesian government that prosecutors would not seek the death penalty.

The Australian Federal Police shared the confidential history of Jessica's troubles: her DUI charges, her multiple suicide attempts, her death threat to her former boss, and the restraining order her ex-boyfriend had issued against her. They also interviewed her former boss, Kristie Carter, for nine hours. Later, Kristie's testimony became vital evidence in the case against Jessica.

Within weeks, Indonesian Police officially charged Jessica with the murder of Mirna Salihin. Dressed in an orange prison jumpsuit and with a sign hanging around her neck with her name on it, police took Jessica back to the Olivier restaurant for a reenactment of the crime.

Indonesian news outlets and social media quickly became obsessed with the case, and Jessica was thrust into the public spotlight. Reporters and cameras followed Jessica's every step, and she seemed to strangely enjoy the attention. Television cameras showed Jessica smiling and waving as if she was unaware of the reason for all the attention.

Despite the agreement between the Australian Federal Police and the Grand Indonesian Police, prosecutors said the agreement not to seek the death penalty would be void if they convicted her on evidence the Jakarta police had gathered. The Indonesian police also argued that Jessica was not an Australian citizen but only a permanent resident. Eventually, the Indonesian police said they would leave it up to the judges for sentencing.

The case quickly became the most notorious case in Indonesian history. The media called Jessica "The Coffee Killer," and the public interest was overwhelming in both Indonesia and Australia. The case played out like a soap opera and was covered every night on the evening news. Everyone in Indonesia seemed to have an opinion of whether Jessica was innocent or guilty.

The broadcast media was criticized for spreading insensitive rumors that Jessica was having an affair with Mirna's husband. A coffee shop in Jakarta advertised non-toxic Vietnamese iced coffee with the slogan, "What doesn't kill you makes you stronger." The Olivier restaurant became a tourist attraction for those who wanted to see where the crime occurred.

The trial started on June 15, 2016, and Indonesian national television broadcast it live. Jessica's wealthy family hired Otto Hasibuan, a well-known celebrity defense lawyer. The defense team questioned the autopsy results, pointing out that they found no cyanide in any of Mirna's organs other than her stomach. They produced forensic and toxicology experts that testified there was no proof that cyanide caused her death.

Jessica took the stand in her own defense, explaining that Mirna was a friend with whom she could laugh, talk, and share secrets. She tried to play on the sympathy of the court,

"My family has been publicly shamed, and I have been treated like the scum of the earth since the case started."

Mirna's friends and family held press conferences to sway public opinion against Jessica.

The prosecution presented forty-six witnesses, including Mirna's father, husband, twin sister, and several employees from the restaurant. The prosecution presented the case with the motive of revenge. They argued that Jessica blamed Mirna for the breakup with her ex-boyfriend and the subsequent chain of events in Jessica's life.

The prosecution alleged that the security camera footage showed her looking around the restaurant to see if anyone was watching while she handled the coffee. They also argued that the murder was pre-meditated – that the use of poison illustrates pre-planning. They also used the interview with Jessica's former employer, where Jessica threatened her life, and the restraining order against her to show her anger consumed her.

Ultimately, the panel of three judges agreed with the prosecution. On October 27, 2016, after almost five months of trial, Jessica Wongso was found guilty of poisoning Mirna Salihin by putting cyanide in her coffee.

Jessica Wongso was sentenced to twenty years in prison. She and her team of lawyers submitted a lengthy appeal, but both the Jakarta High Court and the Supreme Court rejected it. Jessica Wongso had no option but to serve the remainder of her sentence.

CHAPTER 2
CAPTAIN CASH

In the late 1990s, London had a thriving drug trade, and Ken Avery was a top-level heroin dealer living the high life. Avery was well-dressed, making money hand over fist, and known for always having a briefcase full of cash with him, which earned him the nickname "Captain Cash." Avery had been smuggling drugs, selling fake passports, and laundering money on a massive scale. In 1996, he was involved in an elaborate plan to smuggle £40 million worth of marijuana into the UK using a submarine.

Avery was known as a playboy that showered women he was interested in with lavish gifts, once buying a woman a new car when hers couldn't be repaired. When he met London socialite Belinda Bruin, he was instantly smitten. Belinda was the personal assistant of Bob Geldof's wife, Paula Yates, and was also involved in the London drug scene. She had previously been arrested with the trunk of her car full of cocaine.

Avery tried hard to impress Belinda, offering to take her by private helicopter to the Monaco Grand Prix, but she declined most of his offers of affection. Finally, however, she accepted his gift of a £4,000 Cartier watch.

Avery ran a bonded warehouse in London which was a perfect cover for his smuggling business. On June 17, 1998, however, his extravagant lifestyle ended when he was caught with twenty-five kilos of heroin and led police on a high-speed pursuit.

Avery was facing over twenty years in prison, but prosecutors offered him a deal. They offered to reduce his sentence to eight years if he helped prosecute the higher-level drug dealers he worked with. Avery took the offer, and his testimony helped put away twelve criminals in a cocaine ring with a business estimated to be worth over £2 billion.

At his sentencing, the judge said,

"As a result of your co-operation, you will never again be trusted by your former colleagues, so you can't go back [to a life of crime], and the enmity of those people will make your future life precarious... those who turn against former associates should receive a very great reduction in their sentence."

During his incarceration, one of his cellmates said,

 "He knew there were contracts on his life, but he didn't seem to care. His attitude was, 'Come on, then, let's get it over with.' There was no way he was going to live quietly. Believe me, when he goes, He will go out with a bang."

Even though his sentence had been reduced to eight years, Avery served only three and was released in 2002. After his release, he had very few friends and no money. Thus, he legally changed his name from Ken Avery to Ken Regan and moved in with his father in a tiny one-bedroom bungalow.

In July 2002, Regan was looking for a way to create his next fortune when he came across a freight company based at Heathrow Airport called CIBA Freight, owned by a man named Amarjit "Neil" Chohan.

CIBA Freight was a very successful fruit importer. Though forty-five-year-old Neil Chohan was wealthy, he was a very modest man. Having saved over £2 million, he could easily afford a luxurious home, but he and his twenty-five-year-old wife Nancy, mother-in-law, and two baby boys lived in a tiny bungalow near the airport. Though he could afford a fancy car, Neil drove his eight-year-old Ford Escort to work daily. Neil and Nancy had recently started their family, with their oldest son just eighteen months old and the newborn just two months old.

His employees knew Neil as a very easygoing boss. Most of them considered him a friend and described him as happy-go-lucky. His relaxed demeanor came into play when Ken Regan came in to apply for a job. Although Regan was an ex-convict, Neil still gave him a chance. After all, Neil had spent a short time in prison for tax evasion. He believed every man deserved a second chance at life and offered Regan a job as a delivery driver.

Ken Regan was a hard worker and quickly gained the trust of Neil Chohan and the other employees. After working for CIBA for six months, Regan came to Neil with a proposal. He explained that he knew some investors in the Salisbury area, near Stonehenge, who were interested in buying CIBA Freight. They were prepared to offer him £3 million for his business. But the investors were fictional; his story was just a plan to take over CIBA Freight and use it for smuggling drugs again. Regan was determined to regain his drug empire at any cost.

Though Belinda Brewin hadn't contacted Regan during his three years in prison, he was still obsessed with the woman. She had since sold her home in Chelsea, London, and moved to a large country estate in Devon. Regan visited her and took notice of her sprawling ranch. He told her she should make some improvements: cut down some trees, build a nice secure wall with electric gates, and put in some drainage for the muddy roads that meandered through the property. She found it strange that he made all these suggestions for changes but thought nothing further of it.

In early February, Regan drove to see Belinda and told her he had some news. He was planning on taking over CIBA Freight and offered her £72,000 per year to manage it for him. He explained that she would only have to work two days a week and she agreed.

Neil initially wasn't interested in selling the company, but after speaking to his wife, Nancy, about the prospect, they agreed it might be a good idea. She wanted him to retire and the family to move to India so they could raise their children in better schools than the ones the UK had to offer. So, on February 13, 2003, Neil Chohan agreed to meet Regan's associates. That Thursday morning, Neil told his employees he was driving down near Stonehenge for a meeting. That was the last time they saw him.

The following Monday morning, the employees of CIBA Freight were called to an emergency meeting held by Ken Regan. He announced that Neil Chohan had agreed to sell the company, and Belinda Brewin was the new owner. Regan told the employees that Neil wished them well, but Nancy was in ill health; he had decided to retire and move back to India to raise his family.

Regan then showed them a bill of sale for the company, signed by Neil Chohan. The employees were shocked, but ultimately, it was a busy company; they needed to get back to business as usual.

The next day, as Belinda was driving to her new job at CIBA Freight, she was feeling sick and turned around to return home. As she was pulling onto her property, she encountered two men with an older model Jaguar and digging equipment. The men had a backhoe and were digging a large trench on one of the roads on her property. Furious, she stopped the car, confronted the men, and asked what they were doing. She hadn't ordered any work to be done. The men explained that Ken Regan had sent them to put in a drainage pipe and put gravel over the muddy road. Belinda was furious, but Regan eventually convinced her to let him install the drainage.

Twelve thousand miles away in New Zealand, Nancy Chohan's older brother, Onkar Verma, was getting worried. Although he hadn't seen his sister in nine years, the two were still extremely close and spoke on the phone daily.

On February 14, he received a frantic call from his sister. She was terrified. She had received a call from a worker at CIBA Freight that told her Neil had flown to Holland. Nancy knew that that couldn't be true because she knew he didn't have his passport with him. Then she received a voicemail message from her husband in English. The two usually spoke to each other in Punjabi, never English.

The next day, Onkar tried to call his sister and his mother, but there was no reply. All calls after that came to an abrupt halt.

Panicked, Onkar called CIBA Freight and spoke to a manager there named Mike Parr. Parr told him that Neil and his family had sold the company and moved back to India, but Onkar knew that couldn't be true. Nancy and Neil would never do that without telling him. He knew something was horribly wrong. Parr even faxed Onkar a power of attorney document signed by Neil, which only alarmed him more: Neil's signature was nothing more than a scribble.

On February 19, Onkar emailed Scotland Yard to explain his worries, and they referred him to the missing person unit.

 "I spoke to Nancy every day. There's never been a day when we did not speak. My sister rang me twice a day, my mum also, and every day, I would ring them once. All of a sudden, there're no calls, no call to say we're OK or we're going to India."

London police told him they stopped by and did a welfare check, but the house was empty. Police told him that the neighbors and friends confirmed that they had moved back to India. Onkar knew none of this could be true and on March 5, he booked a flight to London.

When he arrived, Onkar got the keys to the family home from Mr. Parr at Neil's office and went to the house.

When he arrived he found clothes still in the washing machine, cooked meals in the fridge, and the boy's feed bottles filled. It was clear they had left in a hurry and Onkar became even more worried.

Because Neil Chohan had been in jail for tax evasion in the past, Onkar believed that the police assumed he was in trouble again and was running from someone.

 "I believe they racially stereotyped him, obviously. The police kept saying he's done a runner because he was in trouble. I never believed the police story because I was very close to my family, and they would have told me about it."

Eventually, he convinced the police to transfer the case to the serious crimes group when he explained that his mother's most precious possession, her prayer book, was still in the house, and she went nowhere without it.

The first person detectives interviewed was the last to see Neil Chohan – Ken Regan. Regan told police that Chohan was a shady businessman and had gotten into financial trouble. He said that his only choice was to flee back to India.

After researching Neil Chohan's business dealings, investigators were skeptical of Regan's story and began investigating him instead. They immediately found his extensive criminal background, then looked into his and Neil's phone records.

Cell phone location tracking showed that Chohan left his home in Hounslow and drove toward Stonehenge on February 13. Regan lived nearby in Wilton, Salisbury, and police noticed that Regan's phone met with Chohan's near Stonehenge, then both phones traveled further south.

Knowing that Belinda was now managing CIBA and the two phones had traveled near her home, detectives called her to tell her that they were driving down to question her. Belinda agreed, but Regan was furious with her. He didn't want the police coming onto her property, so he told her to call them back and tell them she would meet them elsewhere.

Belinda didn't understand why he would want her to do that, but she didn't need to call them after all. Regan always had a plan.

Police suddenly received a lead on the whereabouts of Neil Chohan. That lead came from an associate of Regan, William Horncy. Horncy and Regan had sold stolen passports together years ago, and Regan had testified against him, landing him in prison. At the direction of Regan, Horncy called the detectives. He explained that he knew Neil Chohan was still in the UK because he and Regan had plans to meet him the following week in Newport, Wales. He claimed Chohan wanted to buy five stolen passports from him.

Rather than questioning Belinda, detectives decided to wait a few days and see if Chohan showed up to buy the passports. That meant they called Belinda and told her they wouldn't need to question her after all.

Regan had still been pressing Belinda to put in more drainage on her property, and she had eventually agreed to let him put in a ditch near the horse stables, so she wasn't surprised when the same two men she had seen before showed up again with a backhoe. She took her kids to town for the day while the men worked.

The following Monday, detectives watched Regan and Horncy standing near a bronze statue of a pig in Newport. That was to be the meeting point for the sale of the stolen passports. However, as police watched, Regan received a phone call. It seemed the meeting wasn't happening; detectives had a sinking feeling that Regan and Horncy had tricked them. The meeting had been pure fiction.

On April 22, detectives again wanted to interview Belinda Brewin and drove to her home. During the interview, they asked if she had noticed anything odd about Regan's behavior in the past few days, and she mentioned that she had. When she told Regan the police wanted to interview her, he said,

"If they ask you what I was doing on your land, just tell them I was helping you with your water system."

Detectives asked what he really did on her land, and she told them he had dug a drainage ditch. They knew what that meant and immediately assembled a team to dig up Belinda's property.

———

Later that same afternoon, a father and son were spending the evening on a kayak trip off the coast of Bournemouth when they noticed something floating in the ocean. As they got closer, they could tell it was a body. As evening fell, the boy paddled into shore and alerted the police, while the father waited for three hours on the dark ocean with the bloated body, until police arrived.

The body had suffered severe blunt trauma to the back of the head. Packing tape was still wrapped tightly around the head and jaw. One week after they found it, investigators positively identified the body as that of Neil Chohan. The cause of death was both blunt force trauma and suffocation. Police still had no idea where the rest of the family was, but it was becoming increasingly clear that they were dead as well.

The evidence from the body suggested that Neil Chohan had been buried in the ground, then exhumed at a later date and transported to a boat, where he was dumped into the water.

Detectives brought in forensic archeologists and pathologists to dig through the area of the drainage ditch on Belinda Brewin's property. They had found nothing after five days of painstakingly sifting through the dirt, but the site was huge, so the forensic team continued searching. Eventually, they recovered jewelry that belonged to Nancy Chohan, baby clothes, and evidence of a large bonfire. Unfortunately there were still no bodies, but detectives assumed that they had buried the entire family there at one time.

Further analysis of phone location records revealed a chain of events on the day Chohan went missing. It showed that when Chohan met Regan at Stonehenge, two additional phones were traveling the same route. The phones belonged to William Horncy and another career criminal, Peter Rees.

By this time, all three of the suspects were on the run. Ken Regan and William Horncy had fled into mainland Europe, while Peter Rees was alone and in hiding in the United Kingdom.

Peter Rees had checked into a boarding house and had a guilty conscience. He confessed to a woman at the boarding house that the police wanted him for murder, but he claimed that he didn't do it. He told her that Regan had killed all five of the Chohan family. The woman called the police, and Rees spent three days running but was arrested in a pub in Coleford. When police interrogated Rees, he refused to say anything about the Chohan family or his partners.

One month after Rees' arrest, a second body was found by fishermen floating off the coast of the Isle of Wight. Autopsy results confirmed it was the body of Nancy Chohan.

After two more months on the run in Spain, Regan fled to Belgium, where he was tracked down by police and returned to the United Kingdom. Horncy was still in hiding, but after another month, he became tired of running, returned to the UK, and turned himself in. Just one week later, the body of Nancy's mother, Charanjit Kaur, washed up on the shores of the Isle of Wight.

Detectives collected more evidence in preparation for the trial. Vital details came from the movements of the cell phones, as well as evidence provided by Horncy's own son. A final clue came from Neil Chohan himself.

By tracing the movement of their cell phones, investigators discovered that all four phones traveled from Stonehenge to Wilton in Salisbury. The phones arrived at a small bungalow at the address 3 Forge Close. It was the small home that Ken Regan shared with his father. The men had held Neil Chohan captive there for the next three days.

William Horncy's son willingly gave the police a Lexmark color printer and a gray suitcase. Upon examining the suitcase, the police found ten sheets of blank computer paper with Neil Chohan's signature on them.

Regan threatened Chohan and made him sign the blank sheets of paper while he was being held captive. Regan planned to use the signatures to print documents for the takeover of CIBA Freight and to forge additional documents in the future.

The movement of the phones also showed that on February 15, Regan and Horncy then traveled back to London to the Chohan's home. Prosecutors believed Nancy Chohan, her baby sons Ravinder and Devinder, and her mother, Charanjit Kaur, were all murdered that day. Regan and Horncy then rented a van and transported the bodies south to Belinda Brewin's property, where they buried them in the drainage ditch.

The most vital piece of evidence came from Neil Chohan himself. While he was held captive at 3 Forge Close, Neil Chohan managed to find a letter in the house where he was being held. He carefully folded and tucked the letter into his right sock. Though it was damaged from being buried and then dumped in the ocean, the letter remained intact in his sock.

The letter was from Cheltenham & Gloucester Building Society addressed to:

Mr. KR Regan & Mr. RF Avery,

3 Forge Close,

South Newton, Salisbury Wiltshire SP2 OQG.

The date on the letter was February 22, 2003, the day before he was abducted.

Neil Chohan knew he would be murdered, and although he faced certain death, he wanted to leave a clue as to who killed him.

The trial began on November 8, 2004, and lasted nine months. It was the longest criminal trial in UK history and cost taxpayers over £10 million. Prosecutors presented almost 4,500 exhibits of evidence. All three suspects pleaded not guilty and claimed they were falsely imprisoned.

Peter Rees was convicted of Neal Chohan's murder but cleared of the other four murders and received twenty-three years in prison. Horncy and Regan were both sentenced to five consecutive life sentences without the possibility of parole.

The bodies of eighteen-month-old Devinder and eight-week-old Ravinder were never recovered.

Eleven years later, in 2016, police linked both Regan and Horncy to the death of Michael Schallamach from Southampton. When Schallamach went missing in 1992, police and his family were told that he had run off to Europe and Nigeria with an unknown woman. The family received a handwritten letter from someone, allegedly calling herself Helen, saying they had been living together in Europe. However, the last person to ever see Michael Schallamach was Kenneth Regan.

CHAPTER 3

THE OXFORD MURDER

R achel McLean had traveled back home to Blackpool, UK, to stay with her parents during the summer break of 1990. The eighteen-year-old had just finished her first year at St. Hilda's College in Oxford, UK, where she had a hectic schedule with school and social groups. She was an active environmentalist and a vegetarian, but her friends also knew her to be a party girl that loved heavy metal. During term breaks, she worked part-time jobs and donated her time to local charities.

Late that summer, Rachel and her friends were drinking at the Adam & Eve club when she met John Tanner, a charming bartender with long brown hair.

John was from Nottingham, a few hours away, and was working a summer job in Blackpool. He was good-looking, sociable, outgoing, and funny. John was born in the United Kingdom but immigrated to New Zealand at an early age. After growing up in New Zealand, he returned to the UK to attend university in Nottingham and live with his aunt.

Rachel and John flirted that night and by the end of the evening, she had invited him to her upcoming nineteenth birthday party. John gladly accepted. When he showed up for her birthday party, John and

Rachel instantly hit it off. They slept together that night, and the relationship developed from there.

At the end of the summer, Rachel returned to Oxford, John to Nottingham. Oxford was over two hours away from Nottingham, so they could only see each other during occasional long weekends or holidays. He called her several times a week and wrote her a steady stream of long love letters.

That December, she invited him to spend Christmas with her family. She brought him to Blackpool to meet her parents and gave him a paisley tie as a Christmas present.

Over the months, John grew increasingly infatuated with Rachel, but the distance frustrated him. He became agitated when he called the flat she shared with four other students to find she wasn't home.

But Rachel was a busy girl who was involved with her studies and many social groups. She didn't have time to wait by the phone for him to call. Each time he called, his jealousy stewed. He worried that she was seeing other men. Her roommates noticed that they regularly argued over the phone about his jealousy issues.

Although she wouldn't tell him directly, Rachel felt annoyed by his jealousy and thought he was overly possessive. So on February 11, she mailed him a Valentine's Day card in which she wrote:

"To my one and only John. The one who was with me through the most wondrous moments of my life."

But on the same day, she wrote her true feelings privately in her diary:

"What a joke. I just wrote John's Valentine's card. Full of sweet, pure words. Words that I shoveled out of some fountain inside me. A fountain that dried and cracked. Somehow, I don't think you would have appreciated sweet nothings along the lines of 'you sick childish bastard.'"

Unaware of her true feelings, he professed his love to Rachel that Valentine's day and asked her to marry him. To his disappointment, she turned him down.

In April, Rachel spent the Easter break with her parents in Blackpool. The Saturday after Easter, Rachel's mother drove her back to Oxford. After dropping her off, her mother returned to Blackpool around 4 p.m.; John arrived at 7:30 to spend the rest of the weekend with her.

That Sunday was a lazy day at home for the couple. Rachel's roommates hadn't returned from the holidays yet, so Rachel and John had the flat all to themselves. Rachel had term exams the following week, so she studied in the front room while John watched football. John was an avid Nottingham fan, and they were playing West Ham in the FA Cup semi-finals.

The following evening, John took the 6:55 train back to Nottingham from the Oxford train station.

Later that week, when her roommates returned home, Rachel wasn't there. Her bedroom windows were open, but nothing seemed to be out of place. They thought it was odd, but they knew Rachel was busy with school, so they weren't concerned. John tried to call on Wednesday but got no answer, then tried the following day and, as usual again, left a message with her roommates. The next day, a letter from John arrived in the mailbox. He had mailed it as soon as he returned to Nottingham.

"My dearest, lovely Rachel, thank you for such a lovely weekend. Please excuse the handwriting as I am now sadly wending my way away from your smiling face.

Fancy seeing that friend of yours at the station. At least you didn't have to get a bus home. It was nice of him to give you a lift. But I hate him because he has longer hair than me. Ha ha! It's nice to know you will not be alone for the next few days. I worry for you in that house on your own."

It wasn't until four days later, on April 19, when Rachel didn't show up for an appointment with her tutor, that her roommates knew something was wrong. Rachel never would have missed that appointment. Her tutor reported her missing.

Police initially didn't take the missing person report with much urgency. They received dozens of missing person reports every month in the busy college town.

Investigators began searching for Rachel at the flat she shared with four other students: Victoria Clare, Margaret Smith, Sarah Heaume, and Jo Formby. During the questioning, her roommates showed police the letter John had mailed to Rachel from Nottingham. The letter's contents let them know that John was the last person to have contact with her – except for an unknown man at the Oxford train station.

Nothing seemed out of place during the first inspection of the house. There were no obvious signs of foul play and nothing was out of place. Initial examinations of the floorboards showed no signs of tampering, but when police later found Rachel's diary, they realized that John's letter didn't quite add up. From what Rachel had written in her diary, they could clearly see that John was very possessive of her. In his letter, he wrote of the "long-haired stranger" who gave her a ride back home, but that wasn't John's style. He wouldn't have been tolerant of another man taking her home. From her diary, investigators knew that this mysterious man would have set off John's jealousy. That never would have sat well with John.

A second letter from John arrived at Rachel's flat. It was short and sharp. He wrote,

 "I have tried calling you all week, but I guess you are working. A call would be appreciated."

The following Monday, April 22, police spoke to John Tanner in the first of many interviews. He expressed his concern for Rachel's where-abouts and told detectives that Rachel had woken up earlier than him the previous Monday to study while he slept in until around noon. He then showered and got ready to take the train back to Nottingham. He said they made love in the afternoon and took the bus to the Oxford train station around 4:15 p.m.

John claimed that while they were at Oxford Station waiting for his 6:55 p.m. train, they ran into a friend of Rachel's in the cafe, where the three of them sat and had coffee. He described the man as having long hair, ripped jeans, and a black leather jacket. The description was essentially the same as a description of himself. John explained that he didn't remember the man's name as he didn't think it was important at the time. However, he told the police that the mystery man had offered to take Rachel back to her house, so she wouldn't have to take the bus home.

John said that he and Rachel embraced and kissed on the platform before his train arrived, then he boarded the train back to Nottingham. But detectives didn't buy his story, and he quickly became the prime suspect.

That same day, the Oxford Police went public with the news of Rachel's disappearance. Detective John Bound told reporters,

"Although we could not admit it publicly, it seemed from the outset that some harm had befallen her. There was no reason for her to run away. She was a happy girl with a good background, loving parents, and a bright future."

Police assigned two police officers who befriended John Tanner. They made him believe they were updating him on the search for Rachel, but they were actually watching every move he made. They watched his reactions to the news of the investigation, his body language, and generally all of his movements from day to day.

The search of the neighboring area was extensive. Police went door to door in her neighborhood, asking neighbors if they had seen Rachel or noticed anything suspicious. Officers used sniffer dogs to comb through the nearby scrubland, and divers were sent to drag the nearby River Cherwell. Investigators searched Rachel's house once again, but again, they found nothing.

Nine days after Rachel's disappearance, her parents, Joan and Malcolm McLean, held a press conference in hopes it might help find their daughter. As with many mysteries like this, many calls came to the police with clues, but very few were of any help.

Police asked John to help them put together a sketch of the mystery man from the train station. However, when the drawing was released to the public, no one came forward with any information.

Rachel had been missing for two weeks, and detectives assumed the worst. They believed she was dead and had started searching sewers and cesspits around the Oxford area. Again, their efforts were futile.

Detectives still believed that John Tanner had killed her, but they needed concrete evidence. Surprisingly, Tanner agreed to participate in a press conference and a reconstruction of their last moments together at the Oxford train station. Tanner, however, saw it as an opportunity to portray himself as cooperative and willing to help with the investigation.

Detectives wanted to recruit the help of the media and asked a local television station to present specific questions to him during the press conference to see how he would react. During the press conference, reporters mentioned that his description of the mystery man was much like that of himself. He replied,

"I had nothing to do with her disappearance. I know what people are saying."

As instructed by the police, they asked him directly if he believed she was still alive. His response was,

"I did not kill her. I don't know what happened to her. In my heart of hearts, I know she is still alive."

However, he spoke in the video with a slight smirk on his face. Naturally, that did not sit well with the public or the police.

Finally, when reporters asked if he had a message for anyone that may be holding Rachel against her will, he said,

"I would appeal to them to come forward and tell us, just out of sheer consideration for her mother and father and myself."

During the reconstruction, Tanner and a police officer who played Rachel's role stood on the platform at the train station arm in arm. An actor dressed to match his description of the mystery man met them at the cafe in the station, where they sat at a table and had coffee. Over the next several days, the local television channels repeatedly aired the reconstruction.

When John Tanner took part in reconstructing their last moments together, he thought no one would remember a random couple at a train station two weeks prior, but he was wrong. Two witnesses distinctly remembered John Tanner on April 15 at the Oxford train station. But they placed him alone, not with a girl or another man. An Oxford resident named Jane Wynn-Jones told police she had sat next to him at the station. She described,

"He was agitated and seemed to be shuffling a lot and going in and out of a bag, which was on the floor next to him. He brought out a pad with thin paper and lines on it. He was writing in black ink."

Investigators now believed that this was when Tanner penned the letter to Rachel which he later mailed from Nottingham.

Bit by bit, other parts of John's story started to fall apart. John claimed that he and Rachel had boarded a city bus at 4:15 p.m. that day, but Oxford busses electronically tracked how many people boarded and paid at each stop. On the day and time of that stop, only one person had boarded the bus: John Tanner.

Detectives suspected that Rachel McLean's body was still in her house somewhere. However, it wasn't until they contacted the Oxford Council to get detailed layouts of the home on Argyle Street that they realized the houses on that street were underpinned, meaning there were small cavities of air space beneath the floorboards.

On Thursday, May 2, nineteen days after Rachel was last seen, detectives returned to the house again for a more thorough examination. When they crawled into the cupboards beneath the stairwell and pulled up the floorboards, they found the body of Rachel McLean. Her body had been crammed into a small space only eight inches high. The cold outdoor temperatures at that time of year had slowed the body's decomposition, and the ventilation of the house underpinning allowed any odors to go undetected.

Within an hour of finding the body, John Tanner was arrested in a pub in Nottingham. Initially, Tanner refused to answer any questions posed by the police, but the following day, he broke down and admitted that he'd killed his girlfriend. Tanner explained that on that Sunday evening, after watching the football game, he again asked her for her hand in marriage, but again, she turned him down. Finally, as he begged her, she became aggravated with him and told him she didn't want to be engaged. He wrote in his confession,

> "I was offended. I must have snapped. I flew at her in a rage and proceeded to put my hands around her neck. I think I must have lost control because I have only a vague recollection of the time that elapsed afterwards. I am bewildered why I have done such a terrible thing to a person I love dearly."

Tanner explained that they argued, and during the screaming, she admitted that she had been sleeping with other people. Tanner then called her a "tart." Rachel raised her hand as if she was going to slap him, but instead, he lost control. Tanner recalled lunging at her and moving his hands toward her neck. Medical examiners confirmed evidence of a ligature being used on her neck, but Tanner claimed that, if that happened, he had blacked it out. He said his only other recollection was sitting on the bed with her body on the floor. Police believe he used the paisley tie she gave him for Christmas to strangle her.

Tanner picked up Rachel's dead body and laid her on the bed, then slept on the floor next to her bed.

The following day, he pulled up the floorboards under the stairs and wedged her body into a tiny eight-inch gap beneath the floorboards. He then took a bus to the Oxford train station and caught the 6:55 p.m. train back to Nottingham.

As he waited at the station for the train, he wrote a letter to Rachel to make it appear that he believed her to still be alive and placed suspicion on the mystery man. He mailed the letter when he arrived home in Nottingham. In the days following, he called her home twice and sent a second letter in feeble attempts to solidify his alibi.

Seven months later, in December 1991, John Tanner pleaded not guilty despite his confession. He admitted to killing her, but he claimed it was not murder. Tanner knew that he would be handed a life sentence if he admitted to the murder and would serve about fifteen years. However, if he was convicted of manslaughter on the grounds of diminished responsibility, he would only get about eight years in prison and could be out in four or five. It was an easy choice.

Tanner played the role of the poor boyfriend in court. He tried to convince the jury that he was a loving, caring boyfriend that only wanted to marry his one true love, not the possessive control freak the prosecution made him out to be. He claimed that Rachel provoked him to lose his self-control. He claimed Rachel often teased him because he was unable to perform sexually due to pain from a groin injury.

Ultimately, his pleas didn't help him. After four hours of deliberation, the jury returned with a 10-2 majority guilty verdict.

At his sentencing, Judge Kennedy told Tanner,

"I entirely accept that she was precious to you, but this was a savage attack. And your conduct afterwards, up until the time when her body was found, did nothing to ameliorate the gravity of the offense."

Despite it all, Rachel's mother said that she forgave Tanner,

 "I think we feel the way we have always felt - that this is a tragedy for him in his life as well. Yes, I think we can forgive him because otherwise, it eats into your life and the lives of others around you. If you start on the path of forgiveness, you can start to build a new life, and all the people around you can build new lives."

Twenty-two-year-old John Tanner was sentenced to life in prison, but that's not the end of the story. While in prison, he formed an odd relationship with a 26-year-old woman named Siobahn Howes, who bore a striking resemblance to Rachel McLean. Siobhan visited Tanner at Gartree Prison while studying criminology at Loughborough University.

Siobahn saw Tanner as a victim of a tragic chain of circumstances and a crime of passion. During his time in prison, Tanner referred to Siobahn as his girlfriend, and she looked into the possibility of Tanner finishing his prison sentence in New Zealand.

She eventually moved to New Zealand and taught at Wanganui Collegiate School, the same school Tanner had attended years earlier.

After serving only a little more than eleven years of his life sentence, Tanner was released in 2003 and returned to New Zealand. It is unknown whether Tanner got together with Siobahn Howes upon his return to New Zealand, but he was back in the news again in 2018.

Over a period of six months in 2017, Tanner abused his girlfriend repeatedly and threatened to kill her.

At forty-nine years old, Tanner was sentenced to two years and nine months for punching her with a closed fist and choking his girlfriend during an argument in New Zealand.

During his sentencing, Judge Crayton said,

"Between 1 March 2017 and 27 September 2017, whilst there was an argument, she told you she was leaving you. You, in response, told her that she was not, that you would kill her.

She did not take the threat seriously.

You then jumped on top of her and put both hands across her neck, restricting her breathing. As a consequence, she suffered soreness to her throat area.

You held her down, straddling her. You were yelling at her about her ex-partner. You used your hands to deliver blows, and slaps to her face and head a number of times.

You then punched her twice around the head with a closed fist. At that point, she had suffered a graze and bruising to the left side of her forehead.

She became worried and sat against the headboard on the bed with her knees up. You walked over and pulled her pants down and underwear off, saying you wanted sex.

It was said in a blunt and aggressive manner. You then demanded that she remove her SIM card from her phone, and as she attempted to get away from you, you grabbed her by the shirt, pulling her forward, and punching her several times in the head.

The victim fell onto the floor and attempted to shield her face from the blows. You punched the victim around the head and face several more times.

Mr. Tanner, it is, of course, and never has been acceptable for violence within a family context. You have one significant aggravating factor; it is your previous conviction for murder.

Your uttering of your intent to have sex with her is a disturbing element. That you ripped her clothing off can only be seen in this context as an act of violent domination and control over your victim.

On charge three, injuring with intent to injure, the sentence is one of two years, nine months. On charge one and charge two, there will be one year's imprisonment, concurrent on each."

CHAPTER 4
GOD CHOSE US

The late spring of 1985 was hot in Lexington County, South Carolina, and seventeen-year-old Sharon "Shari" Faye Smith spent the day with her boyfriend, Richard, and a few other friends swimming at nearby Lake Murray.

It was May 31, the Friday before high school graduation, and they were all excited about the graduation ceremony that Sunday. Shari loved to sing and was scheduled to sing the national anthem at their graduation. Immediately afterward, she and her friends had tickets to go on a cruise to the Bahamas.

After leaving the lake, Richard followed behind Shari's car and watched as she turned off the main highway toward her home on Platt Springs Road. The Smiths' home sat back 750 feet from the lonely rural road, with a long driveway leading up to the house. When her little light-blue Chevy Chevette pulled into the driveway at 3:38 that afternoon, her father, Robert, was working in his home office. From his window at the front of the house, he watched as Shari stopped to get the mail from the mailbox on the side of the road, just as she always did before she finished the drive up to the house.

Shari's father continued his work, expecting her to come in the door any minute. But when ten minutes passed and she hadn't come in, he peered out the window again. There at the end of the driveway, he saw the car. The driver's side door was still open but there was no sign of Shari.

Robert got in his own car and drove down the long driveway to see if she needed help. Or maybe she had stopped to talk to someone. But when he got to the end of the driveway, the car was still running with the door still open. Shari was gone.

Bare footprints in the soft dirt led to the mailbox and pieces of mail lay on the ground, but the footprints didn't lead back to the car. Instead, they disappeared near the road. Inside the car, Mr. Smith found her towel, black jelly shoes, and purse, with her medication still sitting on the passenger seat.

Shari Smith suffered from diabetes insipidus, also known as water diabetes. This rare form of diabetes caused her to have an insatiable thirst and a need to constantly drink excessive amounts of water. Unfortunately, this also meant that she had to urinate very frequently. Initially, he thought she might have run across the street into the woods to urinate, but after calling out her name, he got no reply. Knowing that Shari would never go very far without her medication, he panicked. He raced back to the house and immediately called the Lexington County Sheriff.

As with any missing teenager report, police initially assumed Shari had run away from home. However, when Robert explained that her car was left running and that her condition could be fatal if she went without her medication, they sprang into action and put together a search team.

Within hours, Sheriff James Metts, a graduate of the FBI's National Academy, put together the largest organized manhunt in South Carolina history. The Emergency Preparedness Division set up a mobile command center in front of the Smiths' home. They parked a large trailer on their property equipped with radios and telephones and manned the trailer twenty-four hours a day rather than traveling to the local Sheriff's office.

Shari's boyfriend, Richard, and other friends and family were quickly eliminated as suspects. Word spread rapidly through the tight-knit community and the Smith family were overwhelmed with food contributions from neighbors. Anything they could do to help. But Shari's mother, Hilda couldn't eat. She was terrified. She paced the living room floor waiting for word that someone had found her missing daughter.

By Saturday evening, police believed that Shari had been abducted, possibly by a kidnapper hoping to receive a ransom for her safe return. Shari's parents waited by the phone all day that Saturday, but the only call was a cruel prank.

Sunday, the day that Shari was due to sing at her graduation, came and went. The only clue that police had received was from two young men who had driven down Platt Springs Road and recalled seeing Shari at the mailbox. They said they briefly saw a reddish-purple car coming toward them driven by a man in his thirties. They believed the vehicle was possibly a 1982-84 Oldsmobile Cutlass.

Early Monday morning at 2:20 a.m., the phone finally rang. The male caller used an electronic voice distortion device to hide his identity. The man demanded to speak to Shari's mother, Hilda. He wanted to prove that the call was not a hoax and described in detail the clothes that Shari was wearing that Friday. He perfectly described the yellow and black bathing suit she wore beneath her clothes that day. He then told Hilda she would receive a letter in the mail later that day. He informed her that the top of the letter would be dated 6/1/85, and the time would read 3:10 a.m. He then explained that the actual time the letter was written was 3:12, but he decided to round it off. He ended the call by telling her,

"They are looking in the wrong place. Tell Sheriff Metts to get on TV at 7:00 a.m. on Channel 10 and call off the search."

The call was traced to a pay phone twelve miles away from the Smiths' home, but when police arrived, the caller was nowhere to be found. The phone was checked for fingerprint evidence; he had wiped the phone clean, and nobody recalled seeing anyone using the pay phone.

Though the call was not recorded, Mrs. Smith took notes. The caller reassured her that Shari was fine. He told her she ate a little, drank lots of water, and watched TV, but there was no mention of a ransom.

Not wanting to waste precious time for the mail to be delivered, Sheriff Metts called the Lexington County Postmaster and opened the Post Office in the middle of the night so they could sort through the coming day's mail. By 7 a.m., they found a letter addressed to the Smith family. It was a white legal size envelope with a small piece of blue-lined paper pasted on the outside bearing the Smiths' address and no return address.

Inside the envelope were two sheets of lined yellow legal paper. Both pages were handwritten in Shari's handwriting. The first page was titled at the top, "Last Will & Testament."

The text was disheartening,

"6/1/85, 3:10 a.m.

I Love Ya'll

I love you, Mommy, Daddy, Robert, Dawn & Richard, and everyone else and all the other friends and relatives. I'll be with my father now, so please, don't worry! Just remember my witty personality & great special times we all shared together. Please don't ever let this ruin your lives just keep living one day at a time for Jesus. Some good will come out of this. My thoughts will always be with you & in you! (Casket closed). I love you all so damn much. Sorry dad, I had to cuss for once! Jesus forgave me. Richard sweetie - I really did & always will love you & treasure our special moments. I ask one thing though. Accept Jesus as your personal savior. My family has been the greatest influence of my life. Sorry about the cruise money. Some day go in my place.

I am sorry if I ever disappointed you in any way. I only wanted to make you proud of me because I have always been proud of my family. Mom, Dad, Robert & Dawn there's so much I want to say that I should have said before now I love you! I know y'all love me and will miss me very much, but if ya'll stick together like we always did - y'all can do it!

Please do not become hard or upset. Everything works out for the good of those that love the Lord.

I Love Y'all

W/All My Heart

Sharon (Shari) Smith

P.S. Nana - I love you so much. I kind of always felt like your favorite. You were mine! I Love you A lot."

Near the top of the first page, in the left sidebar, she wrote, "God is Love" vertically and "ShaRichard" with a heart.

The letter was sent to the forensic document examiners who searched for clues. Many fingerprints were found on the pages, but they all belonged to Shari. However, the most important clue came from the latent indentations on the pages. The paper had come from a yellow-lined legal pad, and it was clear that the pad had been used in the past, as indentations from previous notes were visible.

Document examiners used an electrostatic detection apparatus (EDSA) to try and read the latent indentations. The device increased the humidity of the paper, which amplified the electrical conductivity. The paper was then placed on top of a brass plate, and a magnetic field was activated. It was then brushed with a black powder, showing the paper's prior indentations.

The process brought out latent indentations of what seemed to be partial phone numbers and a shopping list. The only readable words were "beef sticks," "Mother," "Bob," and the letters "J" and "S."

Later that Monday at 3:08 p.m., the phone rang at the Smith home. This time, investigators were ready to record the call. Shari's twenty-one-year-old sister Dawn answered the phone. Again, the voice was electronically distorted:

Dawn: "Hello."

Kidnapper: "Mrs. Smith."

Dawn: "No, this is Dawn."

Kidnapper: "I need to speak to your mother."

Dawn: "Could I ask who is calling?"

Kidnapper: "No."

Dawn: "Ok, hold on just a second, please."

———————

Hilda: "Hello."

Kidnapper: "Have you received the mail today?"

Hilda: "Yes, I have."

Kidnapper: "Do you believe me now?"

Hilda: "Well, I'm not really sure I believe you because I haven't had any word from Shari, and I need to know that Shari is well."

Kidnapper: "You'll know in two or three days."

Hilda: "Why two or three days?"

Kidnapper: "Call the search off."

Hilda: "Tell me if she is well because of her disease. Are you taking care of her?"

———————

The caller hung up. Investigators traced the call to a pay phone seven miles away at the Lexington Town Square Shopping Center, but the caller was gone by the time they got there, and there were no finger-prints on the telephone.

The search was expanded to include the entire state of South Carolina, the FBI was called in, and an alert went out to all law enforcement agencies nationwide.

That Monday, the Smith family decided to talk to television reporters. They hoped that the kidnapper would see how much suffering he had caused in the family and release Shari. During the press coverage, her father pleaded,

"Whoever has our daughter, Shari, we want her back. We miss her. We love her. Please send her back home. She belongs here with us."

A neighbor, Mrs. Terry Butler, saw the broadcast and contacted the police. She had driven in front of the Smiths' home that Friday and recalled seeing Shari pulling into the driveway. After passing the Smiths' house, she was met head-on by a car coming toward her in her lane. She blew her horn at the car, and the man quickly swerved back into his lane. She said the man was leaning over in the middle of the car and not paying attention to the road. She then watched in her rearview mirror and saw the car pull over near the Smiths' mailbox. Mrs. Butler described the driver as a white male who was slightly balding. Her description seemed to match what the two men had seen, and she helped police produce a sketch of the subject.

———

That evening at 8:07 p.m., the phone rang at the Smith house again. It was the same electronically distorted male voice. Dawn answered,

Dawn: "Hello."

Kidnapper: "Dawn, did you come down from Charlotte?"

Dawn: "Yes, I did; who's calling, please?"

Kidnapper: "I need to speak with your mother."

Dawn: "Ok, she's coming."

Kidnapper: "Tell her to hurry."

Dawn: "She's hurrying. Tell Shari I love her."

Kidnapper: "Did y'all receive her letter today?"

Dawn: "Yes, we did. Here's mother."

Hilda: "This is Hilda."

Kidnapper: "Did you receive Shari Rae's [sic] letter?"

Hilda: "Pardon? I can't hear you. It's not very clear. Speak louder."

Kidnapper: "Did you receive the letter today?"

Hilda: "Uh, yes, I did."

Kidnapper: "Tell me one thing it said. Hurry."

Hilda: "ShaRichard."

Kidnapper: "Do what?"

Hilda: "There was a little heart on the side, ShaRichard written on the side."

Kidnapper: "How many pages?"

Hilda: "Two pages."

Kidnapper: "Ok, and it was a yellow legal pad?"

Hilda: "Yes."

Kidnapper: "And on one side of the front page, it said, 'Jesus is love?'"

Hilda: "No, God is love."

Kidnapper: "Well, God is love."

Hilda: "Right."

Kidnapper: "Ok, so you know now this is not a hoax call?"

Hilda: "Yes, I know that."

Kidnapper: "I'm trying to do everything possible to answer some of your prayers, so please, in the name of God, work with us here."

Hilda: "Can you answer me one question, please? You… you are very kind… and, and you seem to be a compassionate person and… and I think you know how I feel being Shari's mother and how much I love her. Can you tell me? Is she all right physically without her medication?"

Kidnapper: "Shari is drinking a little over two gallons of water per hour and using the bathroom right afterward. I've got to hurry now. Ok, now, this has gone too far. Please forgive me. Have an ambulance ready at any time at your house. And on Shari's request, she requests that only immediate family come and Sheriff Metts and the ambulance attendants. She don't want to make a circus out of this."

Hilda: "Right. Ok."

Kidnapper: "And where she said 'casket closed' in parentheses… if anything happens to me, she said her… one of her requests she did not put in there was to put her hands on her stomach… cross her hands like she was praying in the casket."

Hilda: "We don't want any harm to you. I… I promise. We just want Shari well and all right, ok?"

Kidnapper: "Ok, listen. Listen real carefully. I've got to hurry. I know these calls are being traced, correct? Ok, now listen."

Hilda: "Uh, is Shari with you, or can you tell me that?"

Kidnapper: "I will not say. Ok, now listen to us, please. You're looking in the wrong place. Forget Lexington County. Look in Saluda County. Do you understand?"

Hilda: "Look in Saluda County?"

Kidnapper: "Exactly. Uh, closest to Lexington County within a fifteen-mile radius right over the line… is that understood?"

Hilda: "Yes."

Kidnapper: "Well, tell Sheriff Metts that he... I don't know what the problem is. I told you to forget about looking around your house... Saluda County."

Hilda: "Listen, there are so many people that love Shari, and they just won't give up."

Kidnapper: "I want to tell you one other thing. Shari is now a part of me physically, mentally, emotionally, and spiritually. Our souls are now one."

Hilda: "Your souls are one now with Shari?"

Kidnapper: "And she said she does love y'all, and like she said, do not let this ruin your lives... and well, time's up, and please now have the ambulance ready at any time."

Hilda: "Is her condition getting bad? Is that what you're trying to tell..."

Kidnapper: "Just have the ambulance, and I'll give you the location and tell Sheriff Metts to get all his damn men in Saluda County. Ok, well, God bless all of us."

Hilda: "Will you call me soon?"

Kidnapper: "I will. I've got to be careful. I've got to go now, and, and listen. Please, please, please forgive me for this. It just got out of hand."

Hilda: "Just tell Shari... I know she knows how much I love her. Tell her her Daddy loves her, and her brother and sister love her. God bless you for taking care of her."

Kidnapper: "Shari is protected, and like I said, she is a part of me now, and God looks after all of us. Goodnight."

Hilda: "Good luck to you, too."

Again, the call was traced but their efforts were fruitless. The call came from another pay phone eight miles from the Smiths' home. No clues at all were found at the pay phone.

By this time, several thousand volunteers were helping with the search. The family and Shari's boyfriend were heavily guarded inside the house and not allowed to leave without an officer with them.

The following evening – Tuesday, June 4 – the Smiths received another phone call at 9:45 p.m. Again, Dawn answered.

Dawn: "Hello."

Kidnapper: "Dawn?"

Dawn: "Yes."

Kidnapper: "This is Shari Faye's request. Have your mother get on the other phone quickly."

Dawn: "Get to the other phone, mother."

Kidnapper: "Get a pencil and paper ready."

Dawn: "Get a pencil and paper ready, ok. Mother's not on the phone yet."

Kidnapper: "Ok, now this is Shari's own words. So listen carefully. Say nothing unless you're asked. Ok, and I know these calls are taped and traced, but that's irrelevant now. There's no money demanded, so here's Shari Faye's last request. On the fifth day, to put the family at rest… Shari Faye being freed. Remember, we are one soul now. When located, you'll locate both of us together. We are one. God has chosen us. Respect all past and present requests. Actual events and times… jot this down."

Dawn: "All right, I'm doing it."

Kidnapper: "3:28 in the afternoon, Friday, thirty-first of May, Shari… Shari Faye was kidnapped from your mailbox with a gun. She had the fear of God in her, and she was at the mailbox. That's why she did not return back to her car."

Hilda: "Fear of God?"

Kidnapper: "Ok, 4:58 a.m.... no, I'm sorry. Hold on a minute. 3:10 a.m., Saturday, the first of June, uh, she handwrote what you received. 4:58 a.m., Saturday, the first of June... became one soul."

Hilda: "Became one soul. What does that mean?"

Kidnapper: "No questions now. Last, between four and seven Wednesday, tomorrow, have ambulance ready. Remember, no circus."

Hilda: "Wait, between four and seven a.m.?"

Kidnapper: "Four and seven in the afternoon tomorrow."

Hilda: "In the afternoon, ok."

Kidnapper: "Prayers and relief coming soon... please learn to enjoy life. Forgive. God protects the chosen. Shari Faye's important request... rest tonight and tomorrow. Good shall come out of this. Blessings are near. Remember tomorrow, Wednesday, four in the afternoon until seven in the evening. Ambulance ready... no circus."

Hilda: "No circus. What does that mean?"

Kidnapper: "You will receive last-minute instructions where to find us."

Hilda: "Do not kill my daughter, please. I mean, please."

Kidnapper: "We love and miss y'all. Get good rest tonight, goodbye."

Dawn: "He's gone, Mama."

Within minutes, police arrived at the pay phone that was used for the call, and again, no clues were useable. Police immediately set up roadblocks encircling the area of the pay phone, but after several hours of searching, there was still no sign of the kidnapper.

The following day, on Wednesday, June 5, at 11:54 a.m., the kidnapper called again. This time, Shari's mother, Hilda, answered. The call was extremely brief.

Hilda: "Hello."

Kidnapper: "Listen carefully. Take Highway 378 west to traffic circle. Take Prosperity exit, go one and a half miles, turn right at sign. Masonic Lodge Number 103, go one-quarter mile, turn left at white-framed building, go to backyard. Six feet beyond. We're waiting. God chose us."

Police immediately raced from the Smiths' home to the location described in nearby Saluda County, about sixteen miles away. Shari's decomposing body was found lying on her back, exactly where he explained, in a wooded area directly behind the white building. There was no trace of the killer. She was still wearing the same clothes she wore when she was abducted, but a few pieces of jewelry were missing. There were remnants of duct tape attached to her face, and parts of her hair had been cut where the duct tape had been previously attached. The killer most likely knew that the duct tape could have left clues for the police.

Because of the extreme temperatures of over 100 degrees Fahrenheit during the past few days, her body was already decomposing rapidly, and there were signs of insect infestation. The medical examiner determined Shari had been dead for three to four days. Most likely, she had been killed within twelve hours of her abduction.

Determining the cause of death was a bit complicated. Because of Shari's rare form of diabetes, she most likely died of cardiac arrest caused by extreme dehydration. There were also signs of soft ligature strangulation or smothering. Either way, the medical examiner considered it a homicide,

"The findings present at the autopsy would fit with a number of causes of death. The two most likely causes are extreme dehydration with associated electrolyte imbalance causing cardiac arrest and asphyxia due to soft ligature strangulation or smothering. It is, therefore, my opinion, in light of the history of the case and the postmortem and autopsy findings, the cause of death best be left undetermined. As far as the manner of death, since the death occurred during abduction, the manner of death will still be homicide, regardless of whether it is due to depriving the decedent of water or from some type of homicidal asphyxia."

All previous calls had been placed near the Smiths' home, but the most recent call was placed over forty-five miles away in Saluda County. Police now believed he might be leaving the area, but that assumption changed when the killer called once again. This time, he called a local television reporter for Channel 10, Charlie Keyes. The killer explained that he wanted to turn himself in and be taken alive.

The killer tried to explain his actions. He wanted Keyes to contact Sheriff Metts and arrange for him to give himself up.

"…it just went bad. I know her family and her, and well, I just made a mistake. It went too far. All I wanted to do was to make love to her. I didn't know she had the rare disease, and it just got out of hand. I got scared, and I have to do the right thing, Charlie."

That same evening, at 8:57 p.m., the killer called the Smith home again. This time, he called collect (also known as a reverse charge call). He wanted to let them know how he killed Shari.

In a long and rambling call, the killer explained to Dawn that he had taken photos of Shari while she was standing at the mailbox. He also claimed to have another letter from Shari and that she was at peace when he killed her. He said he was a family friend. Then he explained how he raped and sodomized her before he took her life and wavered between turning himself in and suicide. Dawn and her mother did their best to try to keep him on the line while the police traced the call. What follows are a few excerpts from the long call:

Killer: "Ok, so this is going to have to be the way it is, and she said that uh, she wasn't scared… that she knew that she was going to be an angel, and if I took the latter choice that she suggested to me, that she would forgive me, but our God's going to be the major judgment, and she'll probably end up seeing me in heaven, not in hell. And that uh, she requests… now please remember this. Now, she requests that y'all be sure to take her hands and fold them on her stomach like she's praying."

Dawn: "But Shari was not afraid, and she didn't cry or anything?"

Killer: "No, she didn't do anything, and uh, can you handle it if I tell you how she died?"

Dawn: "Yes."

Killer: "Ok, now be strong, now."

Dawn: "Ok."

Killer: "She said you were strong. She told me all about the family and everything. We talked and… oh God… and I am a family friend. That's the sad part."

Dawn: "You are a family friend?"

Killer: "Yeah, and that is why I can't face y'all. You… you'll find out in the morning or tomorrow."

Killer: "Ok, I tied her up to the bedpost and uh, with electric cord, and uh, she didn't struggle, cry or anything. She let me voluntarily …(conversation missing)… from her chin to her head, ok, I'll go ahead and tell you. I took duct tape and wrapped it all the way around her head and suffocated her, and tell the coroner or get the information out how she died, and uh, I was unaware she had this disease. I probably would have never taken her, and uh, I shouldn't have took her anyway. It just got out of hand, and uh, I'd asked her out before, and she said she would if she wasn't going with anybody…."

Killer: Ok, now, are there any other questions? I've got to go now. Time's running out."

Dawn: "Uh, when... when you killed Shari, was she at peace? She wasn't afraid or anything?"

Killer: "She was not. She was at peace. She knew that God was with her, and she was going to become an angel."

Dawn: "And she wrote that letter to us of her own free will and all that was...."

Killer: "She sure did. Everything I've told y'all has been the truth. Hasn't everything come true?"

Dawn: "Yes, it has. Can... can I ask you one more question?"

Killer: "One more, and that's it."

Dawn: "You told us that Shari was kidnapped at gunpoint?"

Killer: "Yeah."

Dawn: "But she knew you?"

Killer: "Yeah. At first, see, I pulled up and uh, I'm telling you the truth. I have no reason to lie to y'all. I've always told you the truth, right?"

Dawn: "Right."

Killer: "Ok, and I had her... asked her to stand there and took two instant pictures."

Dawn: "You asked her to stand where?"

Killer: "At the mailbox with her car in the background. These pictures, detailed pictures will be with... with the letter that you receive. Since I'm out of town... probably not 'til Saturday. And Charlie Keyes will get a copy, and your family will get a copy, and it's addressed to you unless the mail holds it up."

Dawn: "So, she didn't realize that you were going to kidnap her?"

Killer: "That's exactly right.

Dawn: "...Why on the fifth day did she want us to find her? Why not..."

Killer: "I don't know. She just... she just said that. I don't know. I don't have any idea. I'm telling you exactly how she died, so she died of suffocation. And so... ok anything else?"

Dawn: "Why did you... why did you do that?"

Killer: "She... I gave her a choice... to shoot her or give her a drug overdose or suffocate her."

Dawn: "Why did you have to kill her?"

Killer: "It got out of hand. I got scared because, uh, only God knows, Dawn. I don't know why. God forgive me for this, I hope. And I got to straighten it out, or he'll send me to hell, and I'll be there the rest of my life, but I'm not going to be in prison and electric chair."

Killer: "Oh, yeah. Let me tell you. The other night, they almost caught me. The ignorant son-of-a-guns, I wanted them to catch me. I felt that way at the time, but now...."

Dawn: "When... when was this?"

Killer: "Uh, when I called at 9:45."

Dawn: "When you were over near Jake's Landing?"

Killer: "Yeah, I was at that Fast Fare thing."

Dawn: "Yeah."

Killer: "I pulled out twenty yards in front of two flashing lights."

Dawn: "What color car did you have?"

Killer: "They hit it dead on it, red, and they didn't even... Dawn, I can't get over this. Them ignorant so-and-sos didn't even turn around and follow me, and I cut right at that blinking light down there to go the back way on Old Cherokee Road. And there was a highway patrolman or somebody in front of me and pulled the car in front of me, and he let me turn right on Old Cherokee Road. Can you believe that?"

Dawn: "So, you really wanted to be caught?"

Killer: "At that time, but it's too late now."

Dawn: "What kind of car was it?"

Killer: "Oh, well, they came mighty damn close. Dawn, they're not going to catch me, and I can't give you information because I got to make it back in time, and they'll stop me before I get back if I tell you, but they're right, it was a red one, and I almost got caught three or four times."

Dawn: "Was it a red Jetta?"

Killer: "Dawn, that's irrelevant now. If I die now, or if I die at six o'clock in the morning, it's irrelevant. Well, listen, Dawn."

Dawn: "I really wish you would just think about not killing yourself."

———

Dawn then put her mother on the phone:

Hilda: "Listen, I want to ask you something."

Killer: "This just got out of hand. This got out of hand...."

Hilda: "All you had to do was let her go."

Killer: "I was scared. She, she, was dehydrating so damn bad."

Hilda: "You could have called me for medicine. I would have met you anywhere."

Killer: "Well, that's irrelevant now."

Hilda: "I mean, all you had to do was let her go. Such a beautiful young life...."

Killer: "I know that. That's why I have to join her now, hopefully, and uh, Mrs. Smith, please, uh, ok, well, that's it. I got to go."

Hilda: "Did she know you when you stopped?"

Killer: "Yeah, uh, I took two pictures, Instamatic of, I made her stand... well, before she knew I was going to kidnap her, I asked her to stand at the mailbox, and you'll see by the picture... her car door. I think there's about eight pictures...."

Hilda: "Do you know all of us or just Shari?"

Killer: "I know the whole family, unfortunately, that's why I can't face you.

Killer: "I know this might be selfish, but, uh, you all please, ask a special prayer for me? Your, your daughter said that she was not afraid, and she was strong-willed. She, uh, knew that she was going to heaven, was going to be an angel, and like I told Dawn, she was going to be singing like crazy, and when she said that, she was smiling."

Hilda: "Did you tell her you were going to kill her?"

Killer: "Yes, I did, and I gave her the choice, like, it's on the recording. I asked her if she wanted it to be drug overdose, shot or, uh, uh, suffocated, and she picked suffocation."

Hilda: "My God, how could you?"

Killer: "Well, forgive us, God."

Hilda: "Not us... you."

Killer: "God only knows why this happened. I don't know. It just got out of hand. Goodbye, Mrs. Smith."

(The full transcript is available in the appendix at the end of this book.)

Dawn was able to keep him on the phone for a long time in order to get as many details as possible so they could try and identify the killer.

The call originated fifty miles away in Great Falls, South Carolina. But again, no clues were found at the pay phone.

That Saturday, the Smith family held the funeral for Shari, and everyone in attendance was videotaped. Police believed the killer might show up. Shortly after the family returned home from the funeral, he called again and spoke to Dawn.

This time, he wanted to let her know that he was indeed at the funeral, and the police were too dumb to catch him. Again, he rambled on about killing himself, but Dawn took control of the conversation and put him on the defensive.

The killer tried to make it sound like he and Shari had become best friends. He claimed she was sharing all kinds of personal information with him, but Dawn wasn't falling for it. She was growing sick of him.

(The full transcript of this call is also available in the appendix at the end of this book.)

This time, the call was placed from Augusta, Georgia, about sixty miles away. As per usual, no traces were found at the pay phone.

FBI Profiler John Douglas was called in to provide a prospective profile of the killer. Douglas is now well-known for his work on Netflix's *Mindhunter* series, as well as for being one of the first criminal profilers. He has interviewed some of the worst killers in history, including Edmund Kemper, Ted Bundy, David Berkowitz, John Wayne Gacy, Charles Manson, Gary Ridgeway, and many others. Douglas' analysis came up with a suspect that would be in his late twenties to early thirties, single, a blue-collar worker, lived nearby, had low self-esteem, was overweight, had above-average intelligence, and had a prior criminal record. He also believed that the killer might work with electronics or phone systems because of the voice distortion device used on every call. He also believed the tone of the phone calls indicated that he was an asocial obsessive-compulsive. Finally, Douglas thought the killer felt a strong will to have a sense of power but had never experienced it until this time in his life.

Another week passed, and the killer had not been heard from. Police thought that maybe he had done as he'd hinted and taken his own life. However, exactly two weeks after Shari's abduction, the investigators' worst fears came true. At almost the exact same time of day, it happened again.

Roughly a thirty-minute drive from the Smith home, nine-year-old Debra May Helmick was playing in the front yard of her home with her three-year-old brother, Woody. Their father was just a few feet away inside their trailer home when a neighbor, Ricky Morgan, saw a silver car with red racing stripes drive up. A man got out of the vehicle, grabbed Debra May around the waist, and threw her in the car while she was kicking and screaming. The vehicle then sped away.

Debra May's father hadn't heard his daughter's screams because of the loud air conditioner running in the trailer but was alerted by Ricky Morgan, who had witnessed the abduction. Terrified, little three-year-old Woody only said, "The bad man said he was coming back to get me."

The two men got in their car and went in the direction the abductor's car was going, but they found nothing. Police immediately started an air and ground search. Their fear was that this was the same man that had killed Shari Smith.

Police now had a witness that could give a description not only of the car but of Debra May's kidnapper himself. Ricky Morgan described him as a thirty to thirty-five-year-old white male, approximately five-foot-nine, with a protruding stomach, a short beard and mustache, and brown hair. From this new information, police now drew up another sketch of the suspect.

Eight days had gone by, and there was no sign of Debra May. It had been fourteen days since the Smith family had heard from the killer when he called collect once again. Dawn retook the call, but this time he didn't want to talk about Shari,

Killer: "God wants you to join Shari Faye. It's just a matter of time… this month… next month… this year… next year. You can't be protected all the time… and you know… uh… have you heard about Debra May Hamrick [sic]?"

Dawn: "Uh, no."

Killer: "The ten-year-old… H-E-L-M-I-C-K."

Dawn: "Richland County?"

Killer: "Yeah, uh-huh, ok, now listen carefully… Go 1 north… well… Bill's Grill. Go three and a half miles through Gilbert. Turn right. Last dirt road before you come to stop sign at Two-Notch Road. Go through chain and no trespassing sign. Go fifty yards and to the left. Go ten yards. Debra May is waiting. God forgive us all."

Dawn: "Hey! Listen."

Killer: "What?"

Dawn: "Uh, just out of curiosity, how old are you?"

Killer: "Dawn E., your time is near. God forgive us and protect us all. Goodnight for now, Dawn E. Smith."

Dawn: "Wait a second here, what happened to the pictures you said you were gonna send me?"

Killer: "Apparently, the FBI must have them."

Dawn: "No, sir, because when they have something, we get it too, you know. Are you gonna send them? I think you're jerking me around because you said they were coming, and they're not here."

Killer: "Dawn E. Smith, I must go."

Dawn: "Listen, you said you were gonna... and you did not give me those photos."

Killer: "Goodnight, Dawn, I'll talk to you later."

The killer was clearly now fixated on Dawn. He was now threatening her by calling her "Dawn E. Smith" and telling her that she would soon join her sister.

Police raced to the location given. In the bushes, they found the decomposed body of the tiny, blonde girl. She was clothed in her tank top, shorts, and panties, but over her panties were a pair of silk adult bikini briefs. Like Shari, remnants of duct tape were found in her hair.

Again, the unusually warm temperatures that summer had accelerated the decomposition, and an autopsy was inconclusive. An official cause of death could not be determined, but suffocation was presumed. It also could not be determined if the girl had been raped, though the odd extra pair of panties suggested she had. A pink barrette found near the body with a clump of blonde hair was shown to Mrs. Helmick. She confirmed that it belonged to Debra May.

As expected, the trace of the call resulted in no evidence. The killer was long gone by the time police arrived; there were no witnesses, and the phone had been wiped clean of fingerprints.

Police now worried that the killer had no intention of stopping and that Dawn was going to be the next victim.

Luckily, the forensic document team would soon get their most significant break. The "Last Will and Testament" letter that had been mailed to the family revealed more clues.

Forensic document examiners were able to recover an imprint of a partial phone number from the letter and the name "Joe." The phone number was a Huntsville, Alabama prefix, and the last four digits were only missing one digit, leaving only ten possible phone numbers.

Police called all ten numbers until they found someone with the name Joe. One of the numbers belonged to a young man named Joey Sheppard. When they searched the phone records of Joey Sheppard, they found that he had received calls from a phone in Saluda County, where Shari's body was found.

When investigators called Joey Sheppard, he was quickly eliminated as a suspect. He didn't fit the FBI profile. They asked him if he knew anyone in Lexington or Saluda counties, and he replied, "Yes, my parents live in Saluda County."

On the evening of June 26, police raced to the home of Ellis and Sharon Sheppard, just two miles from where Shari's body was found. They were expecting to find their suspect but were quickly disappointed. The Sheppards didn't fit the FBI profile either.

Detectives decided to question the Sheppards and found that they had just returned from a six-week trip. They explained that they often traveled for extended periods, and a local man that worked for Ellis, Larry Gene Bell, would house-sit for them.

They described Larry Gene Bell as a mid-thirties white male who lived with his parents and had reddish-brown hair, a beard, and a mustache. The description fit the FBI profile perfectly.

Detectives questioned the Sheppards all night until the early morning the next day. During the questioning, they played the tapes of the phone calls for the Sheppards. Despite the electronic distortion of the calls, the Sheppards quickly confirmed that it was the voice of Larry Gene Bell.

They told police that Bell had picked them up from the airport just a few days earlier, when they returned from their vacation. The conversation on the drive home from the airport was dominated by the news of the two murders. Bell seemed to be obsessed with the murders. Mrs. Sheppard mentioned that Bell had mistakenly called her "Shari" on several occasions since they returned from their trip. He had also collected all of the news articles of the murders from the local newspapers. All of this fit the FBI profile of the suspected killer.

Bell had been staying at the Sheppards' home while they were on vacation, so police searched the house. They found that Ellis' .38 caliber handgun was missing.

Bell was due to come to the Sheppards' home that morning at 7:30 a.m. to work. Police arrested Bell as he left his home on the morning of June 27.

After Bell's arrest, a forensic team continued their search of the Sheppards' home. They found Mr. Sheppard's missing .38 revolver underneath the mattress in the bedroom where he had been staying. They also found a blonde hair that DNA later proved was from Shari Smith.

During the interrogations of Larry Gene Bell, he admitted nothing. Hilda and Dawn Smith even came in to try and entice him to confess, but he just mumbled nonsensically and said,

"...this Larry Gene Bell couldn't have done this, but another Larry Bell could have been the one."

Hilda told him that she knew he'd killed her daughter, but she didn't hate him. Bell teared up but still didn't confess.

Bell made a mockery of the trial, blurting out strange comments, refusing to answer questions, and rambling and mumbling nonsense. One of his favorite responses to questioning was, "Silence is Golden," and at one point, he yelled, "I would like Dawn E. Smith to marry me!"

Larry Gene Bell was found guilty of murdering both Shari Smith and Debra May Helmick and sentenced to death. During his incarceration, he repeatedly claimed that he was Jesus Christ.

Bell chose to die by the electric chair rather than lethal injection and was put to death on October 4, 1996.

CHAPTER 5
A UNICORN AMONG BEASTS

L ife on the Hawaiian island of Maui is very relaxed. The North
Shore of Maui, where the big waves can be found, attracts
surfers, beach bums, hippies, and people who just love to enjoy life.
Carly "Charli" Scott was one of those people.

Charli was a fun-loving girl who lived near the North Shore and loved
the laid-back lifestyle of Maui. With her pin-up girl looks, Charli was
known for her quirkiness, taste in music, clothes, and bright red hair.
She loved to sing out loud and often went out of her way to help her
friends and family.

Charli moved to Maui from Woodland, California, in 2004. Even in her
twenties, Charli still had a child-like side to her. She was fascinated
with unicorns, and her favorite movie was 1982's "The Last Unicorn."
She often quoted the Chinese philosopher You Rou, saying she was a
"unicorn among beasts." Unfortunately, the beast she met was named
Steven Capobianco.

Steven Capobianco met Charli in 2009, when she was twenty-two
years old, and he was just nineteen. Charli was smitten with Steven,
and the couple moved in together in the town of Kula, just a few miles
upcountry from the beach town of Paia. Though they lived together for

two full years, Steven often told his friends they were just roommates, even going so far as to avoid having his picture taken with her.

Though Charli openly loved Steven, that love was not reciprocated. Steven never told her he loved her, and according to her friends, he never showed her any affection at all other than sex.

Charli had a motherly side to her as well. She enjoyed making Steven's life comfortable by cooking and cleaning the house, while Steven spent hours in front of the television playing video games or working on his truck. Though the couple lived together, they didn't do many activities together. To their friends' knowledge, Steven was never abusive to her, but behind her back, he would tell his friends, "I hate that fucking bitch."

When Steven and Charli inevitably broke up, they still had an on-again-off-again relationship for the next few years. Charli was still in love, even though she knew Steven didn't care about her, while Steven knew Charli was always there if he needed her for sex. No matter how badly Steven treated her, Charli was under his spell and just couldn't seem to say "no." She came running every time he called.

In the fall of 2013, Steven met a young blonde named Cassandra Kupstas, and the two started dating. Cassandra claimed it was "love at first sight." She was living on Maui when she met Steven but already had plans to move back to her hometown in Pennsylvania.

Though they only had three weeks together before she moved 5,000 miles away, they fell very much in love. Once Cassandra returned to Pennsylvania, she and Steven spoke on the phone via Skype twice a day. She had only been back for a few days before they both realized that they needed to be together, so they made plans for her to move back to Maui the following February.

Neither Steven nor Cassandra seemed to be the faithful type. Early on in their relationship, Steven learned that Cassandra had cheated on him, so he decided to go to a bar in the town of Makawao to drown his sorrows. Steven ran into Charli at the bar. Charli lent a sympathetic ear and invited him over to her place. As usual, Steven was only interested in sex, and Charli knew she couldn't resist.

The cheating was just a minor setback for Steven and Cassandra, as they quickly patched up their relationship and continued with their plans of creating a life together.

That October, just over a month after their hookup, Charli realized she was pregnant. Although this wasn't the ideal situation, Charli had always looked forward to the idea of being a mother.

When Charli told Steven the news, he was less than pleased and told her he wanted to take a paternity test to ensure he was the father. Unfortunately, this pregnancy got directly in the way of Steven's plans with his new love, Cassandra.

He told Charli he wouldn't be there for her baby and insisted she get an abortion. Charli reluctantly agreed, and the two went to Planned Parenthood for a consultation.

During their visit, the director of the local Planned Parenthood noticed the tension between the couple and asked Steven if he was the father. Steven replied,

 "I guess so... but she's not with me."

The director looked at Charli and saw an unmistakable look of pain on her face. Steven then blurted out,

 "We're going to go through with this, aren't we?"

Charli agreed, and they made plans for Charli to come back later for the procedure.

Christmas dinner was held at the home of Charli's half-sister, Fiona, and Charli thought this was the perfect time to announce to her family that she was now three months pregnant and having a baby.

Charli hadn't spoken to Steven since their appointment at Planned Parenthood and had since changed her mind. She'd decided to keep the baby and raise it on her own – with or without Steven's help. She knew that no matter what her situation, she would always have the support of her family and friends.

Jaws dropped, and mouths were wide open around the room. Charli's family was shocked but ultimately overjoyed for her when they saw how excited she was. She had already learned the gender of the baby and had decided she would name him Joshua.

Her half-sister Fiona was curious if Steven knew about the baby, so she sent him a text, "Do you realize you are the father of Charli's child?" Steven replied, "What? How do you know? I thought she had taken care of it?" He had no idea that Charli had changed her mind and decided to keep the baby.

When Fiona spoke to Steven on the phone later that day, he sounded nervous and panicked. He couldn't believe the news. He said that he and Charli had agreed to "take care of it." He told her he had a new girlfriend that he loved, and she was moving in with him in February. However, he worried that this baby would mess up his plans. He ended the conversation by saying, "I need to talk to Charli."

A few weeks had passed before Steven worked up the nerve to break the news to Cassandra during their daily Skype sessions. Steven explained that he didn't know for sure that the baby was his, and he had asked Charli to have an abortion, having even taken her to the clinic himself.

Cassandra, however, was in shock. At only twenty-one years old, she wasn't ready to be a stepmother and told Steven she didn't want to talk for a few days while she processed the news.

Eventually, Cassandra called Steven and told him she didn't want him to be a deadbeat dad and that he should take responsibility for the child. She said he should be there for his son, but she could sense that Steven still wasn't ready to become a father. He told Cassandra he had no feelings for Charli and had never had any feelings for her, explaining "she was just an easy lay."

On the evening of Sunday, February 9, Charli, her mother, and her four sisters gathered at her sister Brooke's house for a relaxed evening watching Disney videos. Brooke had recently found out she was pregnant too, and they talked about their children growing up together on Maui. Brooke later recalled feeling her sister's tummy as Joshua was kicking.

Around 8:00 p.m. that evening, Charli kissed her mother, told her she loved her, and made her way home. Sadly, it was the last time any of her family saw her.

Charli lived only a few miles away from her mother and planned to drop laundry with her on her way to the Hui No'eau Visual Arts Center in nearby Makawao, where she worked as an administrator.

But when Charli didn't show up that morning, her mother, Kimberlyn, called her cell phone. She wasn't surprised when Charli didn't answer. Charli should have been at work by then and typically didn't answer personal calls while working. Kimberlyn then sent her a text message, knowing Charli would respond when she had the time.

As the day progressed, Charli's mother sent a few more texts but received no reply each time. Charli was a very responsible girl, and it was unusual for her to not reply. That was when Kimberlyn started getting worried. By 4:00 p.m., she had already sent her daughter several messages and eventually sent one saying, "Where the hell are you?" By 9:00 p.m., Kimberlyn and the rest of the family were in full-on panic mode.

That evening, Kimberlyn and Charli's sixteen-year-old sister, Phaedra, went to Charli's house. Her Toyota 4Runner wasn't parked outside, and the doors to her home were locked. They knocked, knowing there would be no answer. However, they could hear one of her dogs inside the house. They had keys, so they let themselves in.

Upon entering the house, they found one of Charli's dogs, Zoey, with no dog food or water. Charli would never have left her dogs without food and water. Unfortunately, her second dog, Nala, was missing.

Kimberlyn then remembered that she and Charli shared an app called Life360 that was used for families to track the location of one another, specifically in situations like this. When she checked the app, it showed that the last ping from Charli's phone was at 10:56 p.m. the night before in Ke'anae.

Ke'anae was a remote area along Maui's North Shore, just a short distance from the famous road to Hana. It was a beautiful peninsula with huge waves that crashed against the jagged black rocks of the shoreline, but there was no explainable reason why Charli would have gone there – particularly that late at night when she was five months pregnant.

As the family hypothesized about why Charli would have possibly been that far out in the middle of the night, only one reason came to mind. There was only one person that Charli would see without telling anyone: Steven Capobianco.

At 10:19 p.m. Monday night, Kimberlyn sent Charli one last text, "I'm about to call the police, Charli. Where are you???" When there was still no answer, she called Maui Police and reported Charli missing.

Maui Police showed up at Steven Capobianco's house at 5:30 Monday morning to question him. But he seemed surprised; he claimed it was the first he had heard of Charli's disappearance.

Steven told detectives that Charli had come to his house on Sunday night because he'd asked for a ride to pick up his truck. He said the battery cable had come loose as he drove on the road to Hana the previous day, and he'd left his truck parked on the side of the road. He needed a ride to the truck so he could repair the cable and drive it home. He explained that the vehicle had been stalled just a few miles past Ke'anae at mile marker twenty. It was the exact location where Charli's cell phone last pinged the tracking app.

According to Steven, Charli drove him to his truck that night, and she didn't even need to get out of her vehicle. He claimed she shined her headlights on his truck while he fixed the battery cable and the whole process only took a few minutes. They then drove back toward town in their own vehicles. Steven said Charli followed him on the way back, but he drove faster than she did and lost sight of her headlights near Ulalena Loop in the Twin Falls area, just twenty minutes from her home.

Steven explained that he sent her a text when he got home to thank her, but he didn't receive a reply.

Tuesday at daybreak, the entire family gathered with friends and began their search of the island. They hoped they would find that Charli had rolled her car off the side of the road to Hana and just couldn't get help.

Search crews scoured up and down the road to Hana. They thought she could be anywhere between Haiku and Hana, a forty-mile stretch of twists and turns, one-lane bridges, and sharp cliffs on the ocean side of the road. They were looking for skid marks, broken railings, broken bushes, or any sort of clue at all. By nightfall, however, they'd found nothing.

That evening, friends and family posted on Facebook, and the local news stations picked up the story. Word spread fast around the island that Charli was missing. Just a month prior, another Maui woman, Moreira "Mo" Monsalve, had mysteriously disappeared. Speculation quickly spread that the two cases may have been related.

Wednesday morning, there was a clue. Charli's other dog, Nala, had been found at the Nāhiku Marketplace, an area much further towards Hana. Nāhiku was eight miles past where Steven said his truck broke down and about twenty-five miles from where he said he lost sight of Charli's headlights that night.

The man who found Nala said he found her wandering around Nāhiku Marketplace on Monday morning. Her hair wasn't dirty, and her paws seemed clean and not cracked. Police knew that if a dog had traveled any distance in the rugged area, it would have matted hair and muddy or cracked paws. So, while it was good news that Nala was found safe, it also presented more significant problems. Her family knew that Charli would never willingly leave Nala alone. Also, it left the question of how Nala got that far down the Hana Highway without getting dirty. Someone had to have dropped her off way out there.

That same afternoon, searchers found Charli's vehicle. Her 1997 Toyota 4Runner was located near the famous surf spot, Jaws: it was flipped on its side, completely burned. Forensic experts found the use of accelerants on the passenger side and the rear of the SUV. Everything that wasn't metal had been burned and completely disintegrated. Police questioned two nearby families who said they smelled the toxic smoke burning throughout the night.

Charli's father and several other relatives and friends flew out from the mainland. They all came to help with the search. Local Maui residents came from all over the island to help, donating their horses, search dogs, and helicopters, but families and searchers had a sinking feeling that the chances of finding Charli alive were slim.

On Thursday, a search team found a pair of jeans with bloodstains thrown alongside the Hana Highway. The size matched Charli's, and later analysis showed the blood was hers. Investigators also found a single hair in the pocket of the jeans. DNA taken from the hair was later found to match that of Steven Capobianco.

Late Thursday afternoon, Charli's younger sister, Phaedra, thought it would be best to thoroughly search the Ke'anae area near Nua'ailua Bay, since it was the last ping location of Charli's cell phone. As she and Brooke drove down the road to the area of Paraquat's Beach, they saw lights coming up the dirt road. They instantly recognized them as the headlights of Steven Capobianco's truck. Steven stopped them as they drove down the secluded dirt road and told them he had already searched that area and found nothing. He offered to search the area again with them, but Phaedra and Brooke felt uneasy being alone with him. Instead, they decided to return home and search the area later.

Another of Charli's friends, Adam Gaines, heard a similar story from Steven earlier that day.

Late that evening, when they knew Steven wasn't in the area anymore, Phaedra took two friends back to the area near Paraquat's Beach to do their own search.

The brush in the area was very thick, so the three of them used flashlights and spread out wide enough to where they could still hear each other. Just a few feet into the brush, Phaedra found something. It was a DVD of the movie Twilight. That DVD had been in Charli's car when she went missing.

As they searched deeper into the woods, Molly Wirth found a long black skirt and a blue polka-dot tank top. These were the clothes Charli was wearing on Sunday night, when they saw her last. The skirt, however, had at least 20 puncture marks concentrated around the abdomen area.

As they continued their search, they came to a stream and were overwhelmed by a horrible stench. Something was rotten and decomposing. A green blanket covered with maggots lay on the banks of the stream. It was a blanket that Charli had kept in her vehicle. Nearby were a pair of Perry Ellis jeans, a gray hoodie, and two rolls of masking tape. Terrified at what they had found, the three returned home and contacted Maui Police.

At daybreak, investigators began a full forensic search of the area near Nua'ailua Bay. During their extensive search, they recovered a black bra with cuts in it, five fingernails, skin fragments, clumps of red hair, a body piercing with flesh still attached to it, a bone fragment, and two halves of a lower jawbone. DNA analysis matched them all to Charli Scott.

Forensic analysis of the jawbone showed it was split into two pieces and had marks of dismemberment, blunt force trauma, and removal of flesh with a serrated edge.

Although the search for more body parts continued, it was now clear that Charli had been brutally murdered. The case was now considered a homicide.

Maui prosecutors took their time building their case against Steven Capobianco. Initially, he was only listed as a person of interest – not officially a suspect. During this time, Steven was cocky and convinced he wouldn't be arrested. He spoke with reporters, repeating his story. He said he took a lie detector test but was told he'd failed,

 "They didn't make me take it again. I'm honestly not convinced I failed; I think they might have just said that as a tactic, but I really don't know. I'm walking around right now without handcuffs on."

Four months after finding the jawbone, Maui Police arrested Steven Capobianco for Charli Scott's murder. He was charged with second-degree murder and third-degree arson. Almost every part of Steven's story fell apart as the evidence piled up against him.

Though much of the evidence against Steven was largely circumstantial, his story's sheer volume of inconsistencies was monumental.

The FBI analyzed his cell phone usage: when he claimed his truck had broken down on the road to Hana, his cell phone was actually being used over twenty miles away in Haiku, near his home.

Steven claimed that his friend, Kyle Knight, had picked him up the following morning and given him a ride to work, but Kyle told investigators that was a lie. Security video near his work showed him driving his truck that morning at 6:41 – the same time he claimed the truck was broken down on Hana Highway. That same day, a coworker told detectives he had retrieved a backpack from Steven's truck, parked in the parking lot at his work.

Even Steven's grandfather testified that he left the house that morning in his own truck.

At the trial, local residents who traveled the road to Hana every day testified that they didn't see any vehicles broken down that morning. Steven's story for why the truck broke down didn't make sense, either. If the battery cable had come loose while the vehicle was running, the engine would still run until it was turned off.

Steven made another crucial mistake during interviews with the police and television reporters. He mistakenly referred to Charli in the past tense, before any body parts had been found.

Perhaps his most incriminating inconsistencies were the three different stories he gave for why his hands were injured.

Capobianco had a Skype conversation with his girlfriend, Cassandra, at 2:30 a.m. on Monday, just hours after Charli disappeared. Cassandra told investigators he acted nervous and frantic. He showed Cassandra his scratched and bloody hands and claimed he'd smashed one hand on the hood of a friend's car, then a battery terminal had sliced the other. During the trial, Cassandra testified,

> "He was kind of frantic and wound up, like someone who had just got out of a car accident."

The following morning, referring to the same injury, he told a coworker at Mana Foods that he'd injured his hand working on the window of a friend's car. He claimed the cable that pulls the window up had wrapped around his hand, and he'd lost feeling in it. However, experts testified during the trial that the Honda window cable he referred to was encased in an enclosure that would have made it impossible for the cable to wrap around his hand.

During a police interrogation, Steven told Detective Loo that he had injured his hands at Mana Foods, where he worked as a baker. He also said he'd sliced his pinky while working on the window of his truck, not a friend's car.

Everything about Steven's story was a lie and cell phone data put him in the exact remote location of Charli's death. How she was killed, however, is still a mystery.

On December 28, 2016, a jury returned with a guilty verdict on both counts after twenty-eight days of deliberation. Steven Capobianco was sentenced to life in prison without the possibility of parole.

During his incarceration, Capobianco's aunt, Susan Capobianco, was arrested when visiting Steven at Maui Community Correctional Center. She was caught trying to pass him a package that contained twelve cigarettes, 0.3 grams of methamphetamine, marijuana, hash oil, and rolling papers. She was sentenced to eighteen months in jail and four years of probation.

CHAPTER 6
THE CANAL KILLER

In the late 1700s, London was growing rapidly, and merchants needed a way to get goods to the seagoing ships on the River Thames. A vast series of canals and locks were built throughout the city to bring goods to the Thames using small canal boats. Those canals still exist today, though they are no longer used for trade. Today, the canals offer a peaceful place for walkers, runners, boaters, cyclists, and tourists to enjoy away from the city traffic.

Regent's Canal was built in 1812 and is still one of the most beautiful canals in London. It stretches over eight miles from Paddington to the Thames, encircling the heart of the city. The canal banks are very popular and usually quite busy.

On an afternoon in February 2001, two boys were fishing in Regent's Canal when one of their lines got caught on something on the bottom of the canal. When the boys reeled in the line, they found that it had snagged a duffel bag. They managed to drag the bag to the canal's edge but needed help getting it onto the bank.

Curious, the boys unzipped the bag and found it filled with bricks and ceramic tiles. However, there was also something wrapped tightly with plastic. They opened the plastic and were hit with the sharp stench of decomposition. When they called the London police, investigators confirmed that it was a human body part.

Police were sent in to dredge the canal. Divers found five additional duffel bags, each filled with bricks and each containing more body parts. Six bags were found in total, with ten body parts. The torso had been cut in half, the legs were cut at the hips and knees, and the arms were severed at the shoulders and elbows. The head, hands, and feet were all missing.

An autopsy revealed that the body was female, but not much forensic evidence was available. Bloodwork was sent to the lab, and through DNA, they were able to find out who she was. She was in the system for drug offenses and prostitution.

The body belonged to thirty-one-year-old Paula Fields. Paula was a mother of three who was originally from Liverpool. She had moved to London to try to better her life but became addicted to crack cocaine and turned to prostitution after social services had taken her children away from her.

Police discovered that Paula had been dating a man named Joe Johnson four months earlier. However, they found no record of Joe Johnson, though he had a roommate named Tony Sweeney, who had a lengthy police record. Tony Sweeney's brother, John, also had a record and had been wanted for the attempted murder of his girlfriend in 1994. Before long, investigators realized that Joe Johnson was actually the fugitive John Sweeney.

Forensic analysis of soil found in the duffel bags proved it was identical to the soil from Sweeney's garden, where he lived on Digby Crescent in London. But that wasn't nearly enough to convict him of the murder of Paula Fields.

John Sweeney had been on the run from police for almost seven years, using different names wherever he went. He was working as a carpenter on a construction site in Central London when he was arrested on March 23, 2001.

Sweeney was arrested for the attempted murder of his former girlfriend, Delia Balmer, almost seven years earlier in 1994. Still, police hoped they could also gather enough evidence to link him to the murder of Paula Fields.

At the time of his arrest in 2001, Delia Balmer was still living in London and working as a nurse. She originally met John Sweeney in a London pub in 1991. They had dated and traveled throughout Europe and eventually decided to share a flat in London. However, the relationship soured over time as Sweeney became increasingly aggressive and possessive. By 1994, Delia had decided it was time to end the relationship and changed the locks on their home, but Sweeney didn't take kindly to that.

When Delia walked home from work, Sweeney followed close behind in the shadows. As she opened her door, he ran up behind her and pushed her over the threshold and into the apartment. He held her captive for seven full days. During that time, he tied her to the bed, repeatedly beat her, raped her, and threatened to cut out her tongue if she screamed.

When Delia's friends from work came to her house, they knew someone was inside, but no one would come to the door. Knowing something was wrong, they called the Kentish Town police.

When police arrived on November 14, 1994, Sweeney had Delia open the door ever so slightly while he hid behind the door. The officers could tell by Delia's demeanor that something was terribly wrong and forced the door open. Delia ran out of the door and into the street while police pushed their way in and arrested Sweeney for assault, rape, and unlawful confinement.

Inside, they found evidence that Sweeney had plans to kill Delia and dispose of her body. Sweeney had a "murder kit" containing plastic ground sheeting, orange rubber gloves, rolls of tape, a saw, a bow knife, and a box cutter knife.

Delia told police that while Sweeney had her tied up, he told her that he had murdered his prior girlfriend, Melissa, in Amsterdam. He said she was an American, and he had walked in on her having sex with two German men. He told her that he shot all three of them, sat with their dead bodies for several days, and then dismembered them and dumped them in the canals of Amsterdam. Sweeney taunted Delia, telling her that if she was a good girl then she wouldn't end up like Melissa.

Also inside the flat, police found several firearms and hundreds of paintings and poetry Sweeney had created. Both the artwork and the poetry were violent, dark, and graphic, with images of bloody, dismembered bodies and women being tortured. The poetry seemed to be a confession of his mayhem. One poem read:

"Poor old Melissa

Chopped her up in bits

Food to feed the fish

Amsterdam was the pits"

Police now suspected that Sweeney was a serial killer who had murdered at least one other girl in the same way that Paula Fields was murdered. London police contacted Amsterdam police, but they had no record of a murder matching their inquiry.

Unfortunately, Sweeney was released on bail after only a month in jail for his assault on Delia Balmer, but she wasn't notified of his release. Sweeney wasn't to go near Delia under the terms of his bail, but that didn't stop him. Within hours of his release, he was hiding near Delia's door again, waiting for her to return home from work.

As she approached her front door, Sweeney savagely attacked her with a knife and an axe, slashing her chest and cutting off one of her fingers. Luckily, a neighbor heard her screams, grabbed a baseball bat, and hit

Sweeney across the back. Sweeney ran from the scene, and Delia barely escaped with her life. Her arms were broken, her lung was punctured, and her chest was permanently scarred.

Sweeney went on the run using several aliases and remained undetected by police until his arrest in 2001, after Paula Fields' body was found.

Though police didn't have enough evidence to prove that John Sweeney had butchered Paula Fields and dumped her in Regent's Canal, they had enough to get him into prison while they searched for more evidence. Sweeney was sentenced to serve nine years in prison for the attempted murder of Delia and firearms charges. With Sweeney behind bars, it gave investigators time to find more evidence in the Paula Fields case.

While Amsterdam authorities couldn't find any information about bodies dumped in the canals, they did, however, find something about an American girl named Melissa Halstead. She was reported missing in April 1990 by her family, but unfortunately, they had no more information on her.

Melissa Halstead was a rebellious young American girl who had dated Sweeney in the late eighties. She was a beautiful girl who had worked as a model for Ford Modeling in New York, then moved to London where she took up photography. She and Sweeney had a tumultuous relationship with frequent, violent arguments. On one occasion, he threw a chair at her, which permanently scarred her face. Still, no matter what he did, she always seemed to forgive him.

In 1988, Melissa was deported from the United Kingdom for working without a permit. She left Sweeney and moved to Vienna, Austria. Sweeney followed her, broke into the apartment she shared with a roommate, tied up her roommate, and searched the apartment for evidence that she had another lover. Later that day, he hunted her down and beat her with a clawhammer.

Sweeney was jailed for six months for the attack, but despite the abuse, Melissa again stayed with him. They moved throughout Europe to Stuttgart, Milan, and ultimately settled in Amsterdam. The relationship was still in constant turmoil, and Melissa told her sister that, if she ever went missing, John Sweeney had killed her. Eventually it happened. By April 1990, Melissa Halstead had disappeared.

Although Sweeney was imprisoned in March 2002 for the attempted murder of Delia Balmer, it was only temporary. He would soon be eligible for parole and potentially on the street before they found more evidence on the Melissa Halstead or Paula Fields cases. In 2004, the death of Paula Fields became a cold case.

In 2007, six years after Paula Fields' body parts were found, the London police got a call from the Rotterdam cold case investigation team. They were investigating all of their unsolved cases from 1990 onward.

On May 3, 1990, Rotterdam police had pulled several duffel bags from the Westersingel Canal in Rotterdam. Like Paula Fields, the bags had been weighted down with bricks and contained several dismembered female body parts. The head, hands, and feet were missing.

The Rotterdam team had already spoken to the police in Amsterdam and suspected they were the remains of Melissa Halstead. Melissa had been reported missing just one month before Rotterdam had originally found the body parts. It seemed that, after almost eighteen years, they could identify the body.

In January of 2008, just as time was running out and Sweeney would soon be eligible for parole, Amsterdam, Rotterdam, and London police worked together to exhume the remains of the unidentified body parts from 1990. Using the DNA of her relatives eighteen years after she had been reported missing, Dutch detectives confirmed the dismembered girl was Melissa Halstead.

Despite there being no forensic evidence against Sweeney, the similarities in the cases were all too familiar. On April 26, 2009, John Sweeney was removed from his cell and interviewed. He was officially charged with the murders of Paula Fields and Melissa Halstead, but he made no comment.

During the trial, prosecutors showed the jury his artwork and poetry. There were over 200 images, many depicting severed body parts similar to how the real body parts were found. One painting showed a man with a knife raised above his head, preparing to stab a woman. The caption read, "A romantic weekend for two in Austria." Another showed a female body with its hands, feet, and head cut off.

One of the most damning paintings was an image of Melissa Halstead. Next to her head was a gravestone; the text on the gravestone was covered with white correction fluid. Forensic investigators used ultraviolet light to look behind that correction fluid. He was trying to hide the writing on the gravestone, which read:

RIP

Melissa Holstead [sic]

Born 7 12 56

Died –

Yet another one of his paintings was a self-portrait, where he had a bloody axe tucked into his belt. While he sat in prison, he created several additional paintings with dismembered women's bodies cut up in the same manner as Paula and Melissa.

(Images of John Sweeney's artwork can be found in the online appendix at the end of this book.)

Sweeney often yelled at the prosecution during his trial, arguing that his paintings were random nonsense and abstract. He claimed many were made while he was tripping on LSD and weren't meant to be taken as realistic.

The jury, however, found his paintings and poetry to be confessions to the murders. After ten hours of deliberation, the jury returned with a guilty verdict.

On April 5, 2011, John Sweeney was sentenced to a "whole-life tariff," meaning he would spend the rest of his life in prison without the possibility of parole. The sentence was extremely rare in the United Kingdom, with less than 100 prisoners serving a whole-life tariff.

Prosecutors also believed that Sweeney may have been responsible for the disappearance of several more girls, including a Brazilian named Irani, a Columbian named Maria, and a nurse from Derbyshire, England, named Sue. During his incarceration, Sweeney described them as some of his (thirty to forty) girlfriends that police have been unable to locate.

CHAPTER 7
THE HEAD IN THE BUCKET

In April 2001, Melanie Ovalle walked into a Vancouver, Canada, police station and told officers she needed to talk to someone about a murder. The young woman had a story that was a bit hard to believe, and the detectives assigned to her case didn't know what to make of it.

Melanie was a divorcee who lived with her mother, and from the outset, she admitted to detectives that she was bipolar and had been hanging around local drug dealers. For the police, that didn't help her story's credibility. The detectives knew that people who suffer from bipolar disorder could sometimes have lapses in perception, so what she explained to them might not be the actual truth. Despite their assumptions, Melanie gave a very detailed and persuasive story.

Melanie explained that her best friend, Lee-Ann Price, had shown up at her door three weeks earlier, crying hysterically. Lee-Ann said she had been driving around Vancouver with her boyfriend, Mihaly Illes. While he was driving, Illes repeatedly reached for something in the rear of his van. Finally, he grabbed a white Home Depot bucket just behind his seat. Out of curiosity, Lee-Ann looked into the bucket to see what inside it was so interesting to him, but what she saw shocked her to her core. Inside the bucket was a severed human head.

Melanie explained that Lee-Ann showed up at her house again the following day. This time, she brought her boyfriend with her. Melanie had previously met Illes and his associates, Derrick Madinsky and Javan Dowling, at a bar they frequented.

Mihaly Illes was well-known in certain circles throughout Vancouver as a drug dealer. He was a Hungarian national who had been deported from Canada several times for drug and weapons charges but somehow managed to always get back into the country illegally. He ran an elaborate operation that involved taking marijuana grown in British Columbia over the border into the United States. One pound of the highly potent "B.C. bud" that sold for $1,500 in Canada sold for more than $6,000 in Los Angeles. The DEA estimated that, at the time, the trafficking of Canadian marijuana into the United States was a billion-dollar industry.

But rather than selling the weed for cash, they exchanged it for crack cocaine which they would then smuggle back into Canada. This amplified their earnings exponentially. It was believed that Illes and his friends, Derrick Madinsky, Garry Favell, and Javan Dowling, were making more than $80,000 per deal.

Melanie was shocked when Lee-Ann arrived at her door with Illes in tow. She was terrified when Mihaly insisted that the three of them go for a drive. Mihaly was known as a violent man, and Melanie worried he might hurt her if she didn't go with them.

Melanie rode with them to a garage. Once inside, she recognized another of Illes' associates, Derrick Madinsky. Madinsky was busy cleaning the inside of a van.

Illes suddenly became agitated and pulled Melanie aside. In an attempt to intimidate her, he told her that he wanted to show her what happened to people who betrayed him. He then opened the Home Depot bucket and pulled out the human head. Right away, Melanie recognized the face. It was the head of twenty-seven-year-old Javan Dowling, another drug dealer on Illes' team.

Illes claimed Dowling was addicted to crack and had been skimming from their product. As a result, he had blown a deal with one of their most important clients, and Illes needed to prove to the client that he could take care of the situation. Illes also disapproved of him being homosexual. To make matters worse, Dowling had been living in an upscale high-rise suite in downtown Vancouver's Wall Centre, and Illes didn't like that he lived such an extravagant lifestyle.

———

Melanie continued her story and told detectives that Illes demanded she store the head in her garage. She didn't want to, but she was scared of him and felt she had no choice. That night, Illes moved the bucket with the severed head to Melanie's house and placed it in her garage. She wasn't sure why he wanted the head stored in her garage but assumed it was to make her believe she would be an accessory to the crime.

Illes and Lee-Ann showed up again the next day at Melanie's house, and without a word, they removed the bucket with the head and left. Melanie then spent the next three weeks contemplating if she should call the police.

———

Police thought Melanie's story was difficult to believe but decided to do a little research to try and verify it. The first step was to search police databases for the names of Mihaly Illes, Derrick Madinsky, and Javan Dowling.

A quick search through police computers confirmed that Mihaly Illes was a well-known criminal. They found his prior arrests, deportation, and known drug dealing associates, one of whom was Derrick Madinsky.

Javan Dowling had a police record as well. In addition to several drug-related arrests, Javan Dowling had been reported missing by family members right around the time that Melanie claimed to have seen his head in the bucket. Detectives were beginning to realize that Melanie's story could actually be true.

Luckily for detectives, it wasn't hard to track down Mihaly Illes. He was already in police custody, waiting to be deported back to Hungary again. Before speaking to Illes, however, they wanted to talk to Derrick Madinsky. Madinsky was also well-known to police and had his fair share of drug-related arrests. Yet, when police approached him for questioning, he said nothing. He acknowledged he was friends with Mihaly Illes but said nothing of a murder or a head in a bucket.

Detectives then looked into Melanie's story of the van. She had told police that she had seen Madinsky cleaning the inside of a van. Vehicle records showed that Madinsky had recently sold a van, and police recovered it from a used car sales lot.

A thorough forensic analysis was performed on the inside of the van. In addition to photographs and fingerprint analysis, police used a hema stick to search for the presence of blood. A hema stick is a small stick coated with a blood-sensitive chemical. It indicates the presence of blood when touched to a surface and then sprayed with distilled water. The analysis of the van came back positive for human blood, but police needed to find out if the blood belonged to Javan Dowling.

All three of the drug dealers were avid bodybuilders, and when investigators searched Javan Dowling's home, they found a weight-lifting glove. Inside the glove, police recovered skin cells that matched the DNA from the blood found in the van. There was now no question in the detectives' minds that Melanie's story was credible. They had proof that Dowling had bled in the van, but they didn't have definitive proof that he was dead.

Detectives knew that Derrick Madinsky was involved in the crime, so they got a warrant to wiretap his cell phone. After listening to his phone calls, they realized that Madinsky was still helping Illes run the drug operation from prison. Investigators then assigned an undercover police officer to infiltrate the drug ring. Still, nobody was saying a word about Javan Dowling or a murder.

Unable to get the evidence they needed, the police asked for the help of Melanie Ovalle. Detectives had also wiretapped the phone of Illes' girlfriend, Lee-Ann Price. Reluctantly, Melanie agreed to call Lee-Ann and try to get her to talk about the murder.

Melanie called Lee-Ann's tapped phone and expressed her concern about seeing the head in the bucket. She told Lee-Ann that she was riddled with guilt and considering going to the police with the information. Without admitting anything over the phone, Lee-Ann quickly tried to settle her down and told her that she would call her back. Immediately after hanging up with Melanie, Lee-Ann called Mihaly Illes at the prison.

When Lee-Ann called the prison, the police thought she would speak to Illes about the murder. However, they were shocked to hear her say nothing about her conversation with Melanie or the murder. Instead, she told Illes that the two of them needed to get married. Illes was confused, but she assured him she would explain it later. Detectives realized that Lee-Ann knew precisely what she was doing. She knew that if they were married, she couldn't be compelled to testify against her husband. Two days later, Lee-Ann and Mihaly Illes were married in the prison chapel.

Illes was due to be deported from Canada soon. Detectives needed to quickly come up with evidence that a murder had occurred before he was deported, or they may have lost their chance at a conviction. Melanie was also worried about his release. She knew that Illes was able to run his business from prison; he could easily have her killed. She also knew that he had been deported in the past, but that hadn't stopped him from coming back to the country.

With only ten days left before Illes was due to be deported, he was charged with first-degree murder despite no evidence of a body. The charge gave them some leverage to put on Derrick Madinsky. They gave Madinsky a choice: participate in the prosecution of his friend, Illes, or be charged as an accomplice in the murder of Javan Dowling.

Madinsky was a career criminal and surprisingly unfazed after more than ten hours of questioning. Detectives then offered him complete immunity if he testified against Illes. He accepted the offer and agreed to tell the whole story of what happened to Javan Dowling.

Madinsky told police that he, Illes, and Dowling were planning on going to a movie together. Illes was in the van's back seat while Madinsky drove, and Dowling was in the passenger seat. As they drove through West Vancouver, Illes asked Dowling to reach over on the dashboard and turn off the van's interior light. As Dowling leaned over the middle of the van, Illes pulled out his revolver and shot Dowling four times in the back of the head. After the shots, Illes mumbled,

 "There's not enough room for fags in this world."

Illes then reclined the passenger seat all the way back so the body couldn't be seen from the street, and they drove back to their garage, then parked the van inside.

Once inside the garage, they dragged the body out. Illes instructed Madinsky to clean the inside of the van. Madinsky claimed that Illes took Dowling's body into another room and severed his head.

Illes told Madinsky that, because of Dowling's drug addiction, he shorted a particularly important client. That client threatened Illes, telling him they would seek retribution if he didn't take care of the guy that shorted them. Illes took that to mean they would kill him. He told Madinsky that he severed his head to prove to the client that he'd taken care of the problem employee.

Madinsky told police that he didn't see the body or head of Dowling until a week later when Illes asked for help getting rid of it. Illes had planned to bury the body in the woods and cover it with lime. Illes was under the assumption that lime helped a body decompose more rapidly. Madinsky and Illes then drove forty miles north to a remote wooded area near Squamish, B.C., to bury the body.

The judge in Vancouver told detectives that they had one day to present evidence that Illes had murdered Dowling. Without a body, they would have to deport him back to Hungary.

Police then had Madinsky take them to where they buried the body. In a shallow grave, they found the head of Javan Dowling. The head was well-preserved – Illes had been watching too many mobster movies and had mistakenly covered the head with lime rather than lye. Lye would have sped up the decomposition, but lime actually acted as a preservative. Just as Madinsky had told them, Javan Dowling had four bullet wounds in the back of his head.

During the trial, they turned on each other. Madinsky testified against Illes, and Illes claimed that Madinsky was the one that killed Dowling. In March 2003, a British Columbia Supreme Court jury found Mihaly Illes guilty of first-degree murder. He was sentenced to life in prison without the chance of parole for twenty-five years.

Seven years later, the defense claimed that the judge had made a mistake when instructing the jury and that Illes' rights had been violated. The defense also argued that the prosecution had not disclosed specific evidence. As a result, Illes had his verdict overturned and was awarded a second trial.

During the second trial, the defense argued that letters written to Lee-Ann and other friends of Mihaly Illes were not presented as evidence. They insisted that those letters proved his innocence.

The letters, however, were filled with elaborate conspiracy theories in which he blamed Derrick Madinsky and Melanie Ovalle for the murders.

He claimed Melanie's description of events was motivated by jealousy because her friend, Lee-Ann, was spending all her time with him. He also suspected that Javan Dowling was still alive and in hiding. Another letter claimed that he believed the blood found in the van was from when Javan and his boyfriend got in a fistfight, and he got a bloody nose. Yet another letter claimed that there was no murder at all, and the police were fabricating evidence and playing "KGB mind tricks."

Using yet another letter, the prosecution proved that the prior letters were all written as a ruse, specifically for the intention of the police intercepting them. The letter that the prosecution presented read:

> "There is our defense. The [white] letter says it all. Who killed whom, and why… It will be like an ACE in our pocket. This could decide the case. Make it, or brake [sic] it."

After the second trial, Illes was again found guilty and sentenced to life in prison with no parole for twenty-five years.

Coincidentally, just three months after Javan Dowling's death, Derrick Madinsky was involved in another drug-related murder in California.

Madinsky and his associate, Garry Favell, traveled to Los Angeles for another of their marijuana for crack cocaine deals. This time they brought a new guy with them, Joe Bralic. Bralic was not a career criminal like Favell and Madinsky but was headed in that direction. He'd heard that he could make some quick cash by handling the transaction, and they arranged for him to meet with the Los Angeles buyers.

The three men traveled to Los Angeles together, but Madinsky and Favell were the only ones to return to Canada. On July 5, 2002, Joe Bralic's body was discovered behind a Discount Tire store in Fullerton, California. He had been shot, and his body was wrapped in plastic, found lying between two parked cars. Joe Bralic's killer has never been found.

CHAPTER 8
ARIZONA TORSO
MURDER #1

In 1993, forty-one-year-old Valerie Pape was living in New York City and working odd jobs, with almost no assets to speak of. Living on a shoestring, she rented a car and stayed with friends. She had immigrated from France and cared for an elderly man named Howard Pomerantz when she met his son, Ira Pomerantz.

Ira was a loud, brash, fifty-four-year-old New Yorker. Quite the opposite of Valerie. She was a petite blonde, stood at five-foot-two, and only weighed one hundred and ten pounds. Her friends described her as sweet, gentle, kind, sensitive, and always meticulously dressed. Despite her lack of income, she was obsessed with fashion and wouldn't leave the house without her hair and makeup perfect and dressed smartly.

Despite their thirteen-year age difference, Ira and Valerie hit it off, and within two years they were married. At their wedding on November 18, 1995, Valerie wore a dress from Neiman Marcus, and her close friend from France, Michel Sauvage, gave her away.

That same year, they moved to the posh McCormick Ranch neighborhood in North Scottsdale, Arizona. Valerie enjoyed the year-round warm weather, and the couple quickly became well-known socialites in the area. Valerie was very fit, jogged through the affluent neighborhood daily, and regularly hiked Scottsdale's Camelback Mountain.

Ira Pomerantz opened two bars in nearby Chandler, Arizona, while Valerie attended the Allure Career College of Beauty in Scottsdale. Then in 1997, with the financial help of Ira, Valerie opened her own hair salon and art gallery, the Valerie Pape Beauty Gallery, in the upscale Old Town area of Scottsdale.

Valerie's friend, Michel Sauvage, had followed the couple to Scottsdale and worked at the salon, answering phones and taking reservations. To keep his immigration status and stay in the country, Valerie listed Michel as one of the officers of her company.

Ira Pomerantz was known as a good, friendly man, but he had a drinking problem and a temper. In 1998, he was arrested for DUI. He was also known for not being a very good businessman. He became notorious for refusing to pay his employees, overcharging his customers, watering down drinks, and not obeying liquor laws. Eventually, he was fined by the liquor control board for serving drinks to underage customers and serving drinks after hours.

With stacking debt and business going badly, Ira lost the lease on one of his bars. The closing of the second bar wasn't far behind, and in 1999, he was in the process of filing for bankruptcy.

It didn't help his financial matters that Valerie had grown accustomed to spending their money on her lavish lifestyle. She drove a brand new Jaguar and dressed in only the finest clothes. As a result, the couple constantly argued over their dwindling money supply, and Ira had difficulty controlling his temper.

Michel Sauvage was very close with the couple, and by early 1999, he had moved into Ira and Valerie's 2,900-square-foot home. Michel was a constant third figure in the relationship, rarely leaving Valerie's side. On top of the money problems, Ira became very suspicious that Valerie and Michel were having an affair.

Ira told his friends that he couldn't keep up with Valerie's lavish spending, and she was bleeding him dry. He said he was planning to divorce her.

The arguments between Ira and Valerie got so bad that she took self-defense lessons and learned how to shoot a handgun. Ira had an extensive collection of handguns, and she claimed she was worried he would use one on her.

In September 1999, Valerie needed to get away from Ira, so she and Michel temporarily moved in with her friend, Merle Bianchi. Unfortunately, Merle was having some problems of her own. While Valerie and Michel were staying at her home, Merle reported her husband missing. Valerie and Ira reconciled not long afterward, and they moved back in with Ira.

It was just a week after Valerie and Michel moved out that Merle's husband, Ron Bianchi, was found in the forest eighty miles north of Scottsdale in Payson, Arizona. He was dead.

Once back home, the conflicts between Valerie and Ira continued. During one of their heated arguments in October 1999, Valerie accused him of running into the kitchen, opening a drawer, and throwing kitchen knives at her. Ira denied the allegation, but Valerie was given a court order of protection against him and he was ordered to move out of his own home.

Within a few days, he had violated the court order. She called the police, but a week later they had reconciled. Ira moved back into the house again. She told the court,

 "I have received apologies and want to give him another chance."

Police were called to the couple's house at least six times during the late nineties for assorted reasons, ranging from burglary to aggravated assault and violation of a protective order.

In the early morning hours of January 28, 2000, twenty-five miles away from Scottsdale in East Mesa, a truck driver was dropping off his 5:00 a.m. delivery behind Basha's grocery store on Power Road and McDowell Road. At that time of the morning, he thought it was odd to see a blue Jaguar pull up next to the dumpsters behind the store. He watched as a petite blonde woman wearing high heels, gloves, sunglasses, and a jumpsuit opened her trunk and took out a large object wrapped in plastic. The tiny woman struggled to lift the package over her head and into the dumpster. The delivery driver took down the Jaguar's license plate and watched as the woman drove away.

After the car was gone, the man walked over to the dumpster to peek inside and found what appeared to be a large body part wrapped in plastic sheeting. He immediately called the police.

When police arrived, they recovered the torso of a male body missing its arms, legs, and head. When investigators ran the license plate number of the Jaguar, it came back registered to Valerie Pape.

Police announced the details of the finding,

"The head had been severed at the base of the neck, both arms cut off at the shoulders, the lower half of the body dismembered at the waist."

When police arrested Valerie Pape at her hair salon, her co-workers and friends were stunned. There was no way the petite, sweet woman could have been the one that dumped a human torso, let alone dismembered it.

One of Valerie's close friends was Republican Arizona Senator Russell Bowers. His personal assistant was Valerie's friend, Merle Bianchi, whose husband had also been murdered. Bowers was shocked at the news of Pape's arrest and professed her innocence to reporters,

"Valerie Pape showed my paintings in her salon. She's a very gentle, decent person, and I'm astonished at this. I think highly of Valerie, and it makes me sick to my

stomach to think this could happen to her. I knew her husband beat her up. I've seen her face. It was a sickening thing."

During her interrogation on January 28, Valerie Pape admitted that she dumped Ira's body in the dumpster behind the supermarket but claimed she didn't kill him.

She explained that she came home from work to find Ira dead, face up, and in a pool of blood on the floor. There was a bullet hole in his back and a gun on the floor nearby. She said she only dumped the body in the dumpster to avoid being accused of his murder.

However, she refused to admit to dismembering the body or say where the remaining parts of her husband's body were. She also said that she had found the body on January 24, four days prior, but refused to say what she did with the body during those four days.

Valerie Pape was arrested and charged with first-degree murder. Investigators searched the couple's house and Valerie's 1997 Jaguar. Beneath the back seat of the Jaguar, they found the handgun that was used to shoot Ira in the back.

Police also searched the home of Valerie's friend, Merle Bianchi. They found it all too coincidental that the husband of Valerie's close friend was murdered just four months prior. The ballistics team analyzed the handgun found in Valerie's car against the bullets that killed Ronald Bianchi, but it wasn't a match.

Dismembering and disposing of a body would be a difficult task, particularly for a woman who was only five-foot-two and 110 pounds. Detectives thought she might have had some help, but Valerie didn't say a word.

After searching their home, investigators found the receipt for an electric reciprocating saw and saw blades that Valerie had purchased from a local department store a few weeks before the murder. That, coupled with the fact that she had taken shooting lessons in the prior months, showed that the murder was intentional and premeditated.

Police then searched the Chandler bar that Ira had recently closed. They believed she might have transported the body to the bar and frozen it in the walk-in freezer. A frozen body would have made dismembering the body much more manageable and delayed the decomposition. But, again, there was no way she could have done it alone. She had to have had help.

Valerie Pape was held without bail. Because she was a French citizen, she was placed on an immigration hold – meaning that if she were released for any reason, she would be turned over to the Immigration and Naturalization Service.

Despite their efforts, police found no evidence of Valerie having had help to kill Ira and they never discovered his remaining body parts. There was overwhelming suspicion that Michel Sauvage had a hand in the murder, but a lack of evidence prevented police from bringing any charges against him.

Unfortunately for prosecutors, no blood evidence was linked to Pape, and the bullet that killed him was never recovered. It was believed that the bullet entered the back of his neck and was still in his head, which, again, was never recovered. The saw and blades were also never found.

Additionally, prosecutors were concerned that the claims of domestic abuse might persuade a jury that the murder wasn't premeditated, and she may have been acquitted of a first-degree murder charge. Thus, rather than risk a not-guilty verdict, they offered her a plea deal.

After two and a half years in jail awaiting trial, as part of the plea deal, Valerie Pape admitted she shot Ira Pomerantz during an argument. She pleaded guilty to a lesser charge of second-degree murder with a prison sentence of just sixteen years.

During her time in prison, she served as the prison's beautician and cut the hair of other inmates and prison employees.

In 2006, a Department of Corrections director approved a transfer for Pape to finish her prison sentence in France. She was flown to Oklahoma City in preparation for the move, but Ira Pomerantz's daughters pressured the Department of Corrections to reverse the move. They were concerned because, after her arrival back in France, the country was under no obligation to have Pape finish her sentence. Valerie Pape was then returned to Arizona to finish her sentence.

After serving her sentence, at sixty-three years old, Valerie Pape was released from prison in 2016 and deported back to her native France.

CHAPTER 9
ARIZONA TORSO MURDER #2

The story of Marjorie Orbin is eerily similar to the Valerie Pape story. It occurred just four years and seven months after the Valerie Pape murder in the same city of Scottsdale, Arizona. The body was found in a similar condition – a dismembered torso – and both killers were trophy wives of wealthy men. It makes you wonder if she was mimicking the Valerie Pape case.

Marjorie Orbin led a somewhat extraordinary life. But to hear her say it, calling her just a stripper would be unfairly downplaying her career. Yes, she did some stripping, but in her mind she was also a talented dancer, a showgirl, and a choreographer.

She officially began her dancing career when she was just eighteen in Orlando, Florida, where she danced at a downtown tourist attraction called Church Street Station. She performed line dances, jazz, and clogging routines. Marjorie was extremely ambitious, and within a year she had choreographed the routines and been promoted to manager of another location called Cheyenne Station.

She had always dreamed of being a mother, but at just eighteen, she was diagnosed with endometriosis – a painful disorder that affects the lining of the uterus. Though pregnancy is possible with endometriosis patients, it's unlikely; she was told that she could not have children. This news was a severe disappointment to Marjorie. In that moment, she decided that since she couldn't lead a life for her children, she would live her life solely for herself and her career.

 "I could walk out of any situation. That may sound cold and callous, but the only person I needed to worry about was me."

Relationships came one after another and Marjorie found herself hopping from man to man. By the time she was thirty-five years old, she had been married and divorced six times. Most of the time, she had already found another lover before divorcing her previous husband.

In 1985, before the ink was dry on her second divorce, Marjorie found herself living with a hairdresser named Luke. Luke came from a wealthy family that offered him a condo if he moved back home to Cincinnati. Marjorie quit her job and followed Luke. As they drove across the country, Luke received word that the condo wouldn't be ready for another month, so he suggested they go to Las Vegas temporarily. He had friends there who owned a hair salon that he could work in for a few weeks until the Cincinnati condo was ready for them.

Luke ended up gambling away their $8,000 savings, and the salon job was non-existent. Marjorie packed her car and left, intending to drive back to Florida, but her car didn't last that long. As she drove through Phoenix, Arizona, her car broke down: it needed an expensive part that would take ten days to fix.

Marjorie was wondering how she would pay for the repair work when she noticed a strip club called Bourbon Street Circus and applied for a job. At that point, she had never done any stripping, but it seemed to come naturally to her. Since she was classically trained in dance, she quickly realized she could work the pole better than any of the other girls.

Marjorie was statuesque and beautiful, with platinum blonde hair, long legs, and a flawless body. Within days, she was easily the most popular dancer in the club. The patrons were infatuated with her, and she was pulling in $500-$600 per night. One of those patrons was twenty-six-year-old Jay Orbin.

Jay was a regular at Bourbon Street Circus and almost every other strip club in the Phoenix area. He was well-known by strippers and club management as one of the best customers. But Jay was on the chubby side and didn't have the greatest fashion sense. Known for his balding-yet-thick, curly, black hair, plus rosy cheeks, cowboy boots, and a diamond pinkie ring, he came across as looking much like a used car salesman. According to his friends, however, Jay was funny, charming, and had a heart of gold.

Jay had his own business, Jayhawk International, selling Native American items like turquoise jewelry, kachina dolls, maps, and bows and arrows. His work was profitable and took him all over the country on sales calls. He traveled three out of four weeks per month and spent his free time in strip clubs all over the country.

Jay had dated many strippers throughout the years, but he was utterly captivated by Marjorie. He came in to see her dance and buy her drinks every chance he got. Though he asked to see her outside the club, she refused. Still, he persisted. After about two months, she agreed to go on an afternoon date with him.

Despite his persistence, she still didn't see herself attracted to him. He was very nice but not exactly her type. Eventually, he paid for her car to get fixed and offered to let her move into his home. Marjorie had been living in a hotel, and he offered to let her stay in a spare room at his house for free. He was gone traveling the country most of the time anyway. She agreed and moved in.

Though Jay tried to get her to be romantic with him, at one point even proposing marriage, Marjorie wanted more from her life and eventually moved back to Florida. Through the years, the two of them lost contact.

While back in Florida, Marjorie dated Michael J. Peter. Michael was well-known the world over for transforming the strip club industry. He took the industry from taboo to mainstream. He bought strip clubs all over the world and made billions. For a short time, he and Marjorie were engaged.

Marjorie traveled the world with him, and he gave her a role in his low-budget (unwatchable) movie *No More Dirty Deals*, as well as got her a small spot in Motley Crue's *"Girls Girls Girls"* video. The song became an anthem at strip clubs around the world. Marjorie became the "choreographer" in his clubs, although the strip clubs didn't have much in the way of choreography. Like all of Marjorie's relationships, it didn't last forever. The two stayed on good terms, but Marjorie eventually made her way back to Las Vegas.

Years later, in 1993, Jay was on a business trip driving through Las Vegas when he noticed a billboard for an adult revue at one of the big casinos. He instantly recognized Marjorie in the advertisement and bought tickets for the show that night.

In the years that passed, Marjorie had become a Vegas showgirl and choreographer for adult revue shows. The two met that night, and Jay realized that he still felt the same way he did years before.

Both Marjorie and Jay were making good money by now, but Marjorie still wanted more than anything to have a family. Realizing this, Jay proposed marriage again – but this time, he had a plan. He told her that she could move in with him in Scottsdale, Arizona, quit stripping, and he would pay for fertility treatments until she got pregnant.

Marjorie liked this idea; in 1994, Jay and Marjorie married at the Little White Wedding Chapel in Las Vegas. This was the same little chapel where celebrities like Frank Sinatra, Judy Garland, Bruce Willis, and Britney Spears were married.

Despite her diagnosis, the fertility treatment worked, and they had a son named Noah in August 1996. Although their relationship was doing well, Marjorie had sizable debt and problems paying the Internal Revenue Service. So, to protect Jay's business assets from being seized by the IRS, they divorced while still remaining together.

For almost ten years, Marjorie Orbin lived the life of a typical suburban housewife, raising her son while Jay traveled the country on sales calls. Although the relationship had lasted much longer than her previous six marriages, she became bored like she had with the others and started seeking other men.

Her infidelities started in 2004. Her first affair was with her son's eighteen-year-old karate instructor. The second was with a sixty-year-old bodybuilder, Larry Weisberg, who she met at her gym. With Jay on the road for three weeks every month, it was easy for Marjorie to hide her affairs from Jay. While Jay was gone, Larry lived at the house with Marjorie full-time.

August 28, 2004, was Noah's eighth birthday. After the birthday party, Jay headed back out on the road. This time, he was on his way to Florida for three weeks. However, once Jay got halfway to Florida, Hurricane Francis had grown too large, and he turned around to return home. With this change, he could make it back to Scottsdale to be home by his own birthday, September 8.

On the afternoon of September 8, as he was driving into the Phoenix area, Jay called his parents, as he did several times a week. He told his mother that his trip had been cut short, and he was almost back home, just in time for his forty-fifth birthday. As he pulled into his neighborhood, he told his mother he would call her back later in the day. She never got that call.

Over the next week, when friends and family hadn't heard from Jay on his birthday, they got worried and called Marjorie. Marjorie wasn't worried at all; she said that Jay hadn't come home. She said he'd called and said he had to go on another sales trip and wouldn't be home until September 22. She told them she hadn't seen him since their son's birthday on August 28.

In the weeks that followed, Jay's family and friends were getting more and more worried, but Marjorie showed no concern. On September 20, several of Jay's friends received calls from Jay's cell phone. However, when they answered, there was no one on the other end.

When September 22 rolled around, Jay still hadn't come home or even called, so they pressured her to finally call the police and report him missing. Reluctantly, she called.

Although Marjorie had reported Jay as missing, she was frequently unavailable to discuss the matter with the police. Police needed the license plate number of Jay's Ford Bronco to use plate recognition to search for it, but by September 28, detectives had left three messages for Marjorie. She hadn't returned their calls. When Detective Jan Butcher of the Missing Persons Unit finally got Marjorie on the phone, she was combative:

> Butcher: "I kind of get the feeling that you're really not available and willing to help us out trying to locate…."
>
> Marjorie: "I speak more matter of factly; that doesn't mean that I do not care. Just because I'm not running around crying and in hysteria doesn't mean that I'm not concerned and not doing anything."

Her reluctance to help and defensive posturing made investigators suspicious of her from the very beginning.

When police checked Jay's bank accounts and credit cards, they realized large amounts of money were being pulled out of his accounts. The signatures on the receipts were Jay Orbin's, but they quickly realized that he hadn't actually signed them – Marjorie had. Within days of

Jay's disappearance, Marjorie had pulled out the maximum amount from ATMs each day. When detectives asked about the withdrawals, Marjorie explained she needed the cash to pay the bills. But when investigators noticed that she had bought a baby grand piano for almost $12,000 with the money, it raised even more red flags.

Beginning on September 9, the day after Jay went missing, Marjorie pulled out over $100,000 from Jay's personal bank accounts and over $45,000 from his business account. She was also selling merchandise from Jay's business.

When investigators discovered that Jay had a $1 million life insurance policy with Marjorie as the beneficiary, they knew the situation was going to end badly.

Detective Butcher called Marjorie again to ask her to come in to take a polygraph test, but her tone became combative,

> Det. Butcher: "Can we schedule to take a polygraph tomorrow?"
>
> Marjorie: "She wants me to take a polygraph tomorrow!" (Speaking to someone else in the room.)
>
> Larry: "You tell her to go fuck herself!"
>
> Det. Butcher: "Who was that?"
>
> Marjorie: "None of your fucking business! It's a friend of mine. Is this conversation being recorded?"
>
> Det. Butcher: "Yes, it is."
>
> Marjorie: "It is. Ok. I would like a copy of that."

After phone negotiations proved to be unproductive, Scottsdale police obtained a search warrant for Jay Orbin's house. When the SWAT team broke down the door to the Orbin home, they were attacked by a well-built man. That man was Larry Weisberg, Marjorie's bodybuilder boyfriend. When Larry attacked the SWAT team, they quickly tased and hit him in the face, breaking his nose.

Once inside the house, they found business credit cards and check-books that Jay Orbin typically used on his business trips. Detective Butcher now believed that this was not just a missing person investigation. Everything she knew pointed to it being a homicide.

On October 23, on the corner of Tatum Road and Dynamite Road, a transient was roaming around a piece of Arizona state trust land in the desert, just fifty feet from the road. Though it was desert, it wasn't remote. The roads were busy, and housing developments were only a few hundred feet away.

The man came across a large object wrapped in black plastic garbage bags and sealed with tape. He pulled the tape off and ripped the black plastic. Inside he found a large, blue Rubbermaid storage container. When he opened the lid of the container, he stumbled back in shock. Aside from the horrible stench, he was shocked to see a belt buckle – and what appeared to be the hairy belly of a man. He immediately ran to a nearby store and called the police.

When police arrived, they discovered it wasn't a whole body but only a half-torso. The male body had been cut just below the ribcage, and the legs had been severed at the knees. The internal organs of the lower half of the torso had been removed. The body had been dismembered while clothed, still wearing jean shorts and a brown leather belt.

At the bottom of the container was a .38 caliber bullet, mixed currency totaling $459.10, and a keyring with eleven keys. The Rubbermaid container was new and still had the UPC sticker on the bottom.

During the autopsy, the medical examiner determined that the body had been previously frozen for an extended period before it was dismembered. From the markings on the bones, they could tell that the body had been dismembered with a saw of some sort.

Six weeks after Jay Orbin went missing, they now believed that they had found his remains just a few miles from his home. DNA tests later confirmed their suspicions. They also believed that Marjorie Orbin had placed the torso there because she wanted the body to be found. After all, in order for her to collect the $1 million insurance claim, Jay had to be confirmed dead. She couldn't collect if he was just missing.

Two days after the torso was found, Jay Orbin's green Ford Bronco was found parked in a residential neighborhood just a few blocks from their home. Detectives took the keys that were found in the bottom of the Rubbermaid container, and as they suspected, they opened and started the Bronco. The remaining keys opened the Orbin home and Jay's office. Three witnesses from the neighborhood told police they saw a woman matching Marjorie's description near the Bronco sometime around September 8.

Three weeks after Jay's body was found, police brought Marjorie in for questioning – not for Jay's murder but for forging his signature when she bought computers at a Circuit City electronics store. However, Marjorie explained that she had been signing his name for years and didn't realize there was anything wrong with using his credit cards after his death.

The more investigating detectives did, the more evidence started to pile up. When searching the Orbin home, investigators found a receipt from Lowe's hardware store dated two days after Jay went missing. On the receipt for that purchase was a slew of mops, various cleaning products, black plastic bags, and two fifty-gallon blue Rubbermaid containers. They were precisely the same type as the container in which Jay's disemboweled torso had been found. In fact, the UPC code on the container they found matched the code from the receipt. Still, the most crucial piece of evidence was a videotape they acquired from that Lowes store dated September 10. The tape showed Marjorie at the checkout counter, purchasing the murder clean-up supplies – and it clearly showed her purchasing the large blue containers.

In Jay's office, investigators found an open package of jigsaw blades missing two blades. The medical examiner determined that the cutting pattern on his bones was consistent with that type of blade.

Back at the Orbin home, they discovered that the garage floor had recently been acid-washed, and a thick layer of decorative epoxy had been installed over the cement, eliminating any chance of finding trace forensic evidence.

On December 6, 2004, Marjorie Orbin was arrested at her home and charged with first-degree murder, fraud, and theft. She was held without bail, and their son, Noah, was sent to live with Jay's parents.

Initially, Larry Weisberg was also a suspect. A search of his home and vehicle showed that he had access to the Orbin home. He had a garage door opener for their garage in his vehicle, so he had the means, but there was no hard evidence against him. All of the evidence pointed directly at Marjorie. With a first-degree murder charge in the state of Arizona, she now faced the possibility of the death penalty.

In a controversial move, the prosecution gave Larry Weisberg complete immunity in the case if he testified against Marjorie.

Faced with the overwhelming evidence against her, Marjorie's attorneys advised her to take a plea deal of a lesser charge to avoid the death penalty, but she refused,

 "I will never let my son hear me say that I did this to his father. I'll let them kill me first."

Marjorie spent the next four years behind bars awaiting trial. During the trial, the defense tried to argue that Jay Orbin weighed at least 250 pounds, and it would have been too physically demanding for Marjorie to dismember and move a body that large. But Marjorie wasn't exactly petite: she was a tall, muscular woman that worked out religiously.

The defense also tried to persuade the jury that Larry Weisberg was responsible for Jay's death, but they offered no evidence. They argued that he was aggressive enough to confront a SWAT team, and as a bodybuilder, he was certainly strong enough to dispose of a body.

The prosecutors countered that defense by saying Larry Weisberg was just another in Marjorie's long list of infidelities. They also pointed out that investigators found no evidence that Larry was involved in the murder at all.

The prosecution also brought in the nineteen-year-old karate instructor that she was sleeping with and her former friends, who claimed she often talked badly of Jay. The karate instructor and Larry Weisberg both claimed that Marjorie was skilled in the art of seduction.

The prosecution also called her cellmate from prison, Sophia Johnson, to the stand. Sophia testified that Marjorie had often complained to her that Jay was fat and disgusting. Sophia claimed that Marjorie confessed to her that she shot Jay, froze his body, thawed the corpse, and then cut off his arms, legs, and head.

The only witness called by the defense was a character witness, Marjorie's former billionaire lover, Michael J. Peter. Peter painted a glowing picture of Marjorie as a good, loving mother, but it wasn't enough to sway the jury.

The trial lasted eight months, but it took only seven hours for the jury to come back with a guilty verdict.

As Judge Arthur Anderson handed down the sentence to Marjorie, he compared her case to yet another Arizona killer: Winnie Ruth Judd, who murdered and dismembered her two friends in 1931 and stuffed their remains into steamer trunks.

At the sentencing on October 1, 2009, Marjorie had her son to thank for avoiding the death penalty. The jury chose to sentence her to life in prison without the chance of parole rather than death.

"We all decided that the son is the innocent victim here. We all walked out of there feeling good." - Juror, Stan Brown

"This is what we wanted all along. From the beginning, we didn't want to kill the boy's mother, and we wanted life." - Jay Orbin's brother, Jake Orbin

To this day, Marjorie Orbin claims that Larry Weisberg shot Jay Orbin in the garage of their home, she never saw Jay's dead body, and she certainly didn't dismember or dispose of the corpse. Marjorie admitted that she helped cover up the murder but insisted she didn't kill him.

She claimed to TV crews of the show *48 Hours* that Weisberg was a very violent man and shot Jay in their garage. She said that Larry threatened to kill her son if she told the police he did it. She claimed that Weisberg said,

 "It's just that easy to snap that kid's scrawny neck if you don't do what you're told."

Although she claimed that Weisberg threatened her when in front of TV crews, she never told this story to the police.

Currently, Marjorie's profile on writeaprisoner.com reads:

Growing up in Miami, Florida, the sunshine and water were a big part of my life, playing on the beaches, diving, surfing, sailing, playing beach volleyball.

The little girl in ballet class was the start of a lifelong love of dance. I had quite a career as a professional dancer and choreographer, from Disney World to cruise ships in Las Vegas shows. Paris, Japan,

Germany. Even dancing on Rock videos. Motley Crew "Girl, Girls, Girls." Traveling all over the world. I had many exciting adventures.

Then… one unforeseen incident changed everything. But even now, I do my best to be positive and create a meaningful life for myself.

I am strong and healthy and active. I teach aerobics classes. I am tall, slender and have long blonde hair. I have a pretty silly sense of humor sometimes. I read, watch trashy TV and stay out of drama.

I miss traveling, good food, the ocean, interesting friends and romance. I would love to meet new friends from the real world that might share their adventures or maybe just talk.

Please write to me directly.

Marjorie

CHAPTER 10
THE TACOMA MURDERS

W hen the use of DNA as a crime-solving tool was first introduced in 1986, it was used to convict criminals who left samples of their DNA at a crime scene. Unfortunately, it took a long time to process and was extremely costly.

As time went by and technology improved, it became less costly and took less time to test, but there was still the matter of finding a match. Investigators needed to have a suspect and acquire that suspect's DNA before they could find a match.

Then, in the 1990s, CODIS (Combined DNA Index System) was introduced. The FBI established CODIS as a central database of known DNA samples. This was a considerable advancement: if investigators didn't have a suspect, they could check in CODIS to find a possible match. The only problem was that the person in question had to have been convicted of a crime in the past *and* to have had their DNA taken at that time. Currently, DNA laws vary per state in the United States. Some states take DNA for felony arrests, some for misdemeanors; some apply to juveniles, some don't. However, as of 2019, most states will take DNA for felony arrests.

In the past few years, another huge advancement in DNA crime-fighting has happened. Now, people freely give their DNA in search of their ancestral roots. Sites like 23andme.com (co-founded by Ann Wojcicki, wife of Google's Sergey Brin), GedMatch.com, and Ancestry.com have acquired vast amounts of the general public's DNA, meaning the DNA of people who have not necessarily committed any crimes. With that DNA comes a world of new possibilities. This method was used in 2018 in the high-profile case of the Golden State Killer.

The disappearance of Michella Welch also used this new process. Her case was thought to be linked to a similar murder that happened the same year, but DNA eventually proved there were two separate killers. These two cases are prime examples of the unsettling fact that there are monsters that walk among us, undetected.

On March 26, during Spring Break of 1986, twelve-year-old Michella Welch and her two younger sisters rode their bicycles to Puget Park in North Tacoma, Washington, at around 10:00 a.m.

After a few hours of playing in the park, the girls were getting hungry and Michella decided to ride her bike back home to prepare some lunch and bring it back for herself and her sisters. When she returned to the park, her sisters weren't around. Michella put the brown paper bag with their lunches on a picnic bench, locked her bike up, and went looking for her sisters.

Around 1:15 p.m., Michella's sisters returned and found her bike and the lunches, but there was no sign of Michella. The two sisters wandered around the park, looking for her and calling her name, but they got no reply. Worried and scared, they went home. By 3:10 p.m., the Tacoma Police had been called, and an official search began.

At 11:27 that evening, the police search and rescue dogs found Michella's body near a fire-pit area in the park. She had been sexually assaulted, suffered blunt force trauma to her head, and her throat had been slit.

A classmate of Michella told investigators that he saw a suspicious-looking man beneath the Proctor Bridge looking at young girls, but the man was never found.

In early August of that same year, just five months after Michella was murdered, thirteen-year-old Jennifer Bastian was riding her bicycle in Point Defiance Park. The park was just three miles from the park where Michella had disappeared. Jennifer was practicing for a bike ride she had planned in the San Juan Islands later that summer.

Jennifer took out her new Schwinn eighteen-speed bike, promised her mother she'd be home for dinner by 6:30, and headed for a road called Five Mile Drive.

When Jennifer hadn't returned home by 6:30 that evening, her mother became worried. Two hours later, her terrified parents called the police and reported her missing. Police with sniffer dogs searched the park extensively, but there was no sign of Jennifer.

Three teenage boys that went to school with Jennifer recalled seeing her riding her bike at approximately 4:10 p.m. She was riding her bicycle on Five Mile Drive, as she had told her mother, but they said she didn't seem concerned or in any danger.

The police closed the park for two days and recruited members of the Green River Killer Task Force to help with the search, but they had still found nothing after two days of searching.

Three weeks later, joggers found Jennifer's body in a remote area of the park. Her body had been concealed by brush, and her bicycle was located just a few yards away. Her swimsuit bottoms were pulled down around her ankles, and there was evidence that she had been raped. An autopsy showed that Jennifer died of strangulation.

With both crimes happening in the same vicinity, both girls being similar in age and appearance, and both riding their bicycles in the parks, police assumed it was the work of the same killer.

Thousands of tips were called in of possible suspects seen in the area, and police facial sketches were shown on the nightly news. More than 10,000 hours of police work went into the two investigations, but after all their efforts, no credible leads ever turned up. The killer seemed to have vanished into thin air, and both cases went cold for over thirty years.

Though DNA evidence was found at Michella's scene, DNA forensic science was in its infancy in 1986. Even CODIS was unavailable at that time. Still, police saved the DNA samples, knowing that technology would someday change, and they could eventually catch the killer.

Twenty-five years later, in 2011, the Tacoma Police Department launched a new division concentrated on looking at older cold cases. The cold cases of Michella and Jennifer were part of the reason the new division was created. Detectives pored through dozens of binders of files for the two cases and over 2,300 names connected to the cases.

Though there had been no useable DNA collected from Jennifer's crime scene at the time, they had saved the swimsuit bottoms she was wearing. With new technology that wasn't available almost thirty years prior, they could now recover male DNA from the swimsuit.

It wasn't until 2016, when the two DNA samples from Jennifer and Michella's murder scenes were compared to each other, that detectives made a startling discovery. For almost thirty years, police had believed that the same person had killed both Jennifer and Michella, but now they realized there were, in fact, two different killers.

Armed with the new DNA results from Jennifer's crime scene, police had a list of 160 suspects. They now needed DNA samples to compare to the semen found on Jennifer's bathing suit.

In May 2018, FBI agents knocked on the door of sixty-year-old Robert Washburn, who had lived near Point Defiance Park at the time but now lived in Eureka, Illinois. He was on the list of 160 potential suspects. Washburn voluntarily gave a sample of his DNA, which matched the DNA found at Jennifer Bastian's murder scene. He was arrested and brought back to Pierce County, Washington, to stand trial.

Washburn first came up on the Tacoma Police's radar when he called in to give a tip on Michella's murder.

Friends and family that knew him as an older man found it hard to fathom Washburn as a child killer. They knew him as a doting father and full-time caretaker for his disabled daughter. Even Washburn's ex-wife had no idea,

> "I would have divorced him and turned him in. I am happy for that family, for that little girl... We never saw this coming. He was always gentle."

Robert Washburn pleaded guilty to the first-degree murder of Jennifer Bastian and was sentenced to twenty-six years in prison.

In the case of finding Michella's killer, police caught an extremely lucky break using Genetic Genealogy.

Typically, DNA evidence was only relevant if there was a suspect to compare it to. Databases like the FBI's CODIS only had the DNA of prior criminals, but if investigators were looking for someone who had never been convicted of a crime then they were out of luck.

Using the DNA from Michella's crime scene, police entered the DNA into a public online DNA-matching website, GEDmatch.com. After uploading the DNA, they were able to create a family tree. The family tree limited the suspects down to two brothers who lived in North Tacoma in 1986 near Puget Park, where Michella was killed.

Police followed sixty-six-year-old Gary Charles Hartman from his job as a nurse at Western State Hospital to a restaurant in Tacoma, where he had lunch with a co-worker. Detectives sat at a table in the restaurant and had lunch just ten feet away. They watched as Hartman finished his lunch, wiped his mouth with a napkin, and placed it in a paper bag. Hartman then left the bag on the table and left the restaurant.

Detectives gathered the napkin containing his DNA and submitted it to the police lab for testing. The DNA was indeed a match to the DNA left at the scene of Michella's murder, which led police to arrest Hartman.

Like Washburn, Hartman led an otherwise completely normal life, and news of his arrest for such a heinous crime shocked his friends and family. Hartman was a father of two who collected vintage cars. He worked as a community nurse specialist at Western State Hospital and had no prior criminal record. Acquaintances described him as a pleasant, even-tempered guy. Hartman had lived within a mile of Puget Park at the time of Michella's murder.

In March 2022, Gary Hartman was convicted and sentenced to twenty-six years in prison.

CHAPTER 11
THE KILLER BRIDE

K alispell, Montana, is known as the gateway to Glacier National Park. With a population of only 23,000, it was hurled into the national spotlight during the summer of 2013 as the spot of one of the most absurd murders of the year.

Jordan Graham was a shy, introverted, and deeply religious twenty-year-old when she met twenty-three-year-old Cody Johnson. Cody was quite the opposite. He was very outgoing and social, and although they met at a church picnic, he didn't really have an interest in attending church. He was more interested in fast cars and shooting guns than going to church.

Cody was instantly smitten with Jordan, and the two began dating. Although Cody quickly fell madly in love with Jordan, she didn't feel the same way and was unaffectionate. Because of her religion, Jordan didn't believe in sex before marriage – but her lack of affection went beyond just the absence of sex. Their friends noted that the couple never even held hands or flirted together.

But that didn't deter Cody. He tried hard to win over Jordan's love. When they first started dating, Cody told his mother that she was "*the one*." He told her that he intended to make Jordan his wife.

Church was very important to Jordan, and one of the first things she insisted Cody do was go to church with her every Sunday. If they were going to have any relationship at all, he would need to be a good Christian like her.

They had dated for several months without any sexual contact at all, and Jordan still wasn't interested in showing affection, yet Cody was undeterred. After a year of dating, he asked her to marry him. To Cody's delight, she said "yes," and they started planning their wedding.

Jordan was clearly having second thoughts. She often asked her friends if she was making the right decision. Her friends could tell she was apprehensive, but she continued to plan the wedding regardless. Before the wedding, Jordan confided in her friends that she was excited about the wedding, but she wasn't looking forward to being married.

June 29, 2013, was the big day. It was a warm summer day in Montana. Cody and the wedding guests were excited, but Jordan's mood was somber and emotional. Walking down the aisle, Jordan was crying and looking at the ground. It was obvious that her tears weren't tears of joy; she was terrified. When Jordan got to the altar, the crying continued. She couldn't even look Cody in the eye. She held his hand but could only look at the ground in front of her.

After the ceremony, the newlyweds danced to a song composed by a friend, with lyrics,

 "…you helped me to climb higher for a better view… you're my safe place to fall…."

It was clear that Jordan didn't enjoy the wedding, the reception, or the thought of being married, and she was dreading what was coming next: the wedding night. She sent a text to her matron of honor:

"I should be happy, and I'm just not."

"I just know he's gonna want to do stuff, and I'm not really wanting to."

"I'm using the 'my period started' spiel tonight. I freaking hope it works. Because if I'm forced to do something, I'm goin' to freak out."

"I feel like it's my job to make him happy, even if I'm miserable."

In the days after the wedding, Jordan confessed to friends that they still hadn't consummated the marriage. She told them she was just too nervous and couldn't do it. While she was with friends, she was lethargic and depressed.

Cody also confided to his friends. He told them that even though they were now married, there was still no sex or even affection. Nothing had changed.

A week after their wedding, Jordan sent a text to a friend again,

Jordan: "Oh well, I'm about to talk to him."

Friend: "I'll pray for you guys."

Jordan: "But dead serious, if you don't hear from me at all again tonight, something happened."

And something did happen. Nine days after the wedding, Cody's friends and family became worried when he didn't show up for work. That was entirely out of character for Cody. The last time anyone had seen him was with Jordan on Sunday afternoon after church at the local Dairy Queen.

When Cody's friends spoke to Jordan, she seemed unconcerned about Cody's disappearance. In fact, she was happy – happier than her friends had ever seen her.

Jordan told Cody's friends that he was out in the garage of their home that Sunday evening, then when she went out to see him, he wasn't there anymore. Instead, she saw a dark-colored car with Washington plates driving away. She claimed that she later got a message from him, saying he was going for a ride with friends from out of town.

Despite Jordan's story, Cody's friends knew he wouldn't just take off like that. He certainly wouldn't ignore their texts and calls. Knowing something was wrong, Cody's friends called the police and reported him missing.

Understandably, the first person that police wanted to speak to was the last person to have contact with him: his wife of little over a week, Jordan Graham.

Jordan told the police the same story she told Cody's friends. She claimed Cody had gone out for a drive with some of his buddies.

 "Well, I got a message saying that he was going to go for a ride with some of his out-of-town buddies that were visiting . . . I had no idea who they were . . . But he always told me this one thing, when his friends came to visit, he would take them to Glacier Park."

When asked if she and Cody had been fighting that night, she told police they hadn't. She had also told one of her friends that they hadn't been fighting. When the detectives eventually questioned all her friends, however, one friend had a conflicting story.

When questioning Jordan's matron of honor, Kimberly, they found that Jordan had told her that she and Cody had indeed been fighting. She said Cody had held her down while they argued, and he'd grabbed his keys and scratched her.

Friends and family showed up at Jordan's house to help her look for Cody, but she had no interest in looking for him. Instead, she became frustrated that everyone was so concerned about Cody. She was visibly flustered and, at one point, took off her wedding ring and threw it across the room. Her friends were shocked and confused. They wanted to help her find her husband, but she seemed to want the opposite.

Police noted Jordan's strange actions and the conflicting stories she had been giving. She seemed to give everyone involved a slightly different story. Even her friends were becoming suspicious of her and had no idea why she was behaving so strangely.

Then Jordan suddenly had some news. She told her friends that she'd gotten an email from someone who called himself "Tony the car man." In Tony's email, he wrote that Cody took him to Glacier National Park, and he accidentally fell off a cliff.

> "Hello Jordan, my name is Tony. There is no bother looking for Cody anymore. He's gone."

Her friends thought it was odd that Jordan had shown the email to them but not the police. What they thought was even more strange was that she wasn't crying. Someone had just told her that her husband of a little over a week was dead and she didn't seem the slightest bit upset. Her friend insisted that she show the email to detectives.

Investigators, of course, were immediately suspicious. They weren't suspicious of the mysterious "Tony" and the oddly worded email, but they were wary of Jordan. Detectives knew things just didn't happen that way. There was also the question of her demeanor. It was as if she was relieved by the message rather than saddened. Kalispell Police Detective Cory Clarke told reporters,

> "The email that she provided to us stated that these unknowns that he had taken off with, as well as this Tony person, had seen him fall from a cliff or at least disappear and that she was given explicit instructions to tell the police to call off the search. There was no more need to search for him, and at that point, I think she expected us to just walk away from it."

Four days after Cody's disappearance, she gathered her friends and told them she wanted them to help her look for Cody in Glacier National Park.

Glacier National Park is a massive park that spans over 1 million acres of rugged mountain terrain and has over 700 lakes. As she and her friends drove to the park, Jordan acted like it was a vacation. She drove with her arm out of the window, playing with the breeze and singing along to the songs on the radio. Her friends were sad and confused at her lack of emotion.

When they arrived at the park, her friends diligently searched as best as they could in such a gigantic park, but Jordan was barely making an effort. After a day of searching, they found nothing and drove back home.

The following day, they went to the park again. Within minutes of entering the park, Jordan knew precisely where to go. She told her friends that she thought he was at a particular spot on a trail called the Loop Trail. Along the Loop was a spot with a 300-foot cliff on the other side of a safety wall. Jordan seemed excited and said, "I think he's down here." She hopped over the safety wall and climbed to the cliff's edge, where she could see the bottom. She then yelled to her friends, "He's down there. I can see him!"

Jordan's friends were in disbelief. In a park that spans 13,000 square miles, she knew exactly where to go. When the police arrived, they used a helicopter to get to the bottom of the cliff. At the bottom, they found the body of Cody Johnson in the shallow water beneath a waterfall. Cody's body had extensive damage to his head and arms. It was determined that he had fallen face-first. His forehead had an eight-inch gash, and he was found without his wedding ring.

Aside from relief, Jordan was once again void of emotion. When police asked her how she knew where to find him in such a massive area, she replied,

"The Holy Spirit led me to where he was. It was a place he had wanted to see before he died."

After only a few days of marriage, Jordan Graham was a widow, and she didn't seem to care. She told her friend, Kimberly,

 "Now that we have the body, we can have the funeral, and the cops can be out of it."

Jordan naively thought the police would just drop everything once his body was found.

By the time of Cody's funeral, just sixteen days after the wedding, there was no question in her friends' minds that Jordan was responsible for Cody's death. Jordan's behavior was simply unacceptable, and she showed no emotion at all. During the funeral, as they put Cody's body into the ground, his friends and family were crying, but Jordan was on her phone, texting. That only solidified her friends' suspicions. The police had felt the same and were building their case against Jordan.

After the funeral, Kalispell police brought her back in for more questioning. By this time, the FBI was involved. When agents told her that she was under arrest for killing her husband just eight days after their wedding, Jordan was unmoved. It wasn't until they presented with their evidence against her that she showed any emotion.

Police had subpoenaed Jordan and Cody's cell phone providers. The cell phone records showed they both entered Glacier National Park that Sunday evening. In addition, the security camera at the entrance to the park showed them entering the park in her car.

Police also proved that the email from "Tony the car man" was actually composed by Jordan at her stepfather's home. She had written the email herself to try and hide the crime.

After FBI agents presented the evidence against her, she broke down. She admitted that she had regrets about the marriage and was overwhelmed with negative emotions. She explained that they had been arguing on the night of Cody's death and decided to go to Glacier National Park and the Loop Trail. Jordan then mentioned something that shocked the FBI agents. Out of the blue, Jordan claimed that

Cody told her that he knew the trail so well that he could wear a blindfold.

> "I didn't want to do that trail because I was afraid that he could fall, and he said, 'I could do it with a blindfold on. I could just put it on, take a step, and I wouldn't even fall.'"

This shocked them because police found a black cloth near the body that they believed could have been used as a blindfold. When tested by FBI forensic scientists, human hairs were embedded in it. Unfortunately, however, because the cloth was mishandled during the investigation, they were unable to prove that she had used it as a blindfold.

Additionally, on the Sunday before his disappearance, Cody's friends told police that he had been in a good mood because Jordan had told him she had a surprise. Cody and his friends all assumed that surprise was that they would finally have sex. With this information, FBI agents believed that Jordan brought Cody to the park, blindfolded him, and filled him with the hope that they would finally have sex.

Jordan explained that while on the Loop Trail, they hopped over the safety wall and climbed down a steep, rocky slope. They then made their way to the edge of a cliff with a massive drop below,

> "It kept going through my head that, you know, 'you are going to fall or something,' and then we were arguing some more, and he went to grab my arm and my jacket, and I said, 'no, I am going to defend myself.' So I said, 'let go,' and I pushed, and then he went over."

> "I wasn't thinking about where we were; I just pushed. I don't feel like I killed him; I mean, I pushed him, but it was an accident."

> "I think it's because emotions were running so high. I was frustrated, I was angry, I was every emotion I could

ever think of all at once. And I've never felt like that
before. I've never experienced such high emotions."

Later in the interrogation, she finally admitted that she had shoved
Cody with both hands on his back in a fit of rage. Then, after he fell 300
feet to his death, she simply left the park and went home. On the one-
hour drive home, she sent text messages to friends but mentioned
nothing about what had just happened to her husband. She then made
up stories to her friends and family that Cody had gone on a joyride
with his friends.

Twenty-two-year-old Jordan Graham was charged with first-degree
murder, second-degree murder, and making misleading statements to
police. She faced a potential life sentence.

Initially, she pleaded not guilty, then changed her plea during the trial
just before the case was presented to the jury. She pleaded guilty to
second-degree murder and was sentenced to thirty years in prison
without the possibility of parole.

Jordan Graham offered no apologies or explanations for her crime,

"It was a moment of complete shock and panic. I have
no other explanation."

"I kinda was feeling, 'should we have waited a little bit
longer and then got married?' I wasn't feeling like I was
on cloud nine."

CHAPTER 12
THE LADY KILLER

Neville Heath was born on June 6, 1917, to a modest barber and his wife in Essex, England. The first school Neville attended allowed the "caning" of children as a form of punishment. It's assumed that at this early age is when Neville Heath acquired his fascination for sadomasochism. At age six, he stole one of his teacher's canes and beat a young girl with it.

The Heath family saved every penny so their son could go to Rutlish Grammar School, a well-known private school with famous former pupils including former British Prime Minister John Major.

Despite proper schooling, Neville didn't excel academically. Instead, at fifteen, he trapped a teenage girl in a room with him, kissed her, and held her throat tight enough to leave red scratch marks.

When he was seventeen years old, Neville Heath left his home in Ilford, England, and joined the Royal Air Force. Within a year, Heath had become a flying officer stationed in Duxford. During his time in the military, he realized that women would pay more attention to him if he were wealthy and successful. Neville also knew that if he couldn't achieve riches and success, he could always fake it.

Heath forged checks and embezzled from the military to pay for a more extravagant lifestyle. When caught by military police, he escaped and stole a sergeant's car. He was quickly captured again and dismissed from the military for being absent without leave. He spent time defending himself in court for fraud and robbery charges and was sent to a Borstal school.

Heath was also well-known for impersonating various aristocrats. Some of his favorite fictitious names to use were Lieutenant-Colonel Armstrong and Lord Dudley. He used the money he stole from the military to pay for prostitutes that he hired to whip him.

Banishment from the military didn't deter Heath. He enjoyed military life, and one year later, he applied to join the Royal Army Service Corps. Unfortunately, World War II was imminent; the army willingly accepted him, turning a blind eye to his prior offenses.

In March 1940, Heath was commissioned to the Middle East and given the rank of second lieutenant, where he fought against Italian troops moving into Egypt. He was eventually promoted to acting captain.

The war didn't keep him from continuing his deviant activities. During his time in the Middle East, he frequented brothels that let customers whip a girl for £50 per night. Somehow, he obtained an additional playbook which allowed him to be paid twice for his military service. He passed more bad checks and tried to con his superior officers. Finally, he was arrested but escaped, then was caught again and court-martialed.

Heath was placed in a troopship headed back to Britain. However, as the ship was sailing around the Cape of Good Hope, he jumped ship while docked in Durban, South Africa. In Durban, he started a new life and gave himself a new name: Captain Selway MC of the Argyll and Sutherland Highlanders.

While in South Africa, he met a girl named Elizabeth Pitt-Rivers. She came from a wealthy family, and when she became pregnant, he asked her to marry him. They had a son named Robert.

Under the name Armstrong, Heath joined the South African Air Force and became a bomber pilot, but he was eventually sent back to the Royal Air Force. On May 24, 1944, he was piloting a bomber between the Dutch and German border when it was hit by anti-aircraft fire. Heath bravely allowed his crew to bale out of the plane while he stayed at the control until the last moment, then parachuted to safety.

He returned to South Africa the following year, but inevitably faced yet another court-martial. This time it was for wearing decorations on his uniform that he didn't earn. Heath was finally dismissed from the military for a third time in February 1946 and returned to London.

The war had just ended, and the nightlife in London was back in full swing. Heath was now a handsome twenty-nine-year-old regular at the Soho and Kensington nightclubs. He was tall, good-looking, charming, and always had a girl on his arm. It was no problem for him to find girls that enjoyed the same fetishes he had.

One such girl was named Margery Gardner. Margery was a thirty-two-year-old divorcee who was an aspiring actress and had been an extra in a few British films. Heath and Margery met at the Panama Club in Kensington, and together, they frequented the hot nightspots of London and stayed in nearby hotels. On one occasion, another patron alerted the hotel manager to the screams of their bondage games.

On the evening of June 20, 1946, Neville Heath and Margery Gardner checked into the Pembridge Court Hotel in Notting Hill under the name Lieutenant Colonel Heath.

The following morning, a chambermaid found Margery Gardener dead in room four. Her clothes were soaked with blood, and her ankles were tied together. Ligature marks on her wrists showed that her hands had also been bound, but the bindings were missing. There were seventeen whip marks on her back from a leather woven horse riding crop with a ferrule tip. Her nipples had been bitten entirely off, and a rough item was inserted into her vagina that had been twisted, causing bleeding. Her face and chin were bruised, presumably by a fist. Strangely, her face had been washed, but dried blood was still visible in her nostrils and eyelashes. Neville Heath was nowhere to be found.

The coroner determined that Margery died from suffocation, not from her injuries. Both Margery and Heath were already in police files. Margery was known to associate with pimps and drug dealers and had recently been a passenger in a stolen car.

Police knew precisely who they were searching for, but Heath had fled to Worthing in Sussex. He was there to stay with a nineteen-year-old girl named Yvonne Symonds, who believed she was Heath's fiancée. Heath had met Yvonne just five days earlier in London, where he proposed marriage to her so that he could get her into bed.

Heath explained to Yvonne that he was indirectly involved in a murder and that the police may be looking for him. He told her he lent the hotel room to his friend, Margery Gardner, who was looking for somewhere to take a man she had met that night. When he returned to the room, he found Margery dead in the bed and left immediately. He told Yvonne, "the person that could do such a thing must be a sexual maniac." He then told Yvonne he was completely innocent and would go back to London and talk to Scotland Yard.

But Heath didn't go back to London. Instead, he wrote a letter to Superintendent Tom Barrett:

 "I feel it to be my duty to inform you of certain facts in connection with the death of Mrs. Gardner.

I booked in last Sunday but not with Mrs. Gardner, whom I met for the first time during the week. I had drinks with her on Friday evening, and whilst I was with her, she met an acquaintance with whom she was obliged to sleep. The reasons as I understand them were mainly financial.

It was then that Mrs. Gardner asked if she could use my hotel room until two o'clock and intimated that I might spend the remainder of the night with her. I gave her my keys.

It must have been almost 3:00 a.m. when I returned to the hotel and found her in the condition of which you are aware. I realized that I was in an invidious position and packed my belongings and left.

Since then, I have been in several minds whether to come forward or not, but in view of the circumstances, I have been afraid to.

I can give you a description of the man. He was aged approximately thirty, dark-haired with a small mustache. His name was Jack. I gathered he was a friend of Mrs. Gardner of some long-standing.

I have the instrument with which Mrs. Gardner was beaten, and I'm forwarding this to you today. You will find my fingerprints on it, but you should also find others as well.

NGC Heath"

Heath sent the letter but didn't include the riding crop. He then left Worthing and traveled to Bournemouth, on the southern coast of England. Bournemouth was busy in the summer, with thousands of people soaking up the sun on the beach. Heath checked into the Tollard Royal Hotel under the name Group Captain Rupert Brooks.

Police had alerted the media that they were looking for Neville Heath, but they hadn't presented a photo to the press. Thus, Heath was able to stay in Bournemouth undetected under an assumed name for thirteen days without attracting attention.

Nineteen-year-old Doreen Marshall was vacationing in Bournemouth with her friend, Peggy. Doreen was recovering from a nasty bout of the flu, and her father had thought that a little time in the sun would do her good. Doreen, a former WREN (Women's Royal Navy Service), was walking along the promenade when she met Group Captain Rupert Brooks, Heath's latest assumed name.

Heath struck up a conversation by claiming he had previously met Peggy at a club. Peggy said she remembered him out of courtesy, but she had no idea who he was. As the day progressed, it was clear that Heath had his eye on Doreen, so Peggy left the two alone for the rest of the afternoon.

Heath and Doreen spent the hot July 3rd walking around the town. They had tea at the Tollard Royal Hotel that evening and, later that evening, dinner and drinks.

At the end of the evening, Doreen asked the hotel to call her a cab back to her hotel, but Heath protested. It was a beautiful, warm night, and Heath insisted on walking her back to her hotel. She was staying at The Norfolk, a posh five-star hotel that her father had paid for, but Doreen never made it back.

The night porter at the Tollard Royal Hotel had worked the hotel's front door all night and knew that Group Captain Rupert Brooks had not returned. Concerned, the night porter checked his room at 4:00 a.m. and was surprised to find him safe and asleep inside.

The following morning, when questioned about how he got back into his room, Heath explained that he had played a joke on the night porter. As he returned from dropping off Doreen Marshall, he explained that he saw a ladder leading up to his room that a construction crew had left behind. He said he climbed the ladder back into his room and went to sleep.

Two days later, the management at The Norfolk was worried about their guest, Doreen Marshall. She hadn't shown up for daily meals in two days. The last they had seen her, she was getting into a taxi headed for the Tollard Royal Hotel. So, the manager of The Norfolk called the manager of the Tollard Royal.

The manager of the Tollard Royal had seen Doreen dining with Group Captain Rupert Brooke, aka Heath. He then informed Heath that the girl was missing and he should call the police.

Using his assumed name, Heath spoke to the police and told them that Doreen Marshall had been flirting with an American soldier earlier in the evening before she went missing, and he believed she might have gone off with him.

Detective Constable Souter questioned Heath and noticed he was a bit too calm about the situation. His smooth-talking demeanor didn't sit well with Souter.

Heath explained that he had walked Doreen part of the way home that night and dropped her off at the pier. He even claimed to have seen her the following day in the city. He repeated to the Detective that he had climbed the ladder outside his hotel to play a prank on the night porter, but this only made Souter more suspicious. He wondered if the real reason he used the ladder might have been because he didn't want the hotel staff to know what time he came back to the hotel.

Just as Heath left the police station, Doreen's father and older sister arrived. Heath was visibly shaken to meet them both but particularly her sister, who looked strikingly like Doreen. Souter noticed his nervousness and said, "Isn't your name Heath?" Heath replied, "Certainly not!" Souter continued, "But you look like the pictures in the papers." Heath replied, "I suppose I do."

What Heath didn't know was that there were no pictures in the papers. The police only released photos of Neville Heath to other police stations, not to the press. Souter alerted Scotland Yard, and on July 6, 1946, Heath was arrested in Bournemouth.

Upon Heath's arrival at the Bournemouth police station, he complained that he was cold. He had left his sports coat at the Tollard Royal Hotel, and he asked the police if they would pick it up for him. When detectives picked up his coat, they found three items in the pockets: a cloakroom receipt from Bournemouth Rail Station, the return half of Doreen Marshall's rail ticket, and a single, white, artificial pearl. Heath claimed he found the return railway ticket on a seat in the lounge of the Tollard Royal Hotel.

Police then took the cloakroom receipt to Bournemouth Rail Station and retrieved the suitcase that Heath had checked in. Inside the suitcase, they found a blue wool scarf stained with blood, a hat with the name "Heath" inside, and a riding crop. The riding crop had a diamond crisscross weave and a ferrule-like hard tip, similar to what had created the marks on Margery Gardner's back. The riding crop had been wiped clean but still had a small amount of blood on it. Police also believed the blue wool scarf might have been used to restrain or gag Margery Gardner.

Neville Heath was officially charged with Margery Gardner's death and taken to London, but Doreen was still missing in Bournemouth.

Two days after Heath's arrest, Kathleen Evans was walking her dog through Branksome Dene Chine, a park just west of the hotels in Bournemouth. Her dog was sniffing at something beneath a rhododendron bush. Beneath the bush, swarming with flies, Mrs. Evans found the body of Doreen Marshall, covered with a camel hair jacket.

Doreen's body was naked except for her left shoe. She had been bludgeoned, raped, and mutilated. She was slashed with a knife from her breast to her vagina. A rough object had torn her vagina and was inserted into her anus. Similar to Margery, one of Doreen's nipples had been bitten off. Her hand was sliced as if she'd tried to defend herself from a knife attack.

Her black dress and a makeup compact were found near her body. Also nearby was her broken artificial pearl necklace, with twenty-seven pearls scattered about. The twenty-eighth was the one found in Heath's coat pocket.

The knife was never found. Nor were Heath's bloody clothes. Police believed that, after he murdered her, he ran into the ocean to wash himself and threw the knife into the sea. They believed that he then went back to his hotel and climbed up the workman's ladder to avoid being seen by the night porter.

Heath originally wanted to plead guilty,

> "Why shouldn't I? After all, I did kill them."

But his attorney convinced him to enter a plea of not guilty by reason of insanity.

In England at that time, a person could only be tried for one crime at a time, so he was only tried for the murder of Margery Gardner. At the trial, women lined up for over ten hours outside the Central Criminal Court to catch a glimpse of "the most dangerous criminal modern Britain has known," as the newspapers described.

During the trial, Heath offered no reason for his killings, saying, "I felt my head go tight." The defense brought up evidence from Doreen's murder to emphasize their insanity plea, but their plan didn't work. The trial only lasted three days, and the jury took less than an hour to reach a verdict.

Neville Heath was found guilty and sentenced to death by hanging. While awaiting execution, Heath didn't seem to care about his fate. He spent his time in his cell reading *The Thirty-Nine Steps* several times and writing letters to his mother, in which he said,

> "My only regret is that I have been damned unworthy of you both."

Heath dressed up for his execution. When given the traditional shot of whiskey before execution, he held out his glass and said, "Old boy, considering the circumstances, you might make that a double."

Neville Heath was hanged in Pentonville Prison on October 16, 1946, just four months after the first murder. Within twenty minutes of his execution, Madame Tussaud's Wax Museum in London debuted its latest wax figure: Neville Heath.

CHAPTER 13
APPENDIX: LARRY GENE BELL

The following is the full transcript from the long, rambling telephone conversation from Thursday evening after Shari Smith's body was found. (Chapter 4)

Operator: "I have a collect call for Dawn Smith."

Beverly: "Dawn is not taking any calls. Could I have a name, please?"

Larry Gene Bell: "Put Dawn on the line please."

Beverly: "Dawn can't come to the phone right now. This is her Aunt Beverly."

Bell: "Well, may I speak to Mrs. Smith? This is an emergency."

Beverly: "Well, I'm sorry, she is being sedated and cannot come to the phone. She is asleep."

Bell: "Ok, may I speak to Bob Smith?"

Beverly: "Bob is up at the funeral home. You realize the situation with their daughter? Wait a minute, you asked to speak to Mrs. Smith?"

Bell: "Or Dawn, I'd rather speak to Dawn."

Beverly: "Uh, well, let me see if we can find her."

Bell: "Ok, hurry up."

Beverly: "Ok, they are looking for her right now."

Bell: "Thank you. Ok, thank you, operator. I'll speak to anybody that comes to the phone, now."

Beverly: "This is her Aunt Beverly."

Operator: "Collect from Joe Wilson. Will you accept the charge?"

Beverly: "Yes, we'll accept the charge. This is Shari's Aunt Beverly. I'll be happy to speak to you. Who am I speaking to please?"

Bell: "I want to speak to Dawn."

Beverly: "We're trying to locate her. In the meantime, I'll be happy to speak to you."

Bell: "No, thank you. I'll have to go then if I can't talk to her."

Beverly: "She's coming. Wait one moment, please. She went outside to walk the dog. They are looking for her. Ok, here's Dawn right now."

Dawn Smith: "Hello."

Bell: "Dawn?"

Dawn: "Yes."

Bell: "I'm calling for Shari Faye. Are you aware that I'm turning myself in tomorrow morning?"

Dawn: "No."

Bell: "Well, have you talked to Sheriff Metts or Charlie Keyes?"

Dawn: "Uh, no."

Bell: "Well, talk to them and listen carefully. I have to tell you this, Shari asked me to uh, turn myself in on the fifth day after they found her."

Dawn: "Wait, I'm trying to write this down."

Bell: "Don't write it down. I, uh, got to get myself straight with God and uh, turn myself completely over to him."

Dawn: "Ok."

Bell: "And uh, Charlie Keyes...you'll know what I'm talking about when you talk to him. He will not be able to get a personal interview from me in the morning. I'm uh, there'll be a letter. It's already been mailed. An exact copy for you and for him and it's with pictures."

Dawn: "A copy for me?"

Bell: "Yes, and him at his home of pictures of Shari Faye from the time I made her stand up to her car and took two pictures and all through the thing, and the letter will describe exactly what happened from the time I picked her up until the time, uh, I called and told y'all where to find her."

Dawn: "Ok."

Bell: "And I'll be doing the same in the morning at 6:00 a.m. and tell the sheriff and Charlie Keyes. I used him as a medium today and talked to him."

Dawn: "Ok, at 6:00 a.m., what will you be doing in the morning?"

Bell: "Well, he'll know."

Dawn: "He'll know?"

Bell: "Ok, and also that uh, uh, that I will be armed, but by the time they find me, I won't be dangerous. Do you understand that?"

Dawn: "You will be armed?"

Bell: "But by the time they find me, I won't be dangerous."

Dawn: "What does that mean?"

Bell: "Well, I...Shari Faye said if I couldn't live with myself, and she wouldn't forgive me if I didn't turn myself in or turn myself over to God, so I'm going to have to...this thing got out of hand, and all I wanted to do was make love to Dawn. I've been watching her for a couple of..."

Dawn: "To who?"

Bell: "To...I'm sorry, to Shari. I watched her a couple of weeks and uh, it just got out of hand and Dawn, Dawn, I hope you and your family forgive me for this."

Dawn: "You're not going to kill yourself, are you?"

Bell: "I...I can't live in prison and go to the electric chair. I can't do that. This is the only way I can get myself straight. I'm very sick, and I can't go through..."

Dawn: "We don't want you to die. We want to help you. Don't kill yourself."

Bell: "No, I just uh, you can't take someone's life, and this is the way it's going to have to be. Shari said..."

Dawn: "But listen to me, ok?"

Bell: "Well, listen I have to go."

Dawn: "No, I've got to tell you something. This is important."

Bell: "Well, these calls are being traced."

Dawn: "But God can forgive you and erase all of that."

Bell: "Dawn, I can't...I can't live with myself."

Dawn: "And we can forgive you, too."

Bell: "I can't live in prison for the rest of my life or go to the electric chair."

Dawn: "Listen, Shari is at peace with God. She's better off than any of us."

Bell: "Well, I want to say something to you that she told me."

Dawn: "Ok."

Bell: "Shari...oh, boy. Shari Faye said that uh...she did not cry the entire time, Dawn. She was very strong-willed and she said that uh, she did not want y'all to ruin your lives...and to go on with your lives like the letter said. I've never lied to y'all before, right? Everything I've told you came through, right."

Dawn: "Yes."

Bell: "Ok, so this is going to have to be the way it is, and she said that uh, she wasn't scared...that she knew that she was going to be an angel, and if I took the latter choice that she suggested to me, that she would forgive me, but our God's going to be the major judgment, and she'll probably end up seeing me in heaven, not in hell. And that uh, she requests...now please remember this. Now, she requests that y'all be sure to take her hands and fold them on her stomach like she's praying."

Dawn: "Ok."

Bell: "And that closed casket..."

Dawn: "Yeah."

Bell: "They already made those plans?"

Dawn: "Yes."

Bell: "Ok, and please have Charlie Keyes with Sheriff Metts, and Charlie knows what to do in the morning and have an ambulance and probably before they get there, they might as well have a hearse also and uh, and I'm just going to allow myself enough time to get in the area and get set up. I'm not in the area, now and uh, it'll be six in the morning that I'll call his office and by the time they reach me, I'll be straight with God and uh...Shari said please take the gold necklace that she had on, and she had one earring in her left ear."

Dawn: "Uh-huh."

Bell: "And uh, save those things and treasure them."

Dawn: "Save them?"

Bell: "Yes."

Dawn: "She doesn't want Richard to have that necklace?"

Bell: "Uh, she said something. There was some special jewelry in her room. I forgot what. It might have been the necklace. But uh, yeah, go, go ahead but the rest of her stuff is irrelevant."

Dawn: "What about her high school ring?"

Bell: "Uh, she said everything else would be decided by the family."

Dawn: "But Shari was not afraid, and she didn't cry or anything?"

Bell: "No, she didn't do anything. And I did make love to her and we had oral sex for uh, three different times and uh, can you handle it if I tell you how she died?"

Dawn: "Yes."

Bell: "Ok, now be strong, now."

Dawn: "Ok."

Bell: "She said you were strong. She told me all about the family and everything. We talked and...oh God...and I am a family friend. That's the sad part."

Dawn: "You are a family friend?"

Bell: "Yeah, and that is why I can't face y'all. You...you'll find out in the morning or tomorrow."

Dawn: "Yes."

Bell: "Ok, I tied her up to the bedpost and uh, with electric cord and uh, she didn't struggle, cry or anything. She let me voluntarily...from her chin to her head, ok, I'll go ahead and tell you. I took duct tape and wrapped it all the way around her head and suffocated her, and tell the coroner or get the information out how she died and uh, I was unaware she had this disease. I probably would have never taken her and uh, I shouldn't have took her, anyway. It just got out of hand and uh, I'd asked her out before, and she said she would if she wasn't going with anybody, and uh, she said also that uh...oh yeah, make sure Charlie Keyes...you know him, the reporter on WIS?"

Dawn: "I can't think of who he is right now."

Bell: "Ok, they'll know who he is. He's the one who wears the bow tie on Channel 10. He's the head news fellow on this case for Channel 10. And, oh yeah, I was there Saturday morning for the search."

Dawn: "You were at the search Saturday morning?"

Bell: "Yes, I was…and if…oh God, Dawn. I wish uh, I wish y'all could help me, but it's just too late. Well, I have to go, now, Dawn. I know the…"

Dawn: "Let me tell you something, ok? God can forgive you, and through God we can forgive you also."

Bell: "Well, uh, Dawn…will you forgive me then?"

Dawn: "Yes."

Bell: "Your family? But I'll have to take the other choice that Shari Faye said to me. I just can't live with myself like this. I'm not…"

Dawn: "I just think you need to think about that a little harder."

Bell: "I'm not going to be caged up like a dog. Ok, now, are there any other questions? I've got to go now. Time's running out."

Dawn: "Uh, when…when you killed Shari, was she at peace? She wasn't afraid or anything?"

Bell: "She was not, she was at peace. She knew that God was with her and she was going to become an angel."

Dawn: "And she wrote that letter to us of her own free will and all that was…"

Bell: "She sure did. Everything I've told y'all has been the truth. Hasn't everything come true?"

Dawn: "Yes, it has. Can…can I ask you one more question?"

Bell: "One more and that's it."

Dawn: "You told us that Shari was kidnapped at gunpoint?"

Bell: "Yeah."

Dawn: "But she knew you?"

Bell: "Yeah. At first, see, I pulled up and uh, I'm telling you the truth. I have no reason to lie to y'all. I've always told you the truth, right?"

Dawn: "Right."

Bell: "Ok, and I had her…asked her to stand there and took two instant pictures."

Dawn: "You asked her to stand where?"

Bell: "At the mailbox with her car in the background. These pictures, detailed pictures will be with…with the letter that you receive. Since I'm out of town…probably not 'til Saturday. And Charlie Keyes will get a copy and your family will get a copy, and it's addressed to you unless the mail holds it up."

Dawn: "So she didn't realize that you were going to kidnap her?"

Bell: "That's exactly right. And uh, what else? So tell Sheriff Metts that it's no use in uh…trying to trace these calls to catch me. It's too late now. I won't be taken alive. And also, Dawn, that uh, uh, he can just call off the damn search. It's over now, and I don't want the people out there wasting their time, and everything I've told you is true and this is coming true, also. I just can't live with it. I can't take it anymore. Shari Faye was right. We, I feel like I got close to her and we…she showed me things. She was very…"

Dawn: "Why are you talking to me instead of mom?"

Bell: "She felt like you were strong-willed more than your mother."

Dawn: "Oh, did you start talking to her?"

Bell: "Uh, she said it was your aunt, but it was your mother, correct?"

Dawn: "Uh, no, that was my aunt that answered the phone."

Bell: "Oh, it was? Ok. She said something about your mother being under medication. Shari Faye told me. Remember I told you on the fifth day to let them know where she was so her blessings of the body could be blessed. Right?"

Dawn: "Why on the fifth day did she want us to find her? Why not…"

Bell: "I don't know. She just…she just said that. I don't know. I don't have any idea. I'm telling you exactly how she died, so she died of suffocation. And so…ok anything else?"

Dawn: "Why did you…why did you do that?"

Bell: "She…I gave her a choice…to shoot her or give her a drug overdose or suffocate her."

Dawn: "Why did you have to kill her?"

Bell: "It got out of hand. I got scared because, uh, only God knows, Dawn. I don't know why. God forgive me for this, I hope. And I got to straighten it out or he'll send me to hell, and I'll be there the rest of my life, but I'm not going to be in prison and electric chair."

Dawn: "But I don't think taking your life is the answer to this."

Bell: "I'll think about it. Well, Dawn, I've got to go now. It's been too long and, uh, tell them to just forget about the search. I'll be in the area long enough in the morning for them to, uh, find me, and by the time I call, uh Charlie Keyes will know exactly the set-ups. I hope now, uh, I know why I'm staying on the phone. They are taping this, right?"

Dawn: "Uh-huh."

Bell: "Ok, good, and anything else? Oh, yeah. Let me tell you. The other night they almost caught me. The ignorant son-of-a-guns, I wanted them to catch me. I felt that way at the time, but now..."

Dawn: "When...when was this?"

Bell: "Uh, when I called at 9:45."

Dawn: "When you were over near Jake's Landing?"

Bell: "Yeah, I was at that Fast Fare thing."

Dawn: "Yeah."

Bell: "I pulled out twenty yards in front of two flashing lights."

Dawn: "What color car did you have?"

Bell: "They hit it dead on it, red, and they didn't even... Dawn, I can't get over this. Them ignorant so-and-sos didn't even turn around and follow me, and I cut right at that blinking light down there to go the back way on Old Cherokee Road. And there was a highway patrolman or somebody in front of me and pulled the car in front of me, and he let me turn right on Old Cherokee Road. Can you believe that?"

Dawn: "So, you really wanted to be caught?"

Bell: "At that time, but it's too late, now."

Dawn: "What kind of car was it?"

Bell: "Oh, well, they came mighty damn close. Dawn, they're not going to catch me, and I can't give you information because I got to make it back in time, and they'll stop me before I get back if I tell you, but they're right, it was a red one, and I almost got caught three or four times."

Dawn: "Was it a red Jetta?"

Bell: "Dawn, that's irrelevant now. If I die now, or if I die at six o'clock in the morning, it's irrelevant. Well, listen, Dawn."

Dawn: "I really wish you would just think about not killing yourself."

Bell: "And Shari told me to tell you, please go back to Carowinds. I know you live in Charlotte, and, uh, I know a lot about family, and uh, go back and start singing and give it your best, and that she knows that she'll be singing like crazy. When she said that, she was smiling."

Dawn: "She was smiling and she wasn't afraid the whole time?"

Bell: "No, never."

Dawn: "Because she knew that she was going to be with God."

Bell: "That's exactly right, the whole time, the whole time. She's so damn strong-willed, and, and…"

Dawn: "But, I just wish you would think about not killing yourself."

Bell: "I will, Dawn."

Dawn: "Listen, our prayers will be for you."

Bell: "I'll call you collect…will be for you, ok. Will you be home tonight?"

Dawn: "We are home tonight. Listen, our prayers will be with you, ok? God can do anything and he can forgive you for this."

Bell: "Yeah, but you know what's going to happen to me, Dawn? I'm going to be fried."

Dawn: "You don't know that. God can work miracles. You don't know that'll happen to you. God is merciful no matter what we do."

Bell: "It's time now, it's time. I got to go now, and I'll just…I'll think about it, but I've got a lot of things on my mind, now. I know you know that, right?"

Dawn: "Right."

Bell: "And, uh, you answer the phone every time it rings tonight."

Dawn: "Me answer the phone tonight, every time it rings?"

Bell: "That's right, and if it's collect, and I'll say, Dawn, like the break of day, you'll know."

Dawn: "Ok, now if we're asleep, you let it keep ringing, ok?"

Bell: "I will, I will. Ok, well, God bless us all."

Dawn: "Wait, mother wants to say something to you."

Bell: "All right, just one thing and then I'm gone."

Hilda Smith: "Hello."

Bell: "Just say one thing and that's it. Dawn will tell you, and you listen to the recordings and there will be a letter you'll receive probably the next day with pictures and detailed information from the time I picked Shari up at the mailbox up 'til tonight and my departure from this earth. Sheriff Metts might as well call it off. It's over. I will not be taken alive. Dawn told me to turn myself in or turn myself over to God, or I'll never live in peace and never be forgiven and go to heaven."

Hilda: "Well, turn yourself over to God. That's most important."

Bell: "I am and this is the only way. I'm not going to spend my life in prison and go to the electric chair. Well, uh, Dawn knows everything and, uh, God bless all of us and I hope…"

Hilda: "Listen, I want to ask you something."

Bell: "This just got out of hand. This got out of hand…"

Hilda: "All you had to do was let her go."

Bell: "I was scared. She, she, was dehydrating so damn bad."

Hilda: "You could have called me for medicine. I would have met you anywhere."

Bell: "Well, that's irrelevant now."

Hilda: "I mean all you had to do was let her go. Such a beautiful young life…"

Bell: "I know that. That's why I have to join her now, hopefully, and uh, Mrs. Smith, please, uh, ok, well, that's it. I got to go."

Hilda: "Did she know you when you stopped?"

Bell: "Yeah, uh, I took two pictures, instamatic of, I made her stand…well, before she knew I was going to kidnap her, I asked her to stand at the mailbox, and you'll see by the picture…her car door. I think there's about eight pictures and Charlie Keyes will be receiving a set and a detailed letter, like I told you, at his house, if this mail doesn't slow it down, which it probably will. If you don't get it tomorrow, you'll get it the next day. You'll get exact copies, the pictures that he gets and, uh, exact letters, too."

Hilda: "Do you know all of us or just Shari?"

Bell: "I know the whole family unfortunately, that's why I can't face you. Ok, well, Mrs. Smith, please, uh, if I decide different, I've already told Dawn what's going to happen. Her answer the phone tonight only, and it will be collect, and I'm going to allow myself just enough time to get back in the area to set everything up if you don't hear from me tonight. I knew the calls were traced, and they came real close to catching me three or four different times and they are correct, I am in a red vehicle."

Hilda: "What kind?"

Bell: "I'm sorry, I don't want them to catch me before I meet my maker on Judgment Day."

Hilda: "You think the maker's going to forgive you now?"

Bell: "He'll, he'll do that, or I'll be crucified and go to hell."

Hilda: "That's right."

Bell: "Well, I've got a lot to think about and I'm, I'm gone Mrs. Smith, and uh, please, I know this might be selfish, but, uh, you all please, ask a special prayer for me? Your, your daughter said that she was not afraid, and she was strong-willed. She, uh, knew that she was going to heaven, was going to be an angel, and like I told Dawn, she was going to be singing like crazy and when she said that she was smiling."

Hilda: "Did you tell her you were going to kill her?"

Bell: "Yes, I did and I gave her the choice, like, it's on the recording. I asked her if she wanted it to be drug over-dose, shot or, uh, uh, suffocated, and she picked suffocation."

Hilda: "My God, how could you?"

Bell: "Well, forgive us, God."

Hilda: "Not us, you."

Bell: "God only knows why this happened. I don't know. It just got out of hand."

Hilda: "I thought you were considerate and loving and a kind person."

Bell: "Goodbye, Mrs. Smith."

The next segment is the phone call that occurred immediately after Shari Smith's funeral:

Operator: "I have a collect call for Dawn Smith from Shari, will you pay for the call?"

Dawn: "From who?"

Operator: "Shari."

Dawn: "Yes."

Operator: "Go ahead, please."

Larry Gene Bell: "Is this Dawn Smith, like the break of day?"

Dawn: "Yes, it is."

Bell: "Ok, you know this is not a hoax call, correct?"

Dawn: "Yes."

Bell: "Ok, did I catch you off guard?"

Dawn: "Well, yeah, because they said it was from Shari."

Bell: "No, I said concerning Shari. Everybody's screwed up here. Excuse my French. Ok, listen carefully."

Dawn: "Ok."

Bell: "Uh, Dawn, I'm real afraid, now and everything and…"

Dawn: "You're what?"

Bell: "Real afraid, and I have to, uh, make a decision. I'm going to stay in this area until God gives me the strength to decide which way…and I did go to the funeral today."

Dawn: "You did?"

Bell: "Yes, and uh, that ignorant policeman…the fellow even directed me into a parking space. Blue uniform… outside, and they were taking license plate numbers down and stuff. Please tell Sheriff Metts I'm not jerking anybody around, I'm not playing games, this is reality and I'm not an idiot. When he finds my background, he'll see I'm a highly intelligent person."

Dawn: "Uh-huh."

Bell: "Ok, and I want to fill in some gaps here because now and next Saturday, the anniversary date of Shari Faye."

Dawn: "Yeah."

Bell: "I'm going to do one way or the other, or if God gives me strength before then, ever when, and I'll call you."

Dawn: "Between now and next Saturday?"

Bell: "Yes."

Dawn: "I think you need to make a decision before then."

Bell: "All right, and uh, I could tell her casket was closed, but did y'all honor Shari's request for folding her hands?"

Dawn: "Yes, yes we did, of course."

Bell: "Ok, she'll, she'll like that. That'll please her. Ok, and uh, tell Sheriff Metts and the FBI, damn, that's like the fear of God in you for sure. They treat this like Bonnie and Clyde. They go out and gun you down, and if I decide, if God gives me the strength to just surrender like that, I'll call you, like I said. When I see them drive up, I'll see Charlie Keyes and Sheriff Metts get out of the car, they'll recognize me. I'll approach them, and I'll put my hands straight up in the air and turn my back to them, and they can approach me without shooting me and stuff, all right? I delivered her to Saluda County, I told you exactly how she died and so forth, and when I took the duct tape off of her, it took a lot of hair with it and so, that'll help 'em out. The examiner said they were having problems telling how she died. And, uh...well, hold on a minute now and let's see..."

Dawn: "Where's the duct tape?"

Bell: "Huh?"

Dawn: "Where's the duct tape?"

Bell: "Only God knows, I don't...ok, ok, now listen. Did you receive the thing and the pictures in the mail?"

Dawn: "They're coming?"

Bell: "Unless the FBI intercepts them. It's written to you. I got Shari Faye to address three or four different things, and it's written to you in her handwriting."

Dawn: "What is written to me?"

Bell: "It's addressed to you. Ok, and now, she, she gave me your address in Charlotte, and there's one picture she wanted me to send to you, and you'll get that in about a week or so, to your Charlotte address and it's…this little note is for your eyes only in her handwriting and she said, Richard, don't tell him this, it'll break his heart. She was getting ready to break up with him, because he was over jealous and that, uh, she couldn't go anywhere and talk to any fellows without him arguing with her, and every time he'd come down to the flea market where she worked in the concession stand, he'd get mad because she couldn't talk to him and working. He worked and we talked from, uh, actually she wrote the 'Last Will and Testament,' 3:12 a.m. She kind of joked and said they won't mind if I round it off to 3:10. So, from about two o'clock in the morning from the time she actually knew until she died at 4:58, we talked a lot and everything, and she picked the time. She said she was ready to depart. God was ready to accept her as an angel."

Dawn: "So, the whole time, you told her that she was going to die, right?"

Bell: "Yeah, ok…and uh, all those times and stuff I gave you before were correct and accurate, ok. When are you going to go back to Charlotte and get the letter? Whenever I get strength, and God shows me which way, I'll mail it like a couple of hours before."

Dawn: "Ok, where is Shari's high school ring?"

Bell: "Uh, Shari's high school ring was not with her."

Dawn: "It was not with her?"

Bell: "No, not unless it was in her car or her pocketbook."

Dawn: "She always wears that ring, and if it was, please, you know…"

Bell: "I'm telling you the truth."

Dawn: "The family would really like to have it."

Bell: "I'm returning everything. I mean I don't have anything of Shari's. I don't have that. If I had it, I'd mail it to you. I'm not lying to you. Ok, you said that, uh… Listen, wait, hold on a minute, I'm not finished, now. We talked about it so much. I made clip notes afterward. Uh, she said to tell Robert Jr. That's the brother, right?"

Dawn: "Yeah."

Bell: "Ok, tell him to grow up and meet his goals and pick a sport out, and he's a big boy, and uh, excel in it."

Dawn: "Uh-huh."

Bell: "Ok, and then the last thing, oh yeah, for respect of your family, Shari Faye always told me to respect the family, and I didn't mail Charlie Keyes a set of pictures and letters. I want your family only. So when you find me, uh, if God gives me the strength, ever which way he decides, it'll be in a plastic bag on my body, on my person, because if the media got a hold of this they'll have a field day. I chose Charlie Keyes as a medium because I thought he was very level-headed, and he wouldn't let it get out of hand, and I can trust him, 'cause I kind of know him. Ok, uh, the last thing she said is… a song, she wouldn't tell me, she said, well, I have to keep some things secret with you, and she kind of chuck-led. She said that Dawn would know on her birthday, which is what, June 12, or something?"

Dawn: "On Shari's birthday?"

Bell: "Yeah, June or August…she told me…"

Dawn: "It's June."

Bell: "Ok, well, ever when it is. I think she said the twelfth or something, but anyway, uh, she said to pick her favorite song, and just you and the family, uh, you sing it and, uh, she'll be listening, and uh, put some real feelings behind it. Ok, and let's see, she, dang, let's see, let me go back through it. Ok, I was at the search Saturday morning and also Tuesday morning. I showed up when they called the volunteers off."

Dawn: "You were there?"

Bell: "Yeah."

Dawn: "You were there Tuesday morning also?"

Bell: "Yeah."

Dawn: "Were you there last night?"

Bell: "No, but I was there for the funeral this morning. And, uh, they took license, still, I'm not a damn idiot. I never had any problems before, and it's just something that got out of hand and that's all."

Dawn: "Can I ask you something?"

Bell: "Ok, now ask questions, but hurry."

Dawn: "Uh, I know that you keep telling me that you're telling me the truth, but, uh, you did tell me that you would give yourself up at six o'clock this morning. Well, what happened?"

Bell: "I didn't have the strength."

Dawn: "What?"

Bell: "I didn't have the strength. I was scared. I'm scared as hell. I can't even hardly read my handwriting."

Dawn: "Well, listen."

Bell: "Hurry, I've got to go."

Dawn: "No matter what you've done, you know that Christ died for you so that you could be forgiven, and if you would give yourself up…"

Bell: "Do you know what would happen, Dawn? Do you realize Sheriff Metts…Sheriff Metts would give me help for a couple of months, and then they'd find out I'm sane, and then I'd get tried and sent to the electric chair…put in prison for the rest of my life. I'm not going to, uh…go to the electric chair."

Dawn: "You keep telling us to forgive you…you don't realize what you've put us through. How could you think about what would happen to yourself?"

Bell: "Ok, any other questions? I've filled in all the holes and everything. If the only reason you wouldn't get that letter today or probably Monday, is that the FBI intercepted it."

Dawn: "Can you tell me where her ring is? You really don't know where it is?"

Bell: "No, I don't, Dawn. I would send it to you if I did. I have no reason. I'm not asking for money, materialistic things. I don't have any reason for…she was not wearing a high school ring when she got in the car, so maybe she left it at the pool party she came from.

Dawn: "Uh, can you tell me? Where did Shari die?"

Bell: "I told you, 4:58 in the morning."

Dawn: "No, I know the time, where?"

Bell: "Saturday morning in, uh, Lexington County."

Dawn: "In Lexington County?"

Bell: "Uh-huh."

Dawn: "Where in Lexington County?"

Bell: "Anything else you want to ask me?"

Dawn: "That's what I'm asking you, where?"

Bell: "Uh, anything else?"

Dawn: "You won't answer that for me?"

Bell: "No."

Dawn: "You said anything I'd ask, you'd tell me."

Bell: "Ok, I'll tell you. Uh, number one. I don't know exactly the location. I don't know the name of the highway, 391 or something like that, but right next to the Saluda County line. That's all I can tell you. Ok, anything else? I'm getting ready to go. At 4:58 in the morning, set your alarm wherever you are, and I'll call you. Can you hear me?"

Dawn: "Yes, this morning?"

Bell: "No, next Saturday, on the anniversary date. Ok, I'll call you and tell you the exact location, just like I did Shari Faye's."

Dawn: "I can't believe this because you've never been telling me the truth."

Bell: "Ok, I have. You believe everything because it is the truth. You go back and you go over everything."

Dawn: "I just feel that the best thing for you to do is give..."

Bell: "Well, Dawn, God bless us all."

Online Appendix

Visit my website for additional photos and videos pertaining to the cases in this book:

http://TrueCrimeCaseHistories.com/vol1/

http://TrueCrimeCaseHistories.com/vol2/

http://TrueCrimeCaseHistories.com/vol3/

THANK YOU!

Thank you for reading this Volume of True Crime Case Histories. I truly hope you enjoyed it. If you did, I would be sincerely grateful if you would take a few minutes to write a review for me on Amazon using the link below.

https://geni.us/TrueCrime123

I'd also like to encourage you to sign-up for my email list for updates, discounts and freebies on future books! I promise I'll make it worth your while with future freebies.

http://truecrimecasehistories.com

And please take a moment and follow me on Amazon.

One last thing. As I mentioned previously, many of the stories in this series were suggested to me by readers like you. I like to feature stories that many true crime fans haven't heard of, so if there's a story that you remember from the past that you haven't seen covered by other true crime sources, please send me any details you can remember and I will do my best to research it. Or if you'd like to contact me for any other reason free to email me at:

THANK YOU!

jasonnealbooks@gmail.com

https://linktr.ee/JasonNeal

Thanks so much,

Jason Neal

More books by Jason Neal

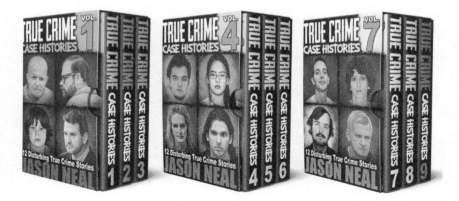

Looking for more?? I am constantly adding new volumes of True Crime Case Histories. The series **can be read in any order**, and all books are available in paperback, hardcover, and audiobook.

Check out the complete series at:

https://amazon.com/author/jason-neal

All Jason Neal books are also available in **AudioBook format at Audible.com.** Enjoy a **Free Audiobook** when you signup for a 30-Day trial using this link:

https://geni.us/AudibleTrueCrime

FREE BONUS EBOOK FOR MY READERS

As my way of saying "Thank you" for downloading, I'm giving away a FREE True Crime e-book I think you'll enjoy.

https://TrueCrimeCaseHistories.com

Just visit the link above to let me know where to send your free book!

ABOUT THE AUTHOR

Jason Neal is a Best-Selling American True Crime Author living in Hawaii with his Turkish-British wife. Jason started his writing career in the late eighties as a music industry publisher and wrote his first true crime collection in 2019.

As a boy growing up in the eighties just south of Seattle, Jason became interested in true crime stories after hearing the news of the Green River Killer so close to his home. Over the subsequent years he would read everything he could get his hands on about true crime and serial killers.

As he approached 50, Jason began to assemble stories of the crimes that have fascinated him most throughout his life. He's especially obsessed by cases solved by sheer luck, amazing police work, and groundbreaking technology like early DNA cases and more recently reverse genealogy.